Lynching in
North Carolina

EDITED BY VANN R. NEWKIRK

New Life for Historically Black Colleges and Universities:
A 21st Century Perspective (McFarland, 2012)

Lynching in North Carolina

A History, 1865–1941

VANN R. NEWKIRK

McFarland & Company, Inc., Publishers
Jefferson, North Carolina

The present work is a reprint of the illustrated case bound edition of Lynching in North Carolina: A History, 1865–1941, first published in 2009 by McFarland.

LIBRARY OF CONGRESS CATALOGUING-IN-PUBLICATION DATA

Newkirk, Vann R., 1962–
    Lynching in North Carolina : a history, 1865–1941 / Vann R. Newkirk.
        p.   cm.
    Includes bibliographical references and index.

    ISBN 978-0-7864-9558-0
    (softcover : alkaline paper) ∞

    1. Lynching—North Carolina.   2. Murder—North Carolina.
3. North Carolina—Race relations—History.   I. Title.
HV6465.N67 N49 2014
364.1'34—dc22   2008040033

BRITISH LIBRARY CATALOGUING DATA ARE AVAILABLE

Cover images © Shutterstock/Clipart

Manufactured in the United States of America

McFarland & Company, Inc., Publishers
    Box 611, Jefferson, North Carolina 28640
    www.mcfarlandpub.com

Table of Contents

Preface

On July 20, 1901, an article published on the front page of the Wilmington *Morning Star* announced that D.B. Jones had been taken from jail and lynched. As reported by the newspaper, "Little can be learned of the LaGrange affair save that during the night ... cries of distress and pistol shots rent the air ... and the would be negro rapist disappeared."[1] While such reports were not uncommon in the last century, the violence that they chronicle has long been an unspoken and for the most part an unwritten part of North Carolina history. Such silence is perplexing considering the role this violence played in shaping North Carolina's political landscape. For instance, during the late 1800s supporters of the Democratic Party used white supremacy, lynching, and mob violence to smash the Republican Party and disenfranchise African American voters.

Yet lynching and mob violence in the Old North State was more than just a political phenomenon. In case after case whites used such violence to remind blacks of their inferior social status. Therefore they lynched their victims for all sorts of trivial matters: casting an unwarranted glance at a white woman, testifying in court, arguing with a white person, or violating a contract. Moreover, North Carolina sanctioned this violence by refusing to arrest or apprehend most of the perpetrators of these crimes.

When I was a child stories of this carnage resonated through my home, thanks in large part to accounts shared by my grandfather. One of particular note was that of Dock Rogers, who was shot, tied to a truck, and dragged through the streets of Burgaw, North Carolina. I could only wonder who was Dock Rogers? What caused this violent act? Was this story real? Over the years the need to answer these questions has led me to write this book. It has also led me to understand my grandfather's central purpose in telling me these stories—namely, that the victims of lynching and mob violence were real people and that the incidents in which they lost their lives actually happened. Most had families, and since most were young one can only wonder what impact they or their offspring might have made on society.

1

However, the very fact that many of the victims of lynching were real people with real lives has led me to understand how even today the propensity for mob violence is never far from the surface. Take, for example, the 1998 lynching of James Byrd in Jasper, Texas; the 1998 murder of Matthew Sheppard in Fort Collins, Colorado; the 2007 rape and torture of Megan Williams in Logan County, West Virginia; or the 2008 murder of Lawrence King in Oxnard, California. In order to understand why crimes like these still exist, we need to look no further than deep-seated divisions that still tear at the hearts of many communities, or to the resurgence of hate groups across the nation. Although many Americans might conclude that such division has always been a part of American society, they cannot deny that such polarization has fostered years of racial and other kinds of violence and conflict.

It is my belief that the key to overcoming division and racial hatred is to ensure that everyone recognizes the central trait that makes us members of our society — our humanity. By chronicling the lives of the victims and the tragic events that led to the deaths of dozens of North Carolinians, I seek to inspire the reader to view the humanity of all people regardless of ethnicity. Some of the photographs in this book are of poor quality but I have chosen to include them because of their historic value. Finally, in recording these tragic events I seek to ensure that the victims will become more than just numbers, as scholars have so often presented them, and that their stories will be preserved for the ages.

Introduction: A Place in Lynching Lore

As night fell on the eighth of September 1891, a mob in Sampson County, North Carolina, kidnapped Mack Bess and carried him to a clearing near the outskirts of Parkersburg. Although Bess defended himself vigorously, he had little chance against men determined to inflict punishment. Holding Bess down, the mob cut off his penis. Then they forced a noose around his neck and hung him from a telegraph pole.[1]

For most of the next day the badly mutilated body remained dangling on the pole where the passengers of a train and hundreds from the surrounding community viewed it. But why did the mob inflict such a terrible punishment on Mack Bess? He was a sharecropper who had no previous legal problems, and there appeared to be no reason anyone would want to harm him, but Mack Bess stood accused of violating the chastity of white womanhood. Two days earlier, as a drunken Bess walked down a country road, he staggered into a woman who claimed he had attempted to rape her.[2] To avenge this transgression, a mob issued the only punishment it considered suitable. Death.

Sadly, Bess's death was not a rare occurrence. In the period between 1865 and 1941, 168 North Carolinians died at the hands of mobs, ranking the state ninth highest in terms of the number of lynching victims. However, for many years most of the world knew little about this violence.[3] Even when newspapers covered lynchings in North Carolina, many of the frightening details were obscured by sensational portrayals of white virgins and ravenous "black brutes" for whom righteous men delivered swift retribution.

In 1909, Ida Wells-Barnett wrote:

> Our country's national crime is lynching. It is not the creature of an hour, the sudden outburst of uncontrolled fury, or the unspeakable brutality of an insane mob. It represents the cool, calculating deliberation of intelligent people who openly avow that there is an "unwritten law" that justifies them in putting human

3

> beings to death without complaint under oath, without trial by jury, without
> opportunity to make defense, and without right to appeal.[1]

The fact that between 1865 and 1900 an average of two persons each year died at the hands of mobs attests to North Carolina's culpability in this national crime, but until the mid–1920s most white North Carolinians refused to take note of the violence spreading across the state. In fact, most whites accepted violence and lynching as a part of daily life.[2]

Nonetheless, in 1893, North Carolina passed a law that classified lynching as a felony, set up a superior court to hear cases in a county adjacent to the one in which a lynching occurred, required that sheriffs secure their jails, and made the county in which a lynching occurred liable for damages. The law, however, did little to reduce mob violence in North Carolina. Sheriffs charged with defending prisoners found it difficult to shoot neighbors and friends to protect a suspect.[3] "Even juries drawn from adjoining counties were likely to have among their number relatives, friends, fellow participants, or sympathizers of the defendants who refused to vote for convictions."[4] With these weaknesses, few were convicted; apathetic sheriffs retained their offices and none of the victims' families ever collected an indemnity.[5] As long as the men who made up the juries believed lynching was a useful method for controlling African Americans and for defending the chastity of white women, lynching remained strong.[6]

Until the early 1900s, few scholars showed an interest in investigating the causes of lynching. Sociologists and psychologists were among the first scholars to devote considerable interest to the study of lynching. Members of both disciplines saw lynching as a well-defined example of a social problem. They were not satisfied with merely attributing lynchings to racial prejudice and the uncontrollable actions of mobs.[7] These scholars felt that whites resorted to lynching not simply to wreck vengeance but to terrorize and restrain a lawless element in the negro population. Thus, lynching represented a sporadic outburst of primeval racism that was fueled by the failure of Southern law enforcement to act decisively at the first sign of violence.[8] The problem with such an interpretation is that it took black vice for granted, and it assumed lynching was a product of Southern backwardness.

The dependency of the South on cotton in the late nineteenth and twentieth centuries led others to examine the economic factors that caused lynching. Led by Arthur Raper these scholars concluded that even a slight decline in the price of cotton could lead to massive unemployment across the South.[9] This undoubtedly increased economic competition between blacks and poor whites. Lynching emerged as a means of reducing black competition and securing white economic security, but it did not just benefit poor whites. Throughout much of the period between the late nineteenth and early twentieth centuries, white planters faced a constant fear that black sharecroppers and poor whites would form a multiracial alliance that could demand better working conditions and improved wages. Since the threat of such a coalition was greatest when the price of cotton was low, planters tolerated lynching because it nurtured enmity and division among workers.[10]

Others attempted to view lynching in the role of honor in the South. Throughout much of the period before the Civil War, Southern planters held an extreme distrust of economic development and the creation of strong local governments that would challenge their hegemony. For this reason, they only supported the establishment of weak governments that barely had enough power to preserve social order.[11] To maintain control they depended on coercion and a code of honor that had at its core the protection and veneration of white women and racial purity. At the end of the Civil War, Southerners transferred these beliefs into an elaborate system of behavior that "required white men to respond to challenges to their honor by acting outside of the law."[12] Sexual acts between black men and white women proved especially bothersome and had to be handled accordingly. Thus, lynching was a response of white men trying to protect the chastity of white womanhood.

After the 1955 murder of Emmett Till, writers issued a plethora of lynching case studies. Unlike earlier comprehensive examinations, case studies provided a voice for local events by showing that they often operated independently of any larger framework. Scholars have used local case studies to give meaning to the broader problem by arguing that a specific case typified some larger issue.[13]

While this framework has it benefits, it also has its pitfalls. For one, since lynching was more common in the Deep South, most case studies have shown a tendency to chronicle this region. This focus has allowed states like North Carolina to gloss over its own guilt. In an editorial published in the *Asheville Citizen*, Walter Adams, longtime editor of the paper, suppresses North Carolina's bloody past by exclaiming, "North Carolina has striven hard to avoid lynching. There is no state in the South which has a better record."[14] Adams was keenly aware of North Carolina's lynching legacy, but because North Carolina law declared that a lynching only occurred when a person was taken from a jail or from the custody of law enforcement officials, the number of recognized lynchings in North Carolina was far fewer than in the Deep South.[15] Due to this fact, Adams proudly proclaimed his state's moral superiority while condemning the Deep South for its lynching problem. Despite this fact, did Tom Jones's soul find comfort that he died in a state where, after he was murdered, a mob composed of men, women, and children cut off his ears and fingers for souvenirs?[16] In the same light, was Powell Green glad that Franklinton police saved him only to see vigilantes overpower the guard and drag him to death?

In blotting out North Carolina's sins, Adams was not alone. Writing in the *State Magazine*, R.C. Lawrence declared, "The lynchers of the law have been put down in Carolina ... and our state now happily enjoys a record second to none of her Southern sisters in securing the triumph of the orderly processes of the law."[17] Prominent North Carolina historian Hugh Lefler was even more misleading in *North Carolina History, Geography, Government*, a widely used textbook: "Nowhere in the South did whites and negroes live together more peaceably than in North Carolina.... Beginning in Aycock's time whites and negroes became more friendly and learned to work together for their own good."[18] Not surprisingly, Lefler conveniently failed to mention that during Aycock's term as governor, North Carolina experienced eleven lynchings.

That historians were unwilling to saddle North Carolina with the baggage of lynching does not remove the state from its responsibility in the death of dozens of its citizens. From the end of the Civil War until the mid–1920s, the culture of lynching prospered in North Carolina, and lynchings were often public spectacles attended by politicians, civic leaders, women, and children alike. However, what set North Carolina apart from the Deep South was the rapid decline of mob violence inside its borders after 1922. That such a decline occurred in the violent period immediately after World War I makes it one of the focal points in America's quest to end lynching.

Yet, despite the notoriety of dozens of cases of mob violence and lynching in North Carolina, due to the passing of time, most have long since slipped into oblivion. Moreover, with the exception of a handful of lynching specialists, even those who concentrate on the study of North Carolina would be hard pressed to identify or recall even the name of one victim. Accordingly, this study has been prepared in the hope of preserving the memories of those who perished at the hands of lynch mobs in North Carolina. This study also seeks to explore the question of why North Carolinians tolerated lynching and mob violence. However, it does not provide insight into a phenomenon that is unique to North Carolina, namely, the rapid decline of mob violence within the state after 1922. For that reason, as its final objective this study will examine the key cases and events that influenced North Carolina to take the lead nationally in ending lynching and mob violence.

It would be a mistake to think that the study of mob violence in one state would guarantee a total understanding of the problem. Moreover, due to factors that are unique to North Carolina, it is impossible to apply everything learned from a study of mob violence in the state to other states. Still, the study of North Carolina lynching history does have many benefits. It allows the chance to feel our way through the fog that surrounds mob violence and to view its long-term ramifications. It also casts light on changing social and political conditions faced by North Carolina in the transitional period that marked the boundary between the Jim Crow era and World War I.

1

Lynching the Carolina Way

It is uncertain when the first lynching occurred in North Carolina; however, what is certain is that the violence that erupted at the close of the Civil War played a major role in shaping race relations in North Carolina. As one prominent scholar of the era stated, "The stresses of the Civil War, such as racism, regional loyalties, political factionalism, [and] economic tension ... inured people to violence in a way that seemed to make lynching increasingly easy to contemplate."[1] This was especially true in North Carolina, where at the close of the Civil War there was considerable fear that freedmen and their Northern carpetbag allies would challenge white hegemony.[2] In response to these fears, violence became a useful tool. To prevent blacks from voting in Edgecombe County, conservatives castrated eleven freedmen who supported the Republican Party.[3] In nearby Chatham County, nightriders administered hundreds of whippings to black citizens.[4] To end the violence, Governor William Woods Holden urged local law enforcement to uphold order.* However, since many local officials were ex–Confederates who had little heart for arresting friends and neighbors, they did not enforce Holden's order.

Emboldened by the governor's weakness, conservatives formed the Constitutional Union Guard, a Klan-affiliated group.[5] "Members of the group promised to work for the overthrow of the Republican regime and to resist by arms any oppression upon their legal rights."[6] The arrest of several blacks for grave robbing presented the Guard with a chance to strike. Using a ruse, sev-

---

*Holden had little support among white conservatives. As a young man he purchased the North Carolina Standard, the official organ of the Democratic Party. As editor he became a champion for political reform. In 1858 he made an unsuccessful bid to become governor of North Carolina by championing states' rights and the expansion of slavery. Several years later, he changed his position to support the Union. However it was his actions at the close of the Civil War that earned him the lasting enmity of whites across the state. In 1865, he was appointed as provisional governor of North Carolina. The next year he organized the Republican Party and subsequently won a full term as governor by a vote of 92,325 to 73,594. However, from the onset he faced enormous challenges such as extending full political rights to blacks — something most whites in the state were unwilling do. He also faced major challenges from the Ku Klux Klan.

eral members entered the Lenoir County jail and removed four African Americans and a white man suspected of supporting the Republicans. A short distance away they executed the men and withdrew into the darkness.[7] Several weeks later, Lewis Cogden, an African American charged with theft, was snatched from a wagon and hung from a nearby tree.[8]

In May 1869, the Constitutional Union Guard assassinated Sheriff O.R. Colgrove of Jones County. Born in New York, Colgrove came to North Carolina as part of the Reconstruction administration. An ardent opponent of the Klan, Colgrove actively challenged and arrested Klansmen throughout Jones County. As a result, on May 1869, the Constitutional Union Guard held a meeting and made plans to kill Colgrove. In short order, members of the Guard collected money for the deed and proclaimed that Colgrove's death would be followed by one of the "best barbecues in the county."[9] Several days later as the sheriff traveled near his home, Klansmen unleashed a fatal blast that killed Colgrove and Amos Jones, a black traveling companion.[10]

Three months later the Klan struck again. This time the target was M.L. Shepperd, a Pennsylvania carpetbagger. After serving in the federal army, Shepperd remained in North Carolina where he gained a seat on the Lenoir County Commission and organized a black militia regiment. However, the presence of armed blacks raised the ire of conservatives. To rid themselves of the regiment, on August 16, 1869, Klansmen secretly entered Shepperd's sawmill and murdered the commissioner.

Following the murders of Colgrove and Shepperd, Governor Holden sent a militia company to Lenoir. Although several Klansmen were arrested, none of the defendants were convicted for the murders. Nonetheless, in response to the attacks, the North Carolina Legislature passed the Shoffner Act in 1869. This law allowed the governor to declare martial law in any county where local officials failed to maintain state law. To punish Klansmen, the law allowed state officials to move the trial of those charged with wearing a mask, murder, or conspiracy to another county.[11]

To test the governor's resolve, in May of 1869 Klansmen murdered prominent Republican leader John W. Stephens in the Caswell County courthouse.[12] Several months later, the Klan murdered Wyatt Outlaw, a black Republican organizer, and hung him in front of the Alamance County courthouse. Stunned by these acts, Holden declared martial law and sent troops into Alamance and Caswell Counties. The governor's actions, however, came too late as intimidation and violence allowed conservatives to garner enough political strength to impeach Holden.

After Holden's impeachment Klan activity declined across eastern North Carolina. But, in the western part of the state, Klan violence remained a serious problem. On April 8, 1871, Klansmen broke into the home of Aaron Biggerstaff, a Republican organizer, and seized the elderly man. A short distance away they hung him from a tree and left him for dead. Fortunately, before he died neighbors noticed his plight and saved him. Although officials arrested several suspects, the presence of Klansmen on the jury ensured their swift release.[13]

At any rate the resurgence of Klan activity in western North Carolina alarmed radical Republicans. Accordingly, in 1870 Congress passed the Ku Klux Klan Act, which made the activity of unlawful "combinations" illegal. In areas where such combinations existed, the law allowed the president to suspend habeas corpus and proclaim martial law. Using the new law officials arrested hundreds of Klansmen, thereby decimating the organization.

Despite this fact, the Klan's reign of terror was effective since Democrats regained control of the legislature and the governor's office. Once in office the Democrats amended the state constitution. This change reduced the political strength of Republicans and their African American supporters by allowing the General Assembly, instead of voters, to select magistrates. The magistrates in turn elected county commissioners. Thus, the legislature, instead of local voters, controlled county taxes and financial policy. This charge also "rendered the Republicans impotent in both state and county financial policy."[14]

A second change prevented Republicans from occupying the office of Superior Court judge. Instead of electing Superior Court judges using a district system, a process sure to seat several Republicans or an occasional African American, the legislature went to a statewide election process. This ensured that "unless Republicans recaptured the Legislature all future Superior Court Justices would be Democrats."[15] This would have dire long-term consequences for North Carolina, since Democratic justices consistently refused to punish lynch mob participants.[16]

Yet, despite the legislation, the year 1880 witnessed a Republican resurgence. After a bitter campaign Republicans recaptured the Second Congressional District seat. They also won fourteen seats in the legislature; the sheriff's office in Craven, Jones, Lenoir, Northampton, and Edgecombe Counties; and a host of lesser offices. This represented a serious setback for conservatives. After all, political life centered around the county seat for whites.[17] Thus, having a black county commissioner or sheriff mattered a great deal more than who represented the area in Washington.

In the wake of these victories conservative newspapers unleashed a succession of articles that raised the specter of black rule. These articles also increased an even greater horror — that of racial equality. To prevent this from happening, violence once again became a useful tool to keep African Americans in their place. Thus, as one Southerner wrote:

> The conviction that the black man must now and then be intimidated in order to keep him from forgetting the bonds Southern tradition have set for him is firmly rooted in the consciousness of many Southern people. So unquestioned

is this philosophy that at times lynchings are planned and carried through not under the fierce compulsion of mob hysteria but by men who have calmly besieged themselves to the performance of a painful duty which according to their rights is necessary for the good of society.[18]

As a result of such beliefs the 1880s would usher in one of the most violent eras in North Carolina history. One of the most notable acts of terror to take place during this period was the 1887 lynching of Benjamin White. While many aspects of the case have been lost, reports suggest that White suffered from mental illness.[19] Possibly maddened by the warm May temperatures, White removed his clothes and ran into the woods. As he wandered through the forest, he noticed a white teenager and her younger companion walking down a road toward Tarboro.[20] Suddenly, White rushed from his hiding place and grabbed the girl. By the standards of the day, touching the girl was enough to warrant a stiff jail sentence. However, as they struggled, he cut the girl and tore her dress, signing his death warrant. Before he could seriously injure the teen, police arrived and placed him in the Tarboro jail. That they did not seriously injure White perhaps attests to the fact that most in Tarboro knew of his mental state.

Nonetheless, as news of the attack spread, a mob gathered outside the jail. To protect White, officials sent the suspect to nearby Williamston for safekeeping.[21] However, this precaution only delayed the attack. Shortly after sunset several men hijacked a train and headed to Williamston. When they reached the town, the vigilantes seized White and leisurely headed back to Tarboro. Marching to the outskirts of the town they hanged the doomed man and unleashed a deadly volley.[22] To explain their actions, the group attached a note to White's body:

> We hang this man not in passion, but calmly and deliberately with a due sense of responsibility we assume. We take executive power in this case and hang this man, because the written law provided no adequate penalty to the crime. And be it understood, we have done this act and will repeat it under similar circumstance.[23]

For African Americans the lynching of White caused considerable concern. R.S. Taylor, the editor of the *Edgecombe Watchman*, demanded a public hearing to identify members of the mob.[24] However, several days later Taylor received a threatening letter that demanded he stop discussing the case or suffer the same fate as White.[25] Afraid for his safety, Taylor fled and the effort to punish the murderers ended.

Less than a year after Tarboro vigilantes killed White, North Carolina mobs struck again, this time in the central part of the state, in Granville County. On September 4, 1888, a mob attacked the Granville County Jail in Oxford and removed three African American sharecroppers, Henry Tanner, John Tanner, and Alonzo Smith, who were charged with setting a string of suspicious fires.[26] When the mob reached the outskirts of Oxford, they hung all three men. The violence, however, could have easily been avoided. Shortly after arresting the men, threats of violence prompted the sheriff to enlist the local militia to protect the jail.[27] With the militia in place, the mob that surrounded the courthouse dispersed, and the siege appeared broken. That being the case, the sheriff dismissed the militia. The next night, the mob hastily reformed and attacked the jail. Although the sheriff quickly recalled the soldiers, it was too late to intervene.

The 1890s would see even more egregious acts of violence as blacks reasserted their political rights by forming a political alliance with poor whites. This resurgence caused considerable concern among Democratic leaders. Perhaps no voice of opposition was greater than that of Charles B. Aycock. Born less than a year before the outbreak of the Civil War, "the experiences of his family during War and Reconstruction supplied him with a lifelong veneration for the people of the South, distrust of the North and distaste for the Republican Party."[28] Moreover, as the son of a slaveholder, "Aycock never lost his conviction that the black race was inferior to the white race."[29]

After graduating from the University of North Carolina in 1881, Aycock opened a law office in Goldsboro. Over the next decade he gained a reputation for his quick wit. In a case brought against the Seaboard Airline Railroad, a plaintiff claimed that the railroad had seriously damaged his hearing. Aycock began his cross-examination by lowering his voice until almost in a whisper he obtained answers from the plaintiff. Suddenly, Aycock shouted, "I thought you couldn't hear."[30] The cross-examination had the desired effect, and the judge ruled for the railroad.[31]

Due to Aycock's skill as a lawyer, he was appointed U.S. district attorney for the Eastern District of North Carolina in 1892. However, the fusion of Populists and Republican Parties and the reemergence of blacks in politics renewed Aycock's interest in Democratic Party politics. As a spokesman for the Democratic Party, Aycock canvassed the state urging the Populists to return to the Democratic Party. However, more importantly he launched a verbal assault against the Republican Party and its black supporters. In a speech given before the Democratic State Convention, Aycock declared:

> We have had two periods of Republican rule in North Carolina — from 1868 to 1870 and from 1896 to 1898. That party contains a large number of respectable white men; the negro constitutes two thirds of its voting strength. Government can never be better than the average of the virtue and intelligence of the party that governs. The Republicans insist that we have never had negro rule in North Carolina; that the Republican Party elects white men to office, and that this fact gives us a government of white men. Governor Russell in his message to the last legislature vindicates himself against the charge of appointing negroes

to office, and proudly boasts that out of 818 appointments made by him, not more than eight were negroes. He misses the point which we made, and make against his party; it is not alone that Governor Russell put eight negroes in office and his party a thousand more, but that the 125,000 negroes put him in office.[32]

In 1898, at Aycock's insistence the Democratic Party unveiled a white supremacy campaign, which relied on speeches, editorials, and threats of violence to shape public opinion to remove blacks from the political process.[33] When he arrived in Concord to promote the campaign, the town was gripped by fear. A few weeks earlier a twelve-year-old girl was murdered as her family attended Sunday school. Officials hastily rounded up two black sharecroppers and charged them with murder. The next day a group of men stormed the jail and lynched the prisoners on the outskirts of Concord. Using this tragedy to his advantage, Aycock declared:

> In the east we have negro juries to interpose between the vicious of their race and the meeting of justice ... why you white men of Cabarrus don't even wait for the law when negroes have dishonored your helpless innocent women.[34]

In large part, due to Aycock and the white supremacy campaign, on election day Democrats swept to victory. However, the tensions stirred up by the campaign refused to abate. On the day after the election, rowdies in Wilmington killed nineteen blacks and burned the building that housed the *Wilmington Record*.[35] The next day Democrats who instigated the riot forced the city's Fusionist leaders to resign in order to make way for the new "white man's" administration.[36]

Following the Wilmington riot, Democrats introduced a bill to end black suffrage. This bill required all North Carolina voters to pass a literacy test and to pay a poll tax before voting. To ease the fear of poor whites, the bill contained a "grandfather" clause that allowed voters to cast a vote regardless of literacy if their grandfather had voted before January 7, 1867. These concessions, however, failed to ease the fear of poor illiterate whites. Aycock, now the Democratic candidate for governor, maintained that the solution to this problem was to educate poor whites.[37] Thus, education for whites as well as white supremacy became the focus of the election.

At a rally held in Forest City to build support for the suffrage amendment, more than four thousand people turned out to hear Alfred Waddell, leader of the recent Wilmington riots. Shortly before the speaker took the podium, a parade led by fifty boys and girls on bicycles and one hundred ladies attired in white, symbols of white purity, marched through Forest City.[38] Waddell told the crowd, "If they found the negro out voting they should warn him to leave and if he refused, kill him [and] shoot him down in his tracks."[39]

Intimidated by Democrats, on election day many blacks stayed away from the polls and the suffrage amendment passed 182,217 to 128,285. Two months later Aycock captured the governor's office with one of the largest majorities ever recorded. Aycock's victory, however, failed to ease growing racial tensions. During his first three months in office, lynch mobs claimed the lives of three African Americans. The most gruesome of these acts was the lynching of James Walker. According to local reports, on March 20, 1902, after prominent Washington, North Carolina, physician Dr. David Tayloe and his family ate breakfast, the family was stricken with an unknown illness.[40] As there was a great deal of concern that Tayloe and his family might succumb, a doctor was summoned, a thorough examination was conducted, and a diagnosis rendered: Dr. Tayloe and his family were suffering from arsenic poisoning.[41]

Charles Brantley Aycock, circa 1902. During the controversial 1898 campaign Aycock played upon racial fears to win the Democratic nomination. Unfortunately, this led to an increase in racial violence and lynching (courtesy North Carolina Collection, University of North Carolina Library at Chapel Hill).

However, the central question remained: who poisoned the family? Suspicion quickly fell on the family's cook. However, when she was found suffering from the same symptoms, the focus of the investigation moved to another employee, eighteen-year-old Jim Walker, the Tayloes' driver. After Walker gave authorities a series of conflicting statements, officials decided to search his clothing. To their surprise, they found a bottle of arsenic and a box of rat poison.[42]

Faced with this evidence, Walker confessed. According to Walker, several days earlier he had gotten into an argument with the nanny. To settle the score, he put a teaspoon of arsenic into the coffee pot and a similar amount in some hash. For some reason, on this day the nanny did not eat her breakfast and Tayloe and his family ingested the tainted food.[43]

For Washington authorities, Walker's confession created a volatile situation as Tayloe's friends and neighbors now had a face and a name to which they could direct their anger. In view of this fact, authorities placed twelve men around the Washington jail to prevent trouble.[44] However, tension remained and the next day authorities transferred Walker to nearby Williamston for safekeeping. Yet, unlike in Washington, officials in Williamston made no provision to protect the jail. In fact, the city did not even have a nighttime jailer, which meant that after dark the jail was unguarded. And so on the night after Walker arrived in Williamston, a mob from Washington traveled to the town. After posting several men near Skewarkee Church to serve as sentinels, the mob broke into the jail. Then, over the next hour, the men methodically busted the hinges on Walker's cell with a sledgehammer.[45]

However, the hammering woke several citizens who lived near the jail. They tried to sound the alarm, but the sheriff was away in Raleigh. Others panicked by the noise contacted the town constable; however he made no effort to stop the vigilantes, claiming that "it was too late even to bother the mob."[46]

Nonetheless, members of the mob were still afraid that authorities would make an effort to rescue Walker. For that reason, they cut the telegraph lines leading to town. Then they made a hasty getaway with their quarry in tow. Upon reaching an isolated spot, they threw a rope over the limb of a gum tree, tied a noose around Walker's neck, and hoisted him into the air.[47] Within minutes, Walker was dead and the mob dispersed.

The next day, as news of the murder spread, hundreds visited the site to view Walker's lifeless body. After several hours of this spectacle, authorities, following the usual course, cut the body down and halfheartedly conducted a coroner's inquest. Then they announced that Walker had come to his death at the hands of unknown parties.[48] No further attempts were made to find Walker's killers.

Yet, despite Walker's death and two other extralegal executions, Aycock did nothing until the Society of Seattle, an antilynching organization offered $500 for the names of persons who committed acts of lynching in North Carolina.[49] Though he declared, "I do not care for outside aid in securing law and order in North Carolina,"[50] Aycock begrudgingly announced that North Carolina would offer a $400 reward for information leading to the arrest of anyone who participated in a lynch mob. The reward, however, attracted little attention since few believed Aycock was serious.[51]

This belief was borne out on June 19, 1902, when Salisbury police arrested two African American men, James and Harrison Gillespie, for the murder and robbery of a white woman. As usual, a mob surrounded the jail, and there was danger of lynching. To prevent such an occurrence, Governor Aycock ordered a company of the National Guard to defend the jail. However, before the militia could muster, the mob stormed the jail and seized the prisoners. A short distance away the mob hung both men.[52] Although the governor offered rewards totaling $300 for the capture of mob participants, not a single arrest was made.

Two months later mob violence struck Wayne County, the governor's home. In late August 1902, a plantation owner's wife saw a man approaching her house. Since it was harvest season and good field hands were hard to find, she invited the man inside. The man demanded that she submit to his sexual advances.[53] When the woman tried to escape, he dragged her to a nearby pine thicket where he raped, beat, and left the woman for dead.[54] When the assailant left, the woman crawled to her home and identified her attacker as Tom Jones, a field hand, who had previously worked for her father-in-law.

Needless to say, after the attack neighbors formed a posse and set out to find Jones. The trail seemed to have gone cold until a farmer spotted a man emerging from a nearby swamp.[55] After a brief chase, he apprehended the man, who was identified as Tom Jones.[56] Within minutes a hostile mob formed and several men threatened to lynch Jones on the spot.[57] Only the quick thinking of a deputy, who announced that Jones would be delivered back to the victim's family — as Southern honor dictated — prevented mob violence. When the suspect reached the plantation, the victim identified her attacker and, according to local reports, Jones acknowledged his guilt.[58] However, considering the fate that awaited a black man charged with rape, it seems improbable that Jones confessed to the crime. In most cases a confession provided the justification for mob action. As Walter Samuel Lockhart maintains in his thesis, this was a ritualistic aspect of lynching that often was done to defend mob action. Often when newspaper reporters made an attempt to verify statements made by victims, they found no one who had witnessed the crimes—yet throughout local communities rumors nonetheless circulated that the victim fully confessed before death. When a victim refused to confess his guilt, newspaper articles often highlighted the special details of the case to justify the actions of the attackers. In this case, when the woman's husband learned of the confession, he struck Jones with a brick and others battered the prisoner with gun butts and sticks.[59]

However, before the situation got out of hand authorities grabbed Jones and retreated to a nearby barn.[60] The situation soon became desperate as the mob descended upon the barn. When one of the officers foolishly opened the barn door, the mob surged inside.[61] In the confusion Jones made a bid to escape and ran toward the door. Unfortunately, he was greeted by the butt of a gun and knocked to the ground.[62] Then several men grabbed the doomed man and forced him into a nearby swamp. Once there the mob tied Jones to a juniper log and unleashed a barrage of gunfire.[63] Surprisingly, he clung to life. This led to perhaps one of the most unusual episodes in North Carolina lynching lore. Over the next thirty minutes, hundreds of people, including women and children, entered the swamp to view the injured man. After thirty minutes of this spectacle, the mob unleashed a second volley that killed Jones.[64]

Immediately afterward a mass of humanity descended upon his lifeless body, removing buttons, pieces of clothing and even body parts.[65] When the sheriff arrived, he formed a jury of inquest. However, as the jury undoubtedly contained many who sympathized with, or quite possibly were part of the mob they hastily drafted a statement of their findings:

> We the undersigned, empanelled as a jury to inquire the cause of the death of Tom Jones find that he came to his death by gunshot wounds inflicted by parties unknown to the jury, obviously by an outraged public acting in defense of their homes, wives, daughters and children. In view of the enormity of the crime committed by said Tom Jones, alias Frank Hill, we think they should have been recreant to their duty as good citizens had they acted otherwise.[66]

The release of the jury's findings ended efforts to investigate Jones's death. However, the violent nature of the attack spurred the efforts of antilynching activists in North Carolina. Perhaps none of the activists was more important than George White, the African American congressman representing the Second Congressional District of North Carolina. In an address to Congress he declared, "I tremble with horror for the future of our nation when I think of what must be the inevitable result if mob violence is not stamped out."[67] On that point White drafted a bill that proposed to make the murder of any citizen by a mob a treasonable offense. Thus, lynching would be a federal offense. The bill, however, was never seriously considered.

That White would even try to introduce this bill surprised many. However, for those who knew him, it fit squarely with his role as the champion of the negro race. Born in rural Bladen County several years before the outbreak of the Civil War, White's political views were shaped by the realities of Reconstruction when violence and terror against blacks were everyday events. To escape these conditions, in 1874 he packed his bags and headed to Washington's Howard University, one of the first institutions of higher education in the nation open to blacks.

The Howard campus, only six years old at the time, was rather small and spartan. In addition to three small brick classroom buildings, the campus contained two resident halls, one for each sex, and the Freedmen's Teaching Hospital. Surrounding the campus was a scattering of residential neighborhoods that had sprung up on land "sold off by the University to support its own precarious development."[68] Despite its drawbacks Howard's location placed White in close contact with many prominent members of the black race such as Fredrick Douglass, noted abolitionist and author; Fannie Coppin, principal of the Institute for Colored Youth in Philadelphia; and Ebenezer Bassett, the U.S. ambassador to Haiti. Without a doubt, these contacts awakened White's interest in the budding effort to improve conditions for blacks. For that reason, after graduation White returned to New Bern, North Carolina, where he launched a career as a lawyer.

Located at the crossroads of the Pamlico Sound and the great swamp belt of eastern North Carolina, New Bern was rather small and isolated. Unlike Washington, D.C., and many points across the South where whites were the majority and Jim Crow laws dominated the lives of African Americans, New Bern had a long history of racial harmony. "During the days of slavery, free blacks lived in New Bern with little open hostility from whites; one wealthy free black, John Stanley, owned some of the town's most desirable land and had at least 18 slaves in 1830."[69] In addition, free blacks operated several businesses and a school for their children.[70]

The Civil War, however, transformed New Bern's racial balance as hundreds of blacks flooded the city in search of freedom and improved economic opportunity. In due time the election of black aldermen, and the establishment of newspapers, schools, and a host of black-owned businesses allowed the city to gain a reputation as the unofficial capital of black North Carolina.[71] Hence, when White arrived, the climate was favorable for the entrance of an ambitious young lawyer. What made his situation so unique was that he was the city's only black lawyer. As a result, White quickly developed a blossoming business.

This success did little to satisfy White's political ambitions. In 1880 he won a seat in the legislature. After serving five years, White became solicitor for the northeastern district of North Carolina. As solicitor his dedication to the job was legendary. Moreover, "his animated and almost florid speaking style and his undeniable eloquence made him an extremely convincing and effective prosecutor."[72] An opposing lawyer gave this description of White:

> Swearing and roaring, the big yellow fellow [White] would rush at the jury Exclaiming, guilty? Yes, gentlemen, of course he's guilty. Why just watch his capers. He waits twell [sic] the moon goes down, then he puts guano sacks under his shoes to hide his tracks, and he slips up to the back of the hog pen and cuts that pig's throat, so he can't squeal and he runs. Now wasn't that just like a nigger?[73]

Despite White's skills as a solicitor, throughout his life he consistently sought higher office. In 1894 he entered the race for the congressional seat of the Second District, a region of intense corruption. As Eric Anderson writes, "For many politically active citizens in the district — white and black — dishonesty had become standard procedure."[74] Accordingly, White's decision to enter the campaign represented a breath of fresh air, and he won the election by a margin of more than four thousand votes. The victory, however, would be bittersweet. Shortly before his victory, South Carolina passed a law that disenfranchised blacks. This swept G.W. Murray, the black representative from South Carolina, from office leaving White as the champion of his race.

And champion of his race White proved to be. In 1897 he urged Congress to enforce the second section of the Fourteenth Amendment. This section required the federal government to reduce the representation of states that denied their citizens the right to vote. He also spoke out against rising racial violence and lynching in the name of protecting white chastity:

> I have examined that question [rape] and I am prepared to state that not more than 15 percent of the lynchings are traceable to that crime [rape] and there are many more outrages against colored women by white men than there are by colored men against white women.[75]

White's statement garnered applause from a large black audience in the Capitol's public gallery. However, in North Carolina the speech brought immediate condemnation. Josephus Daniels, editor of Raleigh's Democratic voice, the *News & Observer*, used White's speech as a platform to call for the expansion of white supremacy in North Carolina:[76] "It is bad enough that North Carolina should have the only nigger congressman.... White justifies assault by negroes on white Women by slandering white men ... appealing to the worst passions of his own race he emphasizes anew the need of making an end of him and his kind."[77]

Despite opposition in North Carolina, on January 20, 1900, White introduced a bill in Congress that made lynching a treasonable offense and created a bureau to investigate mob violence. Accompanying the bill was a petition signed by two thousand citizens from Massachusetts. The bill had little chance at becoming a law. When the Speaker of the House saw the bill, he referred it to the House Judiciary Committee, where it was rejected in committee and never heard from again.[78] For White, the loss represented the beginning of the end of his term in office. Six months after he introduced the antilynching bill, North Carolina passed a constitutional amendment that effectively ended black suffrage by requiring all voters to pay a poll tax and pass a literacy test unless their grandfather had voted before 1867. Angered by this amendment, White decided not to run for re-election, ending his efforts to end mob violence.

Nonetheless, the uproar caused by White and the continuing state of mob violence in North Carolina convinced officials that in order to stop vigilante justice the governor had to do more than call out the militia. To prevent lynching, the governor had to successfully prosecute and convict mob participants so that future mob participants would think twice about the consequences before taking actions. With many calling for stronger action, Aycock's successor, Robert Broadnax Glen, declared during his inaugural address, "Every effort will be made to discourage mob law, and lynching will never be permitted if it is possible for the strong arm of the law with all of its powers at its command to prevent it."[79]

To test the governor's resolve, eight months later vigilantes stormed the Craven County jail and lynched John Moore. Several days earlier a young man entered a small store in Clarks and robbed the proprietor with a meat cleaver.

As he ran from the store, the terrified woman shouted, "That nigger running down the road did the work."[80] Outraged men grabbed their guns and a posse hastily formed. Small groups of farmers scoured the brushes and creeks, and it appeared that the culprit had made his escape. However, when someone noticed John Moore walking toward Clarks they charged him with robbery.*

News of the arrest unleashed a furor as hotheads in the crowd slammed Moore to the ground and bloodied his face before authorities convinced the assailants to let the law take its course.[81] However, when a judge set Moore's bond at only $300, the farmers who formed the posse became enraged. That night they stormed the Craven County jail and hung Moore from a nearby bridge.[82] After a couple of days of excitement, a handful of editorial condemnations and an outrageous verdict by a coroner's jury of "death at the hands of parties unknown," the incident faded into memory.[83]

Governor Glenn made no effort to punish Moore's murderers. Exactly why Glenn did not act is a mystery; perhaps he was waiting for a stronger case or possibly he was concerned that the circumstances behind Moore's death could lead to inability of the state to convict. Whatever the case, the brutality of Moore's death galvanized Glenn, and it made him more determined to put an end to mob violence in North Carolina.

As one of the authors of the white supremacy amendment, Glenn realized that much of the violence spreading across North Carolina stemmed from the white supremacy campaign. In view of this fact, shortly after the election in 1904 Glenn and his supporters split from the main wing of the Democratic Party and formed a liberal wing. Using this group to build a political base, in 1904 he won the Democratic nomination for governor.[84] Once in office, Glenn launched an ambitious plan to attract industry to North Carolina. The jobs that accompanied industrial growth could be used to placate poor whites and thus keep them in the Democratic fold. However, before Glenn could launch his plan, the mob had to be brought under control.

A mob attack in the predawn hours of May 28, 1906, presented Glenn with the case in which to set an example.[85] Shortly after midnight a drunken rabble burst into the Anson County jail and lynched John V. Johnson, a forty-year-old white man. Johnson was charged with murdering his brother-in-law, and he was in jail awaiting trial.[86] Following the lynching, whites across the state called on officials to punish the mob participants. After all, most reasoned that failure to punish the men would lead to greater acts of violence against whites. With this in mind, the governor sent a special judge to Wadesboro so that the matter "would be sifted to the bottom."[87]

Over the next two weeks state officials arrested twenty-two men and

There were many questions surrounding Moore's guilt. When he was arrested, Moore claimed that he was at his home in Dover. Though he maintained that others could verify his whereabouts, officials never attempted to check his alibi.

charged them with lynching. At first few of the men took the charges seriously. As Walter Lockhart writes in his thesis, "Their attitudes were entirely conceivable considering the fate of previous lynch mob members."[88] News of the arrests led many whites to wonder what the world was coming to,[89] while for blacks the arrests represented a new phase in race relations: "This is one time when we all ain't in it."[90]

To ensure that the defendants had no undue influence on the jury, state officials moved the trial to Union County. This made little difference as officials still failed to convict the men. Throughout the trial the prosecution based its case on the 1893 lynching statute, which defined the crime of lynching. Unfortunately, the prosecutor failed to review the 1905 revisions that, while maintaining the essence of the older law, nonetheless altered the 1893 provision. The most important difference between the two codes was the failure of North Carolina to define lynching in the revision. This was extremely important because several years earlier the state's highest court had ruled that a "crime had to be defined within the body of law for prosecution to be valid."[91] Due to this technicality, the men charged with the Anson County lynching escaped jail.

Despite this setback, North Carolina officials were even more determined to make an example of a mob participant. From the moment the Anson County case ended, state officials made plans to ensure that the next opportunity would not be wasted. As a result solicitors across the state were updated on changes in North Carolina lynching laws and urged to prepare their cases more carefully the next time. And they would not have long to wait—a month after the Anson case, intruders broke into the Rowan County home of Isaac Lyerly and murdered the farmer, his wife, and two of his children.[92] Stunned by the carnage, another child escaped and ran from the house to get help. Unfortunately, the horror-stricken girl ran past the nearby homes of Lyerly's tenants and through some woods for help.[93] The child's actions led officials to view the tenants as suspects. Additionally, several days before the murder, Lyerly's wife got into an argument "with Della Dillingham over Della's habit of borrowing washtubs and returning them dirty."[94] In light of these facts, Rowan County officials arrested Lyerly's tenants, Neese, Henry, and John Gillespie and Jack Dillingham.

Two weeks later, when the suspects returned to Salisbury to stand trial, a mob of several thousand angry men surrounded the jail. Only the presence of a company of militia prevented the outbreak of violence. Yet, despite the potential for violence, when the governor asked the sheriff if he could defend the jail, he foolishly replied, yes.[95] As a result the governor dismissed the militia. No sooner had the troops departed than the mob stormed the jail. In the ensuing melee, deputies wounded one of the would-be lynchers and grazed several others. However, since the deputies did not shoot to kill, their attempts to defend the jail did not dissuade the horde. Consequently, the mob battered its way through the jail's door and seized the suspects. After some initial confusion, the mob took the prisoners to a field on the outskirts of Salisbury, where a crowd of more than three thousand watched as they hung and dismembered the men.[96]

News of the attack led Governor Glen to arrest eight men suspected of the crime. But when the men went before a grand jury, only George Hall and G.H. Gentle, both newcomers to Salisbury, were charged with murder.[97] After a short trial, a judge sentenced the men to fifteen years in prison. This turned out to be a Pyrrhic victory because most whites saw the state's case as one designed to punish men who had engaged in a shootout with police rather than a quest to punish mob members. For that reason, most whites felt they had little to fear from North Carolina officials in regard to extralegal violence.

Less than a year after the Salisbury convictions, North Carolina experienced one of its strangest cases of mob violence, which involved the lynching of African Americans by fellow blacks. In this case from Weldon, after receiving news of a sexual assault on a seven-year-old girl, police arrested Dick Whitehead, a hobo who had only recently entered the town.[98] Determined to punish the man, an African American mob seized Whitehead and hung him from a nearby tree.[99] Local officials refused to investigate the murder.[100]

Four years later, a second case that involved an African American mob appeared in newspaper headlines. The victim of this case was a con artist who made a living promoting carnivals and traveling vaudeville shows.[101] In December 1907, the promoter entered the small Johnston County hamlet of Pine Level and sold tickets for a big show. Later that evening when the ticket-holders arrived to see the show, they discovered that instead of the advertised bill, the big show was a one-man act performed by the promoter. Most were dissatisfied, and a few asked for their money back. The promoter refused to grant any refunds, and ticket-holders forced him to flee.

Two days later the man returned and announced he would give another show.[102] This brash display inflamed an already volatile situation and a group of black men seized the man.[103] At gunpoint, they tied him to a heavily used railroad track and returned to their homes. The next day the man's body was found along the railroad tracks.[104] Although officials launched an investigation, a jury of inquiry found insufficient evidence to indict anyone for the murder.[105]

In any case, black-on-black lynchings were extremely rare in North Carolina. Their infrequent occurrence coupled with attacks on outsiders and justifications provided by the mobs suggested a transferal of criminality beliefs, commonly held by whites, to African Americans. Whatever the causes for same-race lynchings, it is important to note that there were only three cases of black on black lynchings in North Carolina. For every black lynched in the state by other African Americans, whites lynched fifty-six blacks.

Election of Woodrow Wilson

After governing America for thirty-three of the forty-one-year period between 1869 and 1909, in 1910 cracks began to emerge in the Republican Party's dominance. The primary cause for this rift was a philosophical disagreement between Theodore Roosevelt and his handpicked successor, William H. Taft. As a progressive, Roosevelt felt that Taft had allowed himself to be influenced by the Republican Party's conservative leadership. Due to this belief, Roosevelt launched a bid to regain the presidency. Although he barnstormed the country and was the overwhelming choice of Republican voters, party leaders chose Taft as the party's nominee. As a result, Roosevelt and his followers bolted the party and formed the Progressive Party, thus setting the stage for the election of 1912.

For the Democrats, this split provided them with their first realistic chance of ending years of Republican dominance. Accordingly, the party nominated New Jersey Governor Woodrow Wilson. To build African American support in several key Northern states, Wilson sent a series of letters to Bishop Alexander Walters, of the African Methodist Episcopal Zion Church, in which Wilson maintained that blacks "could count on [him] for absolute fair dealing.... My earnest wish [is] to see justice done them in every matter, and not merely grudging justice. My sympathy with them is of long standing."[106] This got Walter's endorsement and played a role in influencing William H. Trotter and W.E.B. DuBois to support Wilson.

In the end, however, DuBois, Trotter, and others underestimated Wilson. Once elected he quickly came under the influence of Southern demagogues such as South Carolina's Ben Tillman and Georgia's Hoke Smith.[107] Moreover, pressure from these firebrands combined with Wilson's own racial prejudices convinced the president to reverse many social gains made by blacks. For example, he allowed subordinates in the District of Columbia to pass a law that made interracial marriage illegal. Then he permitted cabinet members to segregate, dismiss, or downgrade the jobs currently held by blacks.[108]

Southern Congressmen followed Wilson's lead, introducing a series of bills that attempted to nationalize Jim Crow. These proposed laws banned interracial marriage, prohibited blacks from becoming military officers, segregated trains and streetcars, and attempted to repeal the Fifteenth Amendment.[109] While such legislation had little chance of becoming law, it nonetheless filled newspaper headlines and colored public opinions. As Josephus Daniels had prophetically predicted during the 1912 campaign, the election of Wilson and Democrats led to the nationalization of Southern racial policy.[110]

In North Carolina, Wilson's election influenced the legislature to actively enforce laws that defined the state's color line. In one of the most colorful cases, *Johnson v. Board of Education*, J.S. Johnson, a white resident of Wilson County, attempted to enroll his children in a school for white children. Although Johnson was white and had no trace of African ancestry, his wife had a trace of African ancestry. The amount of African blood that flowed in his wife's veins was less than one-eighth, which allowed her to be legally classified as white. Nonetheless, due to a 1905 state law that forbade any child with any trace of African American blood, no matter how small, to attend a school for the white race, the school board refused to admit the children. As a result, Johnson filed suit; however, he was unable to overturn the law since in September 1914, the North Carolina Supreme Court ruled in the case that Johnson's children were black, despite the fact both of their parents were legally white.[111] Such cases were only a sideshow to the new reign of negrophobic violence which spread across North Carolina. One of the most notable examples of this violence was the 1913 lynching of Joseph McNeely in Charlotte.

Unlike many of the sparsely populated towns and rural communities of eastern and central North Carolina, where most extralegal violence took place, Charlotte in 1913 was a modern city with a population of more than 34,000. The city had a large and politically active black middle class. It also was the home of the *Star of Zion*, one of the most influential and politically active black newspapers in the South. Perhaps due to this fact, by 1910 the city boasted 154 black-owned businesses and a major black university. However, in August of 1913 none of the city's racial progress seemed important as Judge Lynch showed that even in a relatively enlightened bastion the long arms of vigilante justice could still strike terror. On the afternoon of August 24, 1913, Charlotte police were summoned to arrest Joseph McNeely, a young black man, for firing a pistol at anyone who crossed his path. Just what made McNeely open fire is unknown, but reports printed in the *Charlotte Observer* suggest that he was under the influence of cocaine.[112] Whatever the reason, when Charlotte police officer L.C. Wilson reached the scene, he did not see anything suspicious, but when he started down an isolated side street McNeely dashed from his hiding place and opened fire, wounding Wilson.[113] He turned and attempted to flee, but before he could make his escape, Wilson fired his revolver and wounded McNeely.[114] Fortunately for both men, the sound of the gunfire alerted other officers, who rushed Wilson to Presbyterian Hospital. Then they transported McNeely to Good Samaritan, the city's segregated black hospital.[115]

The officer's shooting raised the ire of many whites. Yet, few were willing to resort to mob violence until they read a story published by the *Charlotte Observer*, two days after the attack. With the headline "Wilson's Recovery Very Doubtful," the newspaper claimed that, contrary to early reports, Wilson was dying.[116] Moreover, according to the newspaper, he was becoming weaker by the hour.[117] This article inflamed an already volatile situation and soon rumors began to circulate that a mob was forming to lynch McNeely.[118]

In many ways such a threat seemed unlikely. Good Samaritan was located in the heart of Charlotte's second ward, a thriving community populated by hundreds of blacks who were prepared to resist white vigilantes—just the sort of environment usually shunned by mobs. However, in this case vigilantes decided to forgo their caution and make a bold attack upon Good Samaritan Hospital. As stated by the *Charlotte Observer*, less than twenty-four hours after McNeely was arrested, a small band of masked men entered the hospital.[119] When one of the officers guarding McNeely made a dash to call for help, several members of the mob surrounded him and took his gun.[120]

Then the vigilantes rushed up the stairs to McNeely's room. At this point they faced their last obstacle, Officer C.E. Earnhardt, who surrendered without firing a shot.[121]* Then several men dragged the doomed man into the street and unleashed a deadly fusillade.[122] Surprisingly, this did not kill McNeely. After lingering near death for several more hours, McNeely died in the county jail, the very place he was supposed to have been transferred earlier in the day.

Not surprisingly, McNeely's death led to public outrage over the performance of the city's police department. In an editorial published in the *Charlotte Observer*, the editor maintained:

> We do not at present undertake to say whether at least morally positive assurance of police non-interference had been received.... There and then two policemen with heavy revolvers in their hands permitted half a dozen mob men coming up a narrow stairway to overpower them without a shot fired on either side. We cannot assume that these policemen displayed moral cowardice for the reason usual in such cases, namely, that the lynching impressed them as a popular demonstration or act. We have no reason to believe that they were physical cowards. Why then, did they permit the mob to work its will? It further transpires that they profess inability to identify any member of the mob. That mob must have been composed of men and boys well known to them practically without exception and those who entered the hospital were masked only just enough not absolutely to compel recognition, while few or none of those outside were masked at all. In light of these facts we can but say that the county was very poorly served by those upon whom the immediate responsibility for averting threatened lawlessness and murder fell.[123]

There were good reasons to suspect police involvement in the murder. For one, on the day that McNeely was placed in Good Samaritan Hospital, the sheriff refused to transfer the suspect from the hospital to the county jail.[124] This decision greatly aided the mob. Another sign of possible police involvement occurred on the day of the lynching. Throughout the day the Charlotte city police and the sheriff had received telephone calls warning that a mob was form-

---

*Since none of the members of the mob knew McNeely, when they charged into the room one of the occupants pointed to the other side of the room: "That's the man ... he's the one you want." However, before the mob could make its move the other man shouted, "For the lord's sake, no ... I'm not the one." At this point several men placed a gun to Earnhardt's head and forced him to identify McNeely. Charlotte Daily Observer, 27 August 1913.

ing.[125] Yet, instead of taking precautions or reinforcing the officers guarding the hospital, the police did nothing.[126]

In the face of possible police duplicity, efforts by city and state leaders to solve the crime increased. The mayor of Charlotte offered a reward of $1,000 for information leading to the arrest and conviction of the men that murdered McNeely.[127] Several days later, Governor Craig announced his intent to vigorously prosecute the members of the mob.[128] Few, however, took the governor's proclamation seriously since the state had never in its history prosecuted a white man for murdering an African American. This belief was borne out several days later when the Mecklenburg Superior Court announced that it was unable to identify any suspects and closed the investigation.

Nonetheless, McNeely's murder was only a precursor of things to come. As the Wilson administration entered its second year in office, social and economic conditions across the country continued to decline for African Americans. As a result, hundreds of African Americans abandoned the farm in search of employment. Apparently, this led Jim Wilson to leave his home and move to Wendell, which lay just fifteen miles from Raleigh. However, instead of finding employment, less than a month later police charged him with the death of Anna Lynch, a thirty-eight-year-old housewife.[129]

Wilson's guilt, however, was less than certain since evidence suggests her husband's possible involvement in the murder. In an account given shortly after the murder, Lynch maintained that upon returning home on January 27, 1914, he was unable to find his wife. This did not cause concern, since his wife had a sick sister in Wendell.[130] A quick check of his sister-in-law's house revealed that his wife had never visited Wendell. Thus, Lynch searched his home and the surrounding area. Surprised when he didn't find his wife, he called his father-in-law and the two men started a new search. Near the door of the barn, they found a bloodstained hood belonging to the missing woman. About twenty yards away lay her lifeless body under a clump of brush. However, it appears that the discovery of his wife's body by her father was more than chance, since prior to the father-in-law's arrival Lynch claimed that he searched the same area but failed to find his wife or the bloody hood that led to her discovery.[131]

At any rate, police were unable to identify a suspect until they came upon a hobo camp one mile from the Lynchs.' When one of the camp's occupants tried to run into a thicket, police arrested the man and charged him with murder.[132] After a stern interrogation, which probably included a beating, the suspect identified as Jim Wilson confessed to the crime.[133]*† The next day however Wilson retracted his story, seriously weakening the case against him.[134] How-

---

*He also implicated James Knott, Sam Cheatham, Petersburg Marcus, and Worth Sanders.

†Law enforcement tactics such as beating a confession from a defendant, presenting evidence known to be false, or suppressing evidence pointing to the innocence of a defendant were not considered violations of a state's criminal defendant's rights in 1916.

ever, just as it seemed the case would fall apart, the victim's husband unbelievably provided police with a motive for the crime. On the day of the murder Lynch claimed he and his wife had visited a store in Wendell. After making a small purchase, he gave his wife a dollar and she headed home.* What surprised Lynch most about the visit to the store was a man that resembled Wilson lurking outside. "Most likely the men mistook the dollar for a large sum and probably followed his wife home."[135] Yet, despite the questions surrounding Lynch, chiefly his whereabouts at the time of the murder and his uncorroborated story, law enforcement officials did not investigate. Instead, the motive he provided became part of the evidence against Jim Wilson.

The murder of Lynch's wife created a frenzy as authorities, perhaps fearing a lynching, moved Wilson to nearby Selma for safekeeping.[136] After a few days in Selma, authorities transported Wilson back to Wendell to stand trial. However, in short order several dozen men surrounded the jail and demanded the suspect. In response the jailer barricaded the door and called a local militia company for assistance.[137] Unfortunately, the news that the militia was on the way panicked the mob, and they burst through the door and snatched Wilson while the jailer who was supposed to protect him cowered in a backroom.[138] A short distance away they tied a noose around his neck and hoisted him toward the sky. However, in their haste they bungled their first attempt to murder Wilson. A branch chosen to hang him was too weak and snapped under his weight. Undeterred, the mob tied the doomed man to a tree and unloaded their shotguns. In the aftermath of this violence, neither the sheriff nor Wendell police attempted to arrest any of his attackers.

On the heels of Wilson's lynching, a chorus of letters called on state officials to take stronger action against mobs. Officials did little until newspapers increased their condemnation of state leaders following the 1916 lynching of John Richards. The origins of this case stemmed from the murder of the prominent Wayne County planter, Anderson Gurley. As Gurley drove home from the sale of a bale of cotton, an assailant struck him in the head with an iron pipe.[139] Searching Gurley's pockets, the robber took thirty-five dollars and then threw his lifeless corpse into the frigid Neuse River. Two days later authorities arrested Jim Richards, a black field hand, as he tried to cash a blood-stained ten-dollar bill.[140] Other than blood-stained money, the sheriff had no conclusive evidence to link Richards to the crime. Undoubtedly, his race and the fact he had a relatively large sum of money were the only reason for the arrest.[141]

In spite of the flimsy evidence many whites remained convinced that Richards was guilty of murder and they began to plot his death. Moreover, the sheriff made it easy for vigilantes to carry out their plans. The day before Richards's death the sheriff declined an offer by the commander of local mili-

---

*Although Lynch claimed he and his wife visited a store in Wendell, deputies failed to explore the possibility that this was a ruse to cover his own guilt.

tia to put troops around the jail.[142] Then in a telephone call to state officials, the sheriff maintained that there was no danger of a lynching and he suggested that reports stating otherwise were greatly exaggerated.[143] Confident in his ability to defend the prisoners, or perhaps in concert with the gathering mob, the sheriff went to bed. The defense of the jail was left to the jailer.[144]

By 10:00 P.M. several hundred rowdies filled the streets of Goldsboro.[145] After shouting threats for a few hours, the mob broke into the jail.[146] In the darkness, several men grabbed the wrong man, who, though terrified, pleaded in desperation for his life.[147] Apparently, this moved the vigilantes, and they placed him back in his cell. The men then seized Richards and threw him into a waiting car.[148]

Driving back to Goldsboro from a possum hunt, the chief of police passed the cars containing the men. Suspicious about the volume of traffic leaving Goldsboro at that time of the night, he turned his car around and attempted to follow.[149] Vigilantes in the trailing cars slowed their vehicles down,[150*] and while the officer was stuck in traffic, others methodically murdered Richards. Analysis of a photograph made after the lynching suggests the mob castrated Richards before ending his life with gunfire.[151] At daybreak hundreds viewed the grisly work of the lynchers while a photographer did a brisk business selling copies of a picture he made of the crime.[152]

Richards's death unleashed an immediate call from newspapers across the state for action to punish the perpetrators and for the sheriff's removal for dereliction of duty.[153] In response, the sheriff maintained that there was little his office could do to protect the suspect considering the mood of the county toward lenient court sentences. Moreover, he pointed to a recent case from Mount Olive, in which an African American shot a white man.[154] When the judge heard the case, he sentenced the man to a long prison term that was later reduced. Edwards maintained the failure to inflict the death penalty in the case had a bad effect upon the county. "And we are now reaping what we have sown."[155]

Nonetheless, in response to the sheriff's actions and damning newspaper editorials, Governor Locke Craig launched a new offensive to punish mob participants. In a letter to a Raleigh newspaper, Craig called into the question the court's failure to indict or punish lynch mob participants despite evidence clearly linking many participants to murders.[156] This unleashed a furor across North Carolina. No voice of opposition was greater than Walter Clark, the chief justice of the North Carolina Supreme Court. Clark placed the blame for lynching on weak criminal laws. Moreover, he maintained that in 1918 there were 274 murders in North Carolina, giving the state the highest murder rate in the nation.[157] Yet, North Carolina laws did little to punish the offenders:

*It is quite possible that the police chief developed this story to cover his involvement in the lynching. Moreover, considering the confusion surrounding the jailbreak it is hard to imagine that members of the mob could identify the police chief or his car at night.

> There would be no lynching if the public were satisfied that they would be pro-
> tected against murder by an efficient administration of law against murder. Our
> people are as much opposed to lynching as any in the world, and they all earn-
> estly desire that crime should be punished by the courts. But the average man
> is not willing that the present carnival of homicide in North Carolina shall con-
> tinue in order that a few lawyers may make cheap reputations and good fees by
> acquitting murderers through the excessive number of challenges and the other
> devices by which justice is cheated in the courts.[158]

Clark did not explain the court's poor prosecution rate for persons charged with the crime of lynching. Instead, his prescription to curb lynching was to suggest a restructuring of state law that would reduce the time needed to convict and execute those charged with murder and rape. In developing this thesis, Clark failed to examine states such as Georgia, which practiced rapid prosecution and execution of criminals charged with murder and rape. Between 1880 and 1927, Georgia executed 487 persons. These executions had no effect on lynching, because mobs murdered 453 victims during the same period.

At any rate, Clark's call for stronger criminal laws was heartily endorsed across North Carolina. Letters poured into the governor's office from members of the legislature, lawyers, ministers, and others calling for a removal of legal challenges in cases of murder and lynching.[159] Therefore, there was little support to investigate Richards's murder. Within a few days, newspapers dropped their coverage and the Jury of Inquiry dropped the investigation. In its final report, the jury maintained that Richards's death came at the hands of persons unknown.

The Jim Crow Era

While North Carolina debated the merits of stronger criminal laws, the legislature passed a series of Jim Crow laws. These laws segregated rail cars, organized the militia in companies separated by race, and required the establishment of separate waiting rooms for whites and blacks. As if this were not bad enough, in 1913, Clarence Poe, editor of Raleigh's *Progressive Farmer*, launched an effort to establish rural segregation throughout the South. The plan he proposed was modeled after South African laws that become the precursor of apartheid. Although the legislature failed to adopt rural segregation, it nonetheless convinced blacks of the danger of not protesting racial inequality. Consequently, across the state blacks lashed out against Jim Crow. Charles Hunter, a St. Augustine school professor, declared there are no negro anarchists, nihilists, or socialists: there are no dynamiters with their bombs.[160] Thus, presumably there was no need for racial violence or laws that discriminated against blacks. Yet, despite rising black dissatisfaction, North Carolina officials did nothing to address these concerns and conditions for African Americans continued to decline.

Two years after Poe launched his rural segregation effort, D.W. Griffith's epic film *The Birth of a Nation* made its North Carolina debut. This was the first Southern showing of the film, which so far had only played in New York, Boston, Philadelphia, Washington, D.C., and Chicago. "That North Carolina enjoyed such favored status was due largely to the desire of Mr. (Thomas) Dixon to bring (the film) within the vision of many who had known him since boyhood."[161] Born in Shelby, North Carolina, several years before the end of the Civil War, Dixon was troubled by what he felt was an unfair depiction of the South.

That being the case, in 1901 after a brief career as a minister, he completed *The Leopard's Spots: A Romance of the White Man's Burden, 1865–1900*. Originally conceived as a response to *Uncle Tom's Cabin*, the book portrayed blacks as unrestrained barbarians who could only be controlled by a heroic Ku Klux Klan. What set the book apart was Dixon's penchant for appropriating actual historical events for the book's inspiration. In his *Leopard's Spots*, Charles Aycock is the model for his hero Charlie Gaston, who transforms into Alfred Waddell for several paragraphs to guide vigilantes during the Wilmington race riot.[162] Since he liberally borrowed historical events, "many readers could not separate fiction from fact and were unaware that Dixon had reversed the outcomes to make African Americans seem powerful and abusive."[163] At any rate the novel became a best seller and sold more than one million copies. The next year Dixon completed *The Clansman, a Historical Romance of the Ku Klux Klan*, which also became a best seller. Like his first book, *The Clansman* explored many of the same themes as *The Leopard's Spots*.

Motivated by the success of his books, "and possibly thinking of the enduring success of *Uncle Tom's Cabin* on stage, Dixon saw a dramatic version of his novels as a means of reaching an ever-wider audience."[164] For that reason, he put together a screenplay based on both books. Yet, like his literary works, the play conveyed his negrophobic view that blacks were not only inferior to whites but that the further removed blacks were from the civilizing influences of slavery the more they rapidly reverted to a state little better than wild beast. In such a state they posed a threat to white society.[165] Accordingly, segregation represented the only acceptable option. "This was the great lesson to be learned from Reconstruction and one that Dixon stressed was equally applicable to his own time."[166] That being the case, when *The Clansman* opened, Dixon boldly proclaimed:

> My objective is to teach the North, the young North, what it has known — the awful suffering of the white man during the Reconstruction period. Almighty God anointed the white men of the South by their suffering during that time immediately after the Civil War to demonstrate to the world that the white man must and shall be supreme.[167]

The volatile nature of the play, however, led critics to condemn the production. Shortly before the play opened in Raleigh, a report arrived from Norfolk that warned that it would inflame passions and destroy racial harmony.[168] Nonetheless, when tickets went on sale, theaters across Raleigh quickly sold out. After viewing *The Clansman*, the editor of the Raleigh *News & Observer* wrote, "It reminds us that the courage and despair of our fathers alone preserved the integrity of our race."[169] Even Governor Robert B. Glenn praised the stage show for its historical accuracy and for its propensity for correcting the unfair distortions of the past.[170]

Though the play gained increasing support, African Americans and a small group of vocal supporters vigorously opposed the production. The editor of the *Star of Zion* condemned Dixon's work, while in Charlotte an unidentified reader wrote, "I fear it will leave behind a new trail of lynchings. Why in the name of heaven should Tom Dixon have written so incendiary a thing?"[171]

Despite opposition, the success of *The Clansman* encouraged Dixon to transform the production into the motion picture *The Birth of a Nation*. Although boycotts were organized, the protests had little impact because Dixon shrewdly gained the support of politicians. For instance, shortly before the national premiere of the film, Dixon held a private showing at the White House for his college schoolmate Woodrow Wilson.[172] Several weeks later he held a showing for congressmen and Supreme Court justices.[173] When New York officials attempted to ban the film, Dixon argued that the film had been shown in the White House and therefore was suitable for general viewing. For that reason, the film became a runaway success. "White audiences wept and cheered the story, and the film spurred the birth of a new Ku Klux Klan."[174] However, perhaps the most enduring legacy of the film was a dramatic increase in racial violence. In Lafayette, Indiana, a white moviegoer murdered a black teenager immediately after he left the theater.[175] In Omaha and Chicago the movie incited mobs to riot.[176]

When the movie opened in North Carolina, public sentiment was much more subdued. In the four cities where the film appeared, most patrons were much more interested in its technical innovations. Additionally, moviegoers were dismayed at the Northern protests that accompanied the film. Since many white North Carolinians had long since accepted the negrophobic ideas of Dixon as truth, most felt there was nothing offensive or inaccurate about the film. Nonetheless, shortly after the film's North Carolina tour, a series of violent lynchings shook the state.

In April 1916, the sexual predation of a young white girl led to one of the most outrageous cases of mob violence in North Carolina history. Details of the case as presented by local newspapers suggest that this attack stemmed from the molestation of a six-year-old girl by an African American teenager. However, oral accounts prevalent in the local African American community suggest that the attack stemmed from an affair between the girl, who was much older, and seventeen-year-old Will Black.[177]

Newspapers from the period consistently printed inflammatory articles that highlighted cases of rape of white women by African American men. The purpose of the articles was to cover up a more complex truth. Throughout the period from 1880 to 1922, sexual liaisons between blacks and whites were not uncommon. "Whites however could not countenance the idea of a white women desiring sex with a negro, thus any physical relationship between a white woman and a black man had by definition to be an unwanted assault."[178] Quite often, however, African American men risked life and limb to maintain relationships with white women.

On that account it is easy to imagine Will Black cautiously making his way to a barn in order to maintain a clandestine relationship. Unfortunately, Black's entrance into the barn did not go unnoticed.[179] Looking out a window in her home, the girl's mother saw him enter the barn. Grabbing a stick she rushed to the barn and struck Black.[180] Unfortunately as he made his escape Black grabbed the stick and knocked the woman senseless.

To escape the inevitable repercussions, Black ran into some nearby woods and made his way home, where his father armed him and urged the young man to make his way out of the state.[181] But before he could get out of the county, a posse discovered Black hiding in a swamp. In the subsequent shootout Black wounded a deputy and the registrar of deeds.[182] When Black's gun jammed, the posse captured him.[183] Battered and thrown into the back of a wagon, the youth was taken by officials to Snow Hill for safekeeping. No sooner had he reached his jail cell when a mob stormed the building.[184] As mob members battered their way through the jail's front door, the sheriff rushed him out of the back door to a waiting car. After a few tense moments, Black and the sheriff reached Raleigh where he was deposited for safekeeping.

Since they were unable to level their anger at Will Black, local whites arrested the teenager's father, Joseph Black, as an accessory.[185] According to Leon Tyson, the girl's father, the elder Black visited his home two days earlier and threatened to kill him if anything happened to his son.[186] Stunned, the judge arrested Black and charged him with attempted murder.[187] However, as word of the arrest spread, hundreds of angry farmers invaded Goldsboro, and the sheriff moved the elder Black to Lenoir County for protection. Even so, news of the transfer reached local vigilantes, and a drunken mob gathered in downtown Kinston.

That night, shortly after 9:20 P.M., scores of men burst into the jail. When Black refused to speak or stand, the mob picked him up and threw him in the back of a waiting car.[188] Suddenly Black cried murder and residents living near the jail got up to investigate. Most however soon realized what was happening and retreated into their homes.[189] The next day the sheriff found Black's badly mutilated body lying beside the road.

Governor Craig immediately launched an investigation to identify and prosecute Black's murderers. Less than two weeks later, officials charged Samuel Stacks, a Greene County farmer, with murder. However, in Stack's subsequent trial, a jury acquitted him of the charges. Perhaps the most important factor in this decision lay in the jailer's inability to identify any of the mob members despite the fact that none wore masks.[190]

As if this were not bad enough, two months after Joseph Black's death, Will Black, guarded by more than a hundred soldiers, returned to Snow Hill. Passions throughout the community remained high, and the troops were necessary to prevent crowds from lynching Black. But apparently state officials predetermined Black's guilt, and his trial was a mere formality since shortly after he entered the courtroom, a judge sentenced him to death for the rape of Mattie Tyson.[191] Twenty days later North Carolina executed the teenager.[192]

Though fear of sexual assaults by black men on white women formed the basis for many of North Carolina's lynchings, merely writing a letter or making contact with a white woman could also be harmful to African American men. Perhaps no case better emphasizes this point than that of Lazarus Rouse. About nine in the evening the mother of Lazarus Rouse, a midwife, peered out of a window and noticed several figures in the darkness. Before she could wake her son to investigate, one of the men knocked on her door and asked for help in delivering a baby. When she opened the door, a man wearing a flimsy disguise of smut smeared across his face placed a gun to her head. Silently the intruders entered the room where Lazarus slept, unleashed a fatal blast,[193] and withdrew. Although many details of the case are sketchy, newspaper accounts maintain that Rouse was murdered for improper comments about a white woman.[194] However, because the case did not involve the forcible removal of a person from the custody of law enforcement, North Carolina officials did not consider the murder a lynching and refused to investigate.[195]* The actions of state officials are best summed by a 1942 address given by A. Phillip Randolph: "The problem of lynching is a specialized one and negroes must take the responsibility and initiative to solve it, because negroes are the chief victims of it."[196]

For most blacks the attitude of A. Phillip Randolph was understandable considering the negrophobic attitudes sweeping the nation. Over the period from 1900 to 1922, race riots erupted across the nation ranging from Atlanta to Wilmington, North Carolina.[197] Additionally, between 1895 and 1919 the nation experienced 1,514 lynchings. It is little wonder most African Americans were cynical of the government's commitment to end mob violence. Such was the case in rural Warren County, North Carolina, where many blacks vowed to protect members of their race from mobs by all means necessary, including

*In North Carolina, lynching was defined as the murder of a person who was taken from a jail or from the custody of law enforcement officials.

the use of firearms. However, such beliefs were nothing new. In November of 1917, when a mob attempted to lynch Russell High, armed blacks in Winston-Salem fought the mob to a standstill. Several years later in Tulsa, Oklahoma, after a white girl charged a black youth with attempted rape, armed blacks came to the jail to protect the youth. Moreover, in the pages of *The Crisis*, W.E.B. DuBois encouraged blacks to fight back. "If we are to die," he maintained after a lynching in Pennsylvania, "in God's name let us not perish like bales of hay."[198] The stage was set for the outbreak of perhaps the most famous case of mob violence in North Carolina history: the case of Matthew Bullock.

2

Norlina

Founded in 1900, Norlina is located just south of the Virginia border in arguably one of the poorest counties in North Carolina, Warren County.[1] Like many small towns, Norlina owed its existence to the railroad. In the late 1830s, organizers of the Raleigh & Gaston Railroad built a coaling station called Ridgeway Junction. To supplement their income, local citizens sold wood and water to the railroad.[2] This led early entrepreneurs to build stores and set up permanent businesses. By the late 1870s, Ridgeway contained several restaurants, two hardware stores, a blacksmith shop, and a taxi service that provided transportation to Warrenton, the county seat.

As the nineteenth century ended, managers of the newly organized Seaboard Airline Railroad reevaluated their station in Ridgeway. Most felt that the station did not fit the needs of a modern railroad. Consequently, in 1900, the Seaboard moved the coaling station two-and-a-half miles farther north and named the new depot Norlina in honor of North Carolina.[3] To serve the needs of people in the surrounding area, eighteen stores of various types, three hotels, a newspaper, a bank, and two churches sprang up along the railroad track.[4]

Since the depot was strategically located at the junction of the Richmond and Jacksonville, Florida, route and the spur track to Norfolk, the Seaboard Railroad stationed train crews and maintenance workers at the new depot. This decision created a volatile situation because most of the railroad workers were an intolerant lot of poor whites, while most of the inhabitants of the area near the depot were black tenant farmers.[5*]

Despite the town's recent origin, Norlina had the look and feel of the Old South.[6] Founded less than four years after the landmark *Plessy v. Ferguson* case,

---

The Seaboard only allowed blacks to fill construction and low-grade skilled positions. To appease white sensibilities, the railroad established a system that placed blacks on the bottom of the employment hierarchy. The top position for African Americans was boiler washer, which served as an assistant to a boilermaker, a job reserved for a white man. Quite frequently a boiler washer performed the same tasks as a boilermaker; however, the railroad paid blacks significantly lower salaries.

which endorsed the concept of "separate but equal," the town rigidly enforced North Carolina laws that separated the races. Town officials established separate waiting rooms at the train depot, and hotel and storeowners refused to let blacks rent rooms or try on clothes.

Moreover, like the Old South, political control of Norlina lay in the hands of a small clique of local business owners. W.F. White, Alex Katzenstein, and H.C. Fleming owned small wholesale and general merchandise stores. Until the mid–1930s, Fleming also supplied Norlina with water and served as the town's fire chief. In addition, his brother Simon P. Fleming served as Norlina's police chief. Other important businessmen were Merrill Early Walker, the owner of Walker Drug Store; Eugene Alston, who ran a meat market; and Charles F. Whitted, who owned the Hotel Norlina. Whitted was the largest taxpayer in town. A former employee of the Seaboard Railroad, Whitted entered the hotel business operating hotels in Henderson, Weldon, and Sumter, South Carolina, before moving to Norlina.[7]

Perhaps the best-known businessman in town was John Curtis Hardy, who owned the *Norlina Headlight*. Born in 1870, Hardy grew up in Scotland Neck, a small town located forty miles east of Norlina.[8] Upon leaving Scotland Neck, he moved to Warrenton where he launched his career as an apprentice for the conservative *Warren Record* newspaper. Over the next decade as printer, reporter, and owner of the *Warren Record*, he gained a reputation as an advocate for white supremacy and the disenfranchisement of blacks.[9] In 1914, he headed to Norlina, where he established the *Norlina Headlight*.[10] One year later, he was elected mayor of Norlina and justice of the peace.[11] Even so, Hardy clung to old convictions that blacks were inferior to whites and he rigidly enforced Norlina's segregationist laws.[12]

By 1920 there were more than two hundred blacks in Norlina, about 33 percent of the total population of 700.[13] Most worked in the town's rail yard as low-paid stevedores or day laborers. A small group of black professionals also called Norlina home. Charlie Smith owned a dry cleaner, and Charles Henderson served as president of Shiloh Institute. Henderson was the best-known African American in town. A graduate of Shaw University, he served for a period as minister before assuming the presidency of Shiloh Institute. That the school was open was a miracle, since shortly before he arrived a severe financial problem almost caused the school to close. However, with Henderson at the helm, trustees purchased fifty acres of land and moved to the outskirts of Norlina. By 1905, enrollment stood at approximately three hundred students.[14]

In addition to the black professionals, there were several farmers who climbed into the ranks of the town's tiny black professional class. One of the best-known African American farmers in Norlina was William Bullock. Born in the turbulent period between 1870 and 1880, Bullock grew up in rural Warren County near the farming hamlet of Drewy.

Throughout the region, farmers maintained a fierce independence derived from the Jeffersonian principle that fiscal freedom lay in farming. In line with this belief, the powerfully built Bullock, standing more than six feet tall and weighing over two hundred pounds, spent much of his early life as a farmer. With little access to formal education, he displayed a passion for reading and memorizing passages from the Bible. While he worked in the fields he often quoted scriptures that pointed to the hope of a better tomorrow, perhaps the only solace available for blacks in the face of a rising tide of hostility and violence.

To improve his lot, in 1905 Bullock moved to Batavia, New York, where he obtained employment in a factory. Ten years later he returned to North Carolina and became a preacher. After settling his family on a two-hundred-acre farm, he gained a reputation as a fiery orator and churches all over Warren and Vance counties sought his services. But first and foremost, Bullock was a farmer. With the help of his thirteen children, by 1920 his assets stood at more than $20,000.[15] This undoubtedly made him one of the wealthiest African Americans in the county. As expected, his success did not go unnoticed. Many blacks maintained that Bullock and his family were "bigshots," while whites, many of whom earned less than $1,000 per year, felt threatened by his success.[16] Yet, somehow until early 1921 there were no acts of violence directed toward Bullock or his family.

Relations between blacks and whites in Norlina and the surrounding area underwent a steady downturn between 1902 and 1912. On August 19, 1902, officials charged six blacks with the murder of Red Stevers, a roadmaster for the Seaboard Airline Railroad.[17] As the southbound train left Norlina, several African American men staged a protest against the squalor of the rail car reserved for blacks and moved into a whites-only coach.[18] When a porter saw the men, he ordered that all the men return to the colored coach. When they refused he summoned the conductor, Red Stevers.[19] Standing over six feet tall, Stevers was an imposing figure. As a fifteen-year veteran of the railroad, he had gained a reputation as an enforcer of order and discipline. Thus, when the porter called for his help, Stevers burst into the coach and struck several of the offending men. Then he threw his arms around Joe Cole, Sr. Unfortunately, he failed to restrain Cole's arms. Twisting his right arm, Cole grabbed his pistol and fired several shots, killing Stevers and mortally wounded a nearby porter. Before Cole and his companions could escape, passengers overpowered the men. There were cries of "kill him, lynch him" on the train.[20]

By the time the train arrived in Henderson, a crowd of angry passengers surrounded the prisoners. After a few minutes of uncertainty, the sheriff took the suspects off the train and placed the men in jail.[21] The real danger, however, was yet to come. When news of the murder reached nearby Norlina, hotheads in the town's rail yard beat several blacks and formed a mob to lynch the men.[22] Fortunately, before the mob made its move, a rumor spread that the prisoner had been transferred to Raleigh. The mob fell apart.

Several years later Norlina faced another crisis. On September 11, 1911, after a white woman reported Norvall Marshall, a thirty-one-year-old black man, had raped her, authorities surrounded Marshall's house. When he refused to surrender to the sheriff, vigilantes threatened to burn the house to the ground. Only the entrance of Marshall's elderly father, who convinced the suspect to surrender, prevented the house from going up in flames.[23] Ten days later when Marshall appeared for his trial, hundreds of outraged whites filled the courtroom.[24] However, the outcome of the case was never in doubt as a jury found Marshall guilty and the judge sentenced him to death. The next day officials transported him to the state penitentiary, where he was executed one month later.[25]

The execution of Marshall failed to ease African American fear of white backlash. Perhaps hoping to soothe tensions, several blacks sent telegraphs expressing sympathy and financial assistance for the victim: "Colored citizens are pained beyond expression to hear that kindly relations have been disturbed by Norvall Marshall.... Should the families need aid we desire the honor through your paper to subscribe."[26] Despite the appeals, after a few days the excitement, the tensions that had erupted after the rape, subsided until the outbreak of the First World War.

When America entered the Great War, Norlina became a key junction on the Seaboard Railroad and recruits filled the town on the way to training bases. For most recruits, the trip through Norlina was uneventful, but for African Americans the trip was less than appealing since local rowdies created a hostile environment in and around the depot. For example, when a black soldier who was returning from the War attempted to assist a white woman who had fallen, rowdies who stood nearby attacked the man for touching the woman. Only the pleas of the woman's husband prevented the mob from killing the soldier.[27]

The end of World War I also did little to ease these tensions. During the war, African Americans in Norlina, like blacks across the county, enthusiastically supported the war effort with their blood and resources. As a reward for these sacrifices, most African Americans expected better treatment at home when the war ended. However, "for those who supported Jim Crow the black man in uniform was like a red flag thrown in the face of a bull."[28] Additionally, across the South supporters of Jim Crow heightened old fears of uncontrollable lust by suggesting that contact with French women increased the likelihood that African American soldiers would assault white women upon return to America. Thus, within the confines of a changed social landscape, violence against African Americans became widespread. As soldiers returned from the war, officials at many Southern railroad stations stripped black soldiers of their uniforms.[29] As if the humiliating treatment of veterans was not bad enough, during the last six months of 1919, mobs lynched seventy-six African Americans.[30]

Out of this number, two of the most horrendous occurred in Franklin County, which lay less than fifteen miles from Norlina. Like Warren, Franklin County was overwhelmingly rural and most residents lived as farmers. The most important cash crop for farmers in 1919 was tobacco. However, the growth of tobacco required constant labor. Farmers rose at dawn and worked late into the evenings. In this regard, W.L. Medlin was like most of his neighbors, rising at sunup and retiring well after midnight. Even so, 1919 was extremely difficult.

In early August, Medlin's wife underwent surgery to solve a serious medical problem.[31] When she returned from the hospital, she was confined to bed and could not help with the harvest. All was well until the night of August 19, 1919, when, shortly before 9:00 P.M. while Medlin worked to harvest his tobacco crop, his wife awoke to find a darkened figure entering her bedroom. However, before she could call for help the intruder pounced on the bed and raped the woman.[32]

After the assault, the woman ran outside screaming hysterically, but the intruder had fled.[33] When authorities arrived, they launched a search for the rapist but had little success until they spoke with a sharecropper who lived near the Medlins. According to Joe Harris, on the night of the attack, Walter Tyler, a twenty-year-old field hand, visited his home where he had dinner.[34]

With this information authorities launched an all-out search for Tyler. The next day they found him at work in a tobacco field, about six miles from the site of the crime.[35] Instead of charging him with the crime, they drove the suspect back to the Medlin farm, where officers determined his footprints matched some found near the house. While it seems improbable today, officials used this flimsy evidence to charge Tyler with murder.[36] Then they placed Tyler in a car and headed to Louisburg. When they reached the Youngsville and Franklinton Road, about two miles away, a car passed and sped away.[37] Officers soon found the reason for the car's haste. As their car went down a small hill they found the highway blocked. Suddenly a mob of armed men rushed from the woods and surrounded the car.[38] At gunpoint they took Tyler and forced him to confess to the crime.[39] It seems odd that Tyler would confess considering the fate that awaited a guilty plea. In any case, it appears mob members announced Tyler's confession as a device to justify their actions.

Completing the interrogation, several men took Tyler into some nearby woods where they tied a rope under his arms, hoisted him, and unleashed a barrage of bullets.[40] The isolated location of Tyler's body failed to attract the attention mob members sought, so they cut the body down and moved it to an area across the road from an African American church.[41]

The next day the Franklin County coroner called a jury to investigate the lynching, and Governor Bickett sent a special solicitor to look into the crime. After several days of testimony, the solicitor concluded that Tyler was responsible for the assault on the victim. "The circumstantial evidence against him would have given the State a fine start towards conviction, even without the confession it is alleged he gave the mob."[42] Apparently, the solicitor failed to consider the fact that only direct evidence he had linking Tyler to the crime was the testimony of Joc Harris. Even the footprints that investigators linked to Tyler created questions. In the course of questioning by police, Tyler maintained that a pack of dogs chased him across a field as he left the Harris home, leaving the footprints.[43] Perhaps more seriously, the solicitor failed to investigate police involvement in the crime. For example, when mob members intercepted the car transporting Tyler, the men did not wear disguises. Instead, they pulled hats over their faces to hide their identities.[44] Officers nonetheless maintained that they were unable to identify any of the mob members. This seems improbable since all of the attackers presumably lived in Franklin County.

In any case, five months after Tyler's death, another lynching in Franklin County caused an even greater outcry. The holiday season of 1919 was especially festive. To celebrate, hundreds visited Franklinton to take in a movie. Inside the theater, whites sat on the main level while African Americans occupied the "crow's nest." However, with so many people stuffed into the small building, noise sometimes presented a problem. So when R.M. Brown, the manager, made his nightly rounds he got into an argument with a black patron, Powell Green, whom he suspected of talking. The intensity of the argument made it difficult for others to enjoy the movie, and Brown demanded that Green leave.[45] When he refused, the manager had police arrest Green.[46] Inexplicably, as the officers marched Green to jail, Brown struck the suspect several times. What happened next surely stunned police for Green pulled a pistol out of his coat pocket and shot Brown.[47] Shocked, police rushed the suspect to the guardhouse.[48]

Soon police were faced with a barrage of threats from a throng of angry moviegoers. Undoubtedly, the belligerent nature of the mob caused concern since the police force only had two officers. To protect Green the police decided to transfer him to the state penitentiary in nearby Raleigh.[49] A car was hired, and officers prepared to place the suspect in the vehicle. However, as soon as the mob saw Green they surged forward and seized the suspect twice before the officers regained control. After this close call officers slammed Green in the car and raced toward Raleigh.[50]

About two miles outside of Franklinton a car loaded with angry men forced the officers off road and attempted to seize Green.[51] Surprisingly he dashed by the mob and made his way into some nearby woods. However, the handcuffs placed on his hands and feet made running difficult and the lynch mob easily caught him. Placing a rope around his neck, they dragged Green several miles behind a car, and then they hung his badly mutilated body from a tree.[52]

Since Green was Franklin County's second victim of mob violence in a six-month period, blacks were outraged by the violence. Several days after Green's death, several hundred blacks, many carrying handguns and shotguns, held mass meetings at Kittrell College and Norlina's Shiloh Institute.[53] They demanded that state officials punish the murderers, or blacks would take action. These threats raised white anxiety since African Americans made up the majority of the population in Franklin, Warren, and Vance Counties. In response, Solicitor H.E. Norris turned Green's body over to local African Americans and the state provided funds for burial.[54] Second, to calm local passions, Norris offered a reward of $400 for the arrest and conviction of Green's murderers.[55] In a press release the governor declared:

> The whole state is shocked and humiliated by this terrible outrage on our laws....
> The members of the mob crucified the elementary principle of justice for which
> white men have fought and bled and died through a thousand years. They have
> assaulted the very citadel of our civilization and all power of the state will be
> exerted to apprehend them and make them suffer the full penalty of the law.[56]

Less than a week later, Norris released the name of a suspect. As in most lynching cases, the names officials chose to connect with the crimes were outsiders. Green's case conformed to this norm as William Haynsworth was a mechanic who recently arrived in Franklin County.[57] Police, however, never arrested anyone and the murder joined a growing list of unsolved cases.[58]

One year later another case of mob violence erupted in Person County, which lay less than forty miles from Norlina. This case stemmed from an attempted sexual assault upon a fourteen-year-old white girl named Mary Ruth Allen. According to published reports, on July 7, 1920, as the girl walked through an isolated area a black man jumped from some bushes and knocked her to the ground.[59] Before he could accomplish his purpose the girl screamed and the assailant fled.

Determined that the man not get away, neighbors formed a posse and tracked the assailant to some nearby railroad tracks. There they concluded that the attacker had boarded a freight train headed for Roxboro. For that reason, members of the posse jumped into their cars and rushed to Roxboro. Arriving at the train depot, the posse arrested Edward Roach, a twenty-four-year-old African American, as he got off the train. To ensure that they had arrested the right man, the posse brought Allen to the jail where she identified Roach as her assailant.[60]

However, Roach denied his guilt. According to Roach he was at work when the assault took place. After leaving work he walked to the Mount Tersa Station to catch the train to Roxboro. Along the way, he passed several white men working on a bridge and, most notably, two men who were searching for the girl's assailant.[61] Yet, despite a host of witnesses who could confirm his alibi, officials made no effort to check his story. Instead they charged him with rape and threw him in the Roxboro jail.

Roach's arrest however could not have come at a more unfriendly location. Following the Civil War members of the Ku Klux Klan in Roxboro routinely beat blacks for even the slightest offenses. Even more violent acts occurred in the town during the election of 1896. As a crowd of blacks attended a Republican rally, a mob of whites attacked the blacks with an assortment of weapons. In the ensuring ruckus "blood flowed freely," and hundreds of blacks were wounded.[62] Thus, it was little wonder that on the morning following Roach's arrest a mob numbering more than 200 men surrounded the Roxboro jail. When the sheriff asked the mob to disperse, the vigilantes pelted him with stones and fired shots into the air to show that they meant business. Instead of returning to the jail where he could have mounted some sort of defense, the sheriff and his deputies retreated, leaving the jail unprotected.[63] With the sheriff out of the way the mob broke the locks off of Roach's cell. Several miles away in the graveyard of an African American church, they hung him in a tree. Then they riddled his lifeless body with bullets.[64]

The next day the solicitor held a cursory hearing during which the sheriff and his deputies testified that they were unable to identify members of the mob. Yet, this seems unlikely since the sheriff passed many of the vigilantes in the street when he evacuated the jail. At any rate, the case did not end at this juncture. The day after Roach's death, his boss, Nello Teer, released a signed statement in which he maintained that Roach was innocent.[65] According to Teer, Roach was at work at 2:30 P.M., the time the alleged crime took place. Moreover, he claimed that Roach worked all day and did not leave work until 5:30 P.M.[66]

Perhaps due to this statement and the violent nature of Roach's death, from across the nation a chorus of condemnations rained down upon North Carolina. From Elizabeth City the editors of the *Independent* wrote, "The unholy lyncher of the innocent negro at Roxboro ... shows just how incapable a mob is of administering justice. And the mob will in all probability go unpunished. It was only a nigger and niggers have no rights that white men may not violate."[67] The *Raleigh Independent* wrote, "The infuriated mob, in the opinion of the contractor, made a ghastly mistake when they dragged Roach from the Person County jail, hanged him to the churchyard tree and riddled his body with bullets, while the brute who committed the crime was allowed to escape."[68] Several days after this editorial appeared in newspapers, James Weldon Johnson of the NAACP sent a letter to Governor Bickett:

> Aside from the brutality of the mob and its inexcusable action, there is no reason why its members should not be punished for this disgrace to North Carolina and the nation. The lynching took place in open daylight. It is neither

possible nor probable that all of the members of the mob were unknown to Sheriff Thompson. He apparently had ample time to recognize at least the ring-leaders and probably a number of the members.... In view of your strong and uncompromising stand against lynching mobs, may we urge you to bring all of the power at your command to force Sheriff Thompson to act in this deplorable case. The punishment of the lynchers in yesterday's mob will stamp you as a man and an executive whom even lawless mobs cannot intimidate and will do much towards wiping out this national evil and disgrace.[69]

The lynching also caused considerable concern among blacks in the sur-rounding area. In the days following the murder, the Durham branch of the National Association for the Advancement of Colored People (NAACP) held a mass meeting and raised more than $40 to investigate Roach's death.[70] How-ever, perhaps the greatest outrage came from the men who worked alongside Roach in the road crew. Following his murder the entire road crew quit.[71]

In response to these concerns Bickett offered a reward of $400 for each suspect apprehended and convicted. Then he ordered the solicitor to conduct a careful investigation.[72] Unfortunately, Solicitor S.M. Gattis made it clear that he had no intention of conducting a thorough investigation. On the morning after the lynching, Gattis, who lived in nearby Hillsboro, drove to Roxboro, conducted a cursory investigation, and exonerated the sheriff. After a few hours he boarded a train for a vacation in Buffalo Springs, Virginia.[73]

One week later the solicitor returned and opened a formal hearing into Roach's death. After a brief description of the events leading up to the murder, Gattis issued a statement to the throng of blacks who filled the courtroom: "Two wrongs never make a right ... and the facts are that today there are men who are murderers. They have violated a higher law than did the victim of their anger because they took over the power of the state, which ought never to be violated."[74] Then in an effort to placate blacks he expressed hope that some-day the perpetrators of the crime would be brought to justice. Then he directed the coroner to dismiss the jury.[75]

However, many whites still felt that blacks would attempt to retaliate in some manner. Perhaps to reassure themselves, local newspapers conducted a series of interviews with African Americans. According to the News & Observer, blacks held "no feeling of animosity toward the crime.... Their chief concern was over the lynching of Roach in the church yard ... and several approached the solicitor to find out what could be done about it."[76] However, Gattis, in a response sure to go down in the annals of lynching lore for its hypocrisy, replied, "Find out the guilty party and we will prosecute them."[77]

Nonetheless, the murders of Green, Tyler, and Roach caused many African Americans to reexamine their role in resisting mob violence. In the period before the deaths many African American leaders urged their followers to prac-tice deference and restraint in the face of mounting violence. In return, these leaders hoped that North Carolina officials would reward their sacrifices with stronger antilynching laws and through the prosecution of mob participants. North Carolina officials, however, were indifferent to these concerns and only halfheartedly attempted to prosecute mob participants. Yet, in the wake of North Carolina's inability to prosecute anyone for the Green, Tyler, and Roach lynchings despite the presence of hundreds of witnesses, even the most docile black concluded that new methods must be utilized to end lynching. These included a restoration of African American voting rights, the placement of blacks on juries, and the adoption of a militancy that was determined to break the stranglehold of Jim Crow.*

Foremost in this effort was the fledgling NAACP. The NAACP sought to end segregation, improve education for black children, and repeal voting restrictions by campaigning for the enforcement of the Fourteenth and Fifteenth Amendments of the United States Constitution. To carry out its work, the NAACP established branches across the country.[78] Between 1918 and 1921, the NAACP added five branches in North Carolina: Fayetteville, Winston-Salem, Asheville, Rocky Mount, and Weldon.[79] However, as organizers traversed the state, tension increased as whites sought to limit the influence of so-called outside troublemakers. The *Charlotte Observer* pushed black elites to guard against the infection of the NAACP while in other cities officials banned the *Crisis*.[80]

As it had in the rest of the state, the arrival of the NAACP sent ripples across the Warren County.[81] The *Warren Record* accused the NAACP organizers of trying to promote social equality, which the editor determined would lead to problems.[82] As if these tensions were not enough, at the same time that the NAACP was making its way into Warren County, blacks in the area began to push for an end to lynching and racial equality. Unfortunately, just as many Warren County African Americans sought change, whites seemed more determined to maintain unity behind the tenets of white supremacy.

The new attitude displayed by many blacks evolved as a direct result of World War I, when African Americans began to proclaim their unhappiness with segregation and discrimination. For example, at Emancipation Day ceremonies in Raleigh in 1919, an assembly of 3,000 blacks passed a strongly worded resolution that "condemned lynching, demanded the boycott of Jim Crow facilities and urged parents and teachers to instill race pride in black children." Crow, Escott, and Hatley, A History of African Americans in North Carolina, 125.

3

The Lynching of Plummer Bullock

As the sun began to set on January 18, 1921, twenty-one-year-old Mathew Bullock, a World War I veteran, and his sixteen-year-old brother, Plummer, drove from Drewy to Norlina in search of girls.[1] However, few girls dared to brave the cold January temperatures. As they prepared to return home, Plummer stopped by J.P. Williams's general store to purchase some apples. Inside the store, the owner kept two barrels of apples, premium grade and inferior quality. After surveying both barrels, Plummer paid ten cents for premium grade apples.[2] However, once outside the store the youth realized that the clerk had cheated him by substituting inferior, half-rotten apples for the premium brand.[3] When Plummer discovered the clerk's deception, instead of observing the tenets of Jim Crow that required submission and passivity, he returned to the store and demanded a refund.[4] "Not after they have been in your black hands will I take them back," Brady Traylor angrily replied.[5] Soon shouts of "lynch the nigger" filled the air, and Plummer beat a hasty retreat.

For the next few days, Norlina remained quiet, and it appeared the town would avoid trouble. Accordingly, on Saturday night, young blacks from all over the region, including Plummer and Matthew Bullock, headed to the Norlina train depot to hang out.[6] Shortly after midnight, news reached local whites that the Bullock brothers were at the train depot, and a mob formed. Just what happened next is subject to some controversy. According to reports printed in the Raleigh *News & Observer*, Raby Traylor, a brother of the store clerk, confronted Matthew Bullock. While they were talking, Jerome Hunter, a companion of Bullock, walked up in the darkness and shot Traylor several times. In the ensuing gunfight, five whites and three blacks were wounded.

Oral reports from Norlina present another picture. According to these reports, on the day of the riot, Traylor and a mob of drunken whites surrounded the depot and threatened to hang Plummer Bullock. When Matthew Bullock and Jerome Hunter stepped forward to defend Plummer, Traylor fired his gun. This set the stage for the ensuing gunfight.[7] Whatever the case may be, when authorities reached the depot, they arrested Jerome Hunter and Robert Moss, who had been wounded in the gunfight. Next, the posse marched to a nearby black neighborhood and invaded its hub, Charlie Smith's dry cleaners. At gunpoint they forced Smith to reveal the names of others who had participated in the riot.* Over the next few hours the posse rounded up twelve more suspects including seventeen-year old Plummer Bullock.[8]

Raby Traylor in 1973, fifty-two years after the Norlina riot. Traylor moved to Norlina with his parents in 1919. As a young man, he worked for a time in his father-in-law's drugstore. He later opened his own appliance store. In 1947, he opened the Peoples Bank and Trust Company of Norlina and became chairman of the bank's board (courtesy *Warren Record*).

For William Bullock, the arrest of his teenage son represented a serious threat. The courts in Warren County were known to give stiff sentences to blacks for even minor infractions. Accordingly, he rushed to Warrenton to hire an attorney. Reaching the town, Bullock headed to the offices of perhaps the most noted attorney in the county, Tasker Polk. Born in 1861, Polk was a nephew of James K. Polk. After graduating from Bethel Military Academy, he launched a career as a politician serving as mayor of Warrenton, solicitor of the County Courts and as a representative for the upper house of the North Carolina General Assembly.[9] In 1890 he single-handedly rounded up enough support to get Warren County to pass the White Supremacy Act. Hence, when Bullock entered his office Polk angrily scoffed, "If you niggers don't go home and mind your own business we are going to take everything you have away from you."[10] Needless to say he refused

---

*The next day J.C. Handy formally charged all African Americans at the depot with rioting and a host of other charges. However, Hardy only charged one white participant, Raby Traylor, with a crime. Three weeks later, Handy dropped the charges against Traylor.

The Warren County jail, June 2002. The Warren County jail is where vigilantes seized Plummer Bullock and Alfred Williams. Photograph by the author.

to take the case, leaving Plummer and the other suspects to their fate in the Warrenton jail.

Located less than six miles from Norlina, Warrenton was noticeably different. Unlike Norlina, which was less than two decades old, Warrenton, founded in 1779, was one of the oldest towns in North Carolina. During the antebellum era, the town prospered as the center of a region dominated by planters. Many of the most important figures in North Carolina history called the town home, including Nathaniel Macon, vocal opponent of the Jay Treaty; Governors William Hawkins, James Turner, and Thomas Bragg; and Braxton Bragg, perhaps the most controversial general in the Confederacy.

Despite its past, by 1921 Warrenton's heyday had long since passed. At the center of the town stood the Georgian-styled Warren County Courthouse, which was built in 1906. Surrounding the courthouse stood a handful of buildings containing two banks, three lawyers' offices, a clothing store, and several drygoods stores. One block north of the town square stood a building that housed the *Warren Record*, the town's only newspaper.

However, like many small Southern towns at the start of the twentieth century, Warrenton was really two towns. Inside the city limits, whites made

Warren County jail, June 2002. Little has changed in Warren County since the lynching of Plummer Bullock and Alfred Williams. Photograph by the author.

up the majority of the population. To maintain control, they gerrymandered the town's borders to keep blacks outside of the city limits. They also employed an all-white police force and militia company to enforce Jim Crow traditions.

Regardless of this fact, the sheer number of African Americans living just outside of the city limits meant that blacks performed many of the important functions in the town. The most important were firefighter and jailer.[11] In

Above: Oak Level Cemetery, site of Plummer Bullock's grave. *Below:* Oak Chapel AME Church. Located 100 yards from the Warren County jail the church was the site of African American efforts to defend Plummer Bullock and Alfred Williams. Both photographs by the author.

Above: The lynching of Plummer Bullock and Alfred Williams (illustration by Nathaniel Allen, March 2008). *Below:* Matthew Bullock in a photograph in the *Toronto Sun* taken shortly after his first arrest in 1922 (courtesy Sun Media Corporation).

addition, Warrenton was home to several black merchants and a handful of black educators, of which the most import were John S. Plummer, who owned a delivery stable; John Watkins, who owned a restaurant; and Gillis Cheek, who organized the Warren County Training School, the first public high school for blacks in Warren County.[12]

However, Warrenton was very much a Southern city and the news of the riot and subsequent arrests led many whites to seek immediate justice. The day after the arrests, a mob surrounded the jail and rumors spread that the throng planned to storm the building. To prevent this from happening, the mayor of Warrenton called Governor Morrison and asked for troops. Instead of sending soldiers the governor ordered the mayor to deputize a sufficient force to protect the jail.[13]

While the mayor struggled mightily to protect the suspects, a small group of African Americans gathered in the basement of Oak Chapel A.M.E. Church.

Since the church was about one hundred yards from the jail, officials feared the outbreak of a second gunfight. Yet, instead of focusing on the mob that surrounded the jail, a more immediate danger, officials sent the home guard to disarm the blacks in the church. Under the command of Tasker Polk, the home guard entered Oak Chapel A.M.E. Church with military precision, disarming the men who had assembled in the basement. No sooner had they disarmed these men than Tasker Polk received word of a second gathering of African Americans in a nearby restaurant. Again, he rushed his men to the scene and disarmed those who were assembled. But instead of hurrying back to the jail, Polk, perhaps in collaboration with the mob leaders, inexcusably allowed the home guard and local police to scatter without further orders.[14] By nightfall, only the jailer, John Green, a middle-aged African American, stood between the mob and the prisoners.[15]

Shortly after midnight a knock on the door of the jail awakened Green. Perhaps thinking it was the police chief returning, he cracked the door and in a flash, masked men burst inside.[16] Before they could complete their task, a determined African American launched a last-ditch effort to protect the prisoners. Slipping through the cordon set up by the vigilantes, a black bystander attempted to burn the getaway car. However, before he could start the fire, a hail of bullets sent the man running for his life.[17] Surmounting this obstacle, the horde dragged Plummer Bullock and his forty-two-year-old cousin, Alfred Williams, into the back seat of the car and sped away. Two miles away the mob riddled both men with bullets and left their bodies beside the road.[18] At daybreak, outraged blacks gathered at the site and demanded justice, and county officials hastily summoned a jury of inquiry. However, as expected, the coroner ruled that the deaths occurred at the hand of persons unknown.[19]

The next day, to prevent further outbreaks of violence, Warrenton officials moved the remaining riot suspects to Central Prison in Raleigh, and the home guard patrolled the town. In nearby Norlina the mayor procured rifles from Henderson and deputized thirty citizens to patrol the town.[20] However, the overwhelming display of troops and firepower failed to provide the internal security most whites sought.[21] Rumors soon began to spread that blacks planned to burn Norlina and Warrenton. As if to confirm these rumors, on February 24, 1921, the *Warren Record* newspaper reprinted a letter, which supposedly was addressed to Warrenton Police Chief E.L. Green:

> Let me say to you Mr. Green I am a colored man but I want to let you know that the colored people is fixing to burn Norlina and Warrenton in March and is now getting the guns and all ready. I write because I don't want no trouble tis the young niggers and they say they is going to kill you because you kept them from shooting the men that took the two out of jail that night. Wach [*sic*] out in March. There is five white men they say they is going to kill and if this is done I am afraid you all will kill us all.[22]

While it is highly unlikely any African American wrote the letter, Tasker Polk nonetheless used it as a tool to maintain white unity and to rid the community of undesirable blacks. In a rebuttal printed in the *Warren Record*, Polk maintained that he had heard the rumors that blacks planned to burn Norlina and Warrenton. He blamed these threats on northern influence and European decadence, which had corrupted blacks that served in the army during World War I. These blacks, he maintained, "returned home with an exaggerated idea of their own importance claiming much for themselves and conceding little to others in a continual menace to the peace of the South."[23] As a warning Polk advised black leaders to control young hotheads, or they would be held accountable. "If the threats are carried out, or attempted to be carried out, the leaders will be held personally responsible and punishment swift and certain will be meted out."[24]

Jarred by Polk, the next day J.K. Ramsey, the pastor of the Tabernacle Baptist Church, issued a statement that urged his members to observe restraint: "Let us go down on record as condemning such violation of law and order."[25] Several days later members of the Greenville Baptist Church also issued their own resolution that condemned violence or any act that would mar friendly relations in Warren County.[26] However, to many whites the resolutions did not go far enough. On the same day that Greenwood Baptist Church issued its resolution, the *Warren Record* printed an editorial that urged

> colored leaders of the South to do their own thinking and quit listening to advice of those who haven't their true interest at heart, and who reside north of Mason's and Dixon's line — with nothing at stake here in the South. If this crowd of advisors and so-called leaders residing in the North will let the colored race in the South alone, they will work out their own salvations in friendship and good will with the white race."[27]

In the face of growing hysteria, a new threat surfaced as a rumor spread that Percy Adams, the principal of the Episcopal school for negroes in Warrenton, had armed blacks in an attempt to protect the lynching victims. The basis of these rumors concealed a more complex truth. As a graduate of Boston University, Adams stood as a shining example of a "New negro," who merely by his education challenged the tenets of Jim Crow. To rid themselves of Adams, Tasker Polk sent a letter to the Episcopal Bishop: "He will have to leave here. The peace of this community demands it, we had rather that he be induced to leave peacefully and quickly." Despite these pleas the Episcopal church refused to remove Adams. Thus, the apprehension and capture of Matthew Bullock gained special significance.

Just how Matthew Bullock escaped capture is the subject of myth and legend. Accounts provided by members of Oak Level Church of Christ suggest that after the riot, Matthew made his way to Ridgeway where he hid in stables belonging to German immigrants. Several days later, with the help of the Germans, Matthew made his way to South Hill, Virginia.[28] While this story has merit, others in Norlina maintain that after the riot and subsequent lynching of Plummer Bullock, O.C. Green, a local mortician, put Plummer's body inside a sack while he placed Matthew in his brother's coffin. Then by pretending he was traveling to a gravesite in nearby Virginia, Green smuggled Matthew out of the state where friends helped the fugitive reach Petersburg.[29] Finally, others, including many local newspapers, claimed that Matthew made his escape by driving the family car to Washington. This sounds least likely since local officials set up roadblocks and telegraphed notices to police as far north as Petersburg, Virginia.[30] Despite the conflicting accounts of Bullock's flight, he somehow reached Buffalo, New York.[31] After a few weeks in the city he fled to Canada.[32] With Bullock's entrance into Canada, the horror of lynching that had tragically taken the lives of his brother and cousin exposed one of North Carolina's best-kept secrets, namely, mob violence.

4

A Well-Deserved Punishment

Unable to locate Matthew Bullock, Warren County officials prepared to unleash their fury on the remaining riot suspects. As the *Warren Record* put it, "In the recent trouble from Norlina the aggression came from armed colored men.... You know that your race must suffer more, yes a thousand fold more than my race."[1] And suffer the men would.

However, before the community's anger could be unleashed, county officials had to at least give the men a trial, which had the outward appearance of fairness. To prosecute the men, authorities hired Tasker Polk and B.B. Williams, a local attorney, to assist the solicitor Garland Midyett. Next, officials tried to hire counsel for the suspects. However, one by one lawyers across Warren County found an excuse to remove themselves from the case. Finally, the state appointed John Exum Woodard to represent the men.

Woodard was one of the most noted lawyers in eastern North Carolina, although at sixty-six he was nearing the end of his career. The son of a prominent planter, Woodard was born in Wilson, North Carolina. After attending the Richmond Law School, in 1877 he was appointed solicitor of the Inferior Court of Wilson County.[2] In 1884, he won a seat in the legislature where he helped pass a law that required elected officials post bonds before assuming office. This law had an adverse impact on black office holding, since most African Americans were poor and few could afford the cost of paying a bond.[3] In 1901, Woodard moved up the political ladder by winning election to the upper house of the state legislature. However, in this role his service was unimpressive — other than playing a minor role in passing a law that segregated public schools, he accomplished little.[4] Due to that fact, in 1903 he returned to Wilson where he became little more than a country lawyer, handling minor cases. Thus, when officials offered him the chance to defend the men charged with the Norlina riot, he eagerly accepted the invitation.

Woodard's appointment, however, was viewed with suspicion by blacks across the region. After all, he had played a major role in limiting black political power and returning the state to white conservative rule. Thus, when T.S. Inborden, the president of Bricks Agricultural School, a black college attended by many of the suspects, heard about the charges he sent a newspaper clipping and a letter to the NAACP requesting help and legal assistance for the men:[5]*

> You have already seen accounts in the newspapers of the Norlina-Warren lynching. A resident just from there who was an eye witness tells us to believe absolutely nothing the white papers are saying about it relative to the colored people being the aggressors in the affair. One negro at least lynched had nothing to do with it and was absolutely innocent of taking any part. Several who are in jail were either former students here or have relatives here in school. It is an awful mess.[6]

Several days after receiving Inborden's letter, the NAACP received another letter seeking help from Framingham, Massachusetts. This letter, out of fear of reprisal, was simply signed Rev. J.W.M.:

> I wish to bring to the attention of the Association a copy of a letter just received by me, in which an account of two lynchings and imprisonment of a number of negroes in the community where the lynching occurred. I have the original letter in my possession and any copy that may be made of it but I am keeping it because I do not wish harm to come to the writer of the letter. Of course the negroes that are in prison who are coming up for trial is our greatest concern in this instance. I hope there is some way the Association can make its influence felt.[7]

However, the NAACP had little interest in the case. It was heavily involved in two major cases—the recent Tulsa race riots and the defense of sharecroppers charged in the Arkansas riot cases. Additionally, the fledgling group was involved in the push to introduce antilynching legislation to Congress.[8]

At any rate, without the NAACP's help a fair trial for the men was impossible since the men had already been tried and convicted in the front pages of the local newspaper and in the minds of local whites. Howard Jones, the editor of the *Warren Record*, maintained, "It is this badly advised type of colored; this ungodly type which is a handicap to good feeling between the races," while the *Norlina Headlight* published a series of columns asking for prompt and immediate reckoning for the perpetrators of such a vile and wicked crime.[9]

On May 24, 1921, nearly five months after the Norlina riot, troops and

---

*For the NAACP, Inborden's letter was one that could not easily be dismissed. Born in 1865 in a small cabin in Loundon County, Virginia, Inborden had long shown that he was dedicated to the advancement of African Americans. After graduating from Fisk University he became a missionary, and he started an elementary school in Helen, Arkansas. After several years in Arkansas he later started schools in Georgia and South Carolina, before moving to North Carolina to start a school for the American Missionary Association-the Bricks School-in 1885. By 1921 the school had sixteen buildings and an enrollment of more than three hundred students. More importantly, Inborden had a long list of influential supporters that included Francis J. Grimke, Booker T. Washington, George White, and W.E.B. DuBois.

heavily armed authorities transported the suspects from Central Prison to Warrenton to stand trial. Although the sheriff feared the outbreak of more violence, the presence of soldiers and several machine guns prevented any disorder. The soldiers, however, did little to deter spectators as a huge crowd filled the courtroom. Those who could not get a seat gathered outside by the windows, which had been opened so the people could hear the proceedings.

When the men went before the judge, they stood in stark contrast to each other. With three gold teeth in the front of his mouth, twenty-year-old Jerome Hunter was identified as the leader of the men.[10] To many whites he was considered a mean negro. Alongside Hunter was his twenty-one-year-old brother, James Hunter, and rail-thin brothers Ben and Richard Crosson. Beside the Crossons was thirty-six-year-old sharecropper Charlie Rodwell, fifty-four-year-old Elias Alston who worked as a stevedore for the railroad, and thirty-six-year-old field hand Alex Milan. Pressed next to Milan was Arthur Kearney, Eddie Lee Jones, John Bracy, Walker Perry, Henry Jones, Norman Smith, Claudie Jones, and Robert Moss and his twenty-year-old son Robert.[11] Noticeably absent was Charlie Smith, who was stricken with tuberculosis and not expected to live.[12]

With the suspects in the courtroom, the prosecution charged Jerome Hunter with secret assault and rioting.[13] Then the solicitor brought the remaining suspects before the court and charged them with rioting. Instead of a prolonged legal battle, the trial turned out to be anticlimactic since Woodard offered no challenge to the state. Instead he convinced each of his clients to plead guilty.[14] Whether the men felt that a successful defense was hopeless is unknown; however, one can be sure that the fear of remaining in the Warren County Jail, where two of their friends were taken from cells and lynched, convinced the men to follow Woodard's advice.

The judgment of the court was that Jerome Hunter, who was charged with the most serious crime, serve eight years in the state penitentiary while Eddie Lee Jones, Richard Crosson, Alex Milan, Ben Crosson, Claudie Jones, Robert Moss Jr., and Charlie Rodwell serve terms ranging from six months to a year on a local chain gang.[15] As for the remaining suspects, Warren County officials dropped the charges. However, for many Warren County whites the sentences only represented a consolation prize, since they were unable to locate Matthew Bullock, the man they most wanted to punish.

5

Canada, O Canada

From the earliest days of the Dominion, Canada has served as a haven for those in need of escape from American jurisprudence and persecution. In the seventeenth century, remnants of various Algonquin groups took refuge in Canada. A century later, the American Revolution forced thousands of loyalists to move north. In the nineteenth century, Tecumseh, Crazy Horse, Sitting Bull, and a host of lesser-known Native American leaders entered Canada to escape the American military. However, by far the largest migration was that of blacks, slave and free.

At the close of the American Revolution, more than three thousand blacks arrived in Canada. Most were freemen or escaped slaves who had answered Lord Dunmore's call to join the British army. When Great Britain and the United States fought in the War of 1812, the movement of blacks to Canada accelerated. To demoralize America, Britain offered freedom to any slave who settled in Canada. This led several thousand bondsmen to make their way north. Moreover, it established Canada's reputation as a safe haven for blacks.

With the passage of the Fugitive Slave Act in 1850, the movement of blacks to Canada increased significantly.[1] The new law, which imposed stiff penalties for aiding runaway slaves, meant that the Northern states were no longer safe for fugitive slaves. Three months after Congress passed the law, more than three thousand blacks entered Canada. From Buffalo, almost the entire congregation of the black Baptist church sought refuge in Canada. Baltimore's oyster industry ground to a halt as black oystermen, who dominated the market, fled to Canada. By 1859, approximately fifty thousand blacks called Canada home. Important communities sprang up in York, London, Kitchener, Windsor, Amherstburg, Saint Catherines, and Hamilton.

At the center of the black community lay the church. By 1840, several churches—most notably the African Methodist Episcopal Church (AME)— had enough members to form a Canadian Conference. Others formed the British Methodist Episcopal Church (BME). The primary factor in the BME's development was a desire to sever connections to the United States. This severance would allow the members of the new denomination to strengthen their relationship with British ideas and government. There was also a practical reason, as many fugitive slaves felt it would be easier to gain justice from extradition if they belonged to a British church filled with British citizens.[2]

The formation of separate churches and social institutions, coupled with the shared history of oppression, allowed blacks to develop a sense of community; achievement for one meant success for all. Those who observed the tenets of good behavior, hard work, and sobriety while avoiding idleness gained legitimacy and could expect the support of the community in times of crisis.

Perhaps no case better represents this trend than that of Matthew Bullock. As fugitive slaves had done earlier, Bullock sought refuge in the black church, regularly attending Saint Paul's African Methodist (AME) church. Possibly through this association, he gained employment with a local construction company where employers recognized his hard work. Thus, he gained legitimacy in the eyes of the black community. Unfortunately, as Bullock become more familiar with his surroundings, he became careless and word soon spread that he was a fugitive. In due time, a letter with his picture reached Warren County officials. With this news, Warren County officials wired Hamilton police and asked them to arrest the fugitive. However, because he had broken no local laws, police charged Bullock with vagrancy and with entering the country illegally. The latter charge posed serious problems since it meant that Canada could deport him without the need of holding an extradition hearing.[3]

As news of Bullock's arrest spread, Canadians rallied to his defense. Foremost in this effort was Reverend J.D. Howell, pastor of Saint Paul's AME church. Howell was recognized as the leader of Hamilton's black community and at his urging, the congregation of St. Paul's formed a committee of defense.[4] He also hired attorney Freeman Treleaven to represent Bullock.[5]

NAACP Leader Walter White in 1942 (courtesy Robert W. Woodruff Library of the Atlanta University Center).

Yet, the addition of Treleaven failed to give Howell much comfort since he realized that Hamilton's small black community lacked the necessary resources and political influence to stop Bullock's extradition. To increase public support, Howell sent letters to newspapers across Canada.[6] He also wired details of the case to the National Association for the Advancement of Colored People (NAACP).[7]

Several days after Howell's telegram reached the NAACP, the civil rights group received another request for help, this one from Anna Henderson, a black secretary for the Canadian Department of Immigration. Aware of Bullock's predicament and afraid that his return to North Carolina would end in lynching, Henderson's letter introduced the case to W.E.B. Du Bois. However, she penciled a message across the bottom of the page: "I secured the evidence in conjunction with my work, and if the facts were known, I shall in all probability lose my position."[8] Finally, in mid–January 1922, Walter White, the Assistant Secretary of the NAACP, arrived in Hamilton. Only twenty-eight at the time, White's affiliation with the NAACP dated back to his college days at Atlanta University, where he was secretary of the local branch. What set him apart from others was his charming manner and his ability to "pass" for white. These attributes proved especially useful in investigating riots and lynchings across the South.

However, the arrival of White had little to do with answering the plea for help and more to do with changing political conditions. Almost one year earlier, the NAACP had received numerous letters seeking help for Matthew Bullock.[9] In response to these letters, the NAACP issued a reply that, although offering legal advice, was noncommittal. The reasons for this cautiousness are not difficult to fathom. Several months before Matthew Bullock made his way north, the NAACP had launched a campaign to get Congress to pass antilynching legislation introduced by Congressman Leonidas Dyer.[10] Given that many legal experts felt the constitutional basis for such legislation was marginal, the NAACP lobbied congressmen to build support.[11] Indeed during the six months between the introduction of the Dyer Anti-Lynching Bill and its passage by the U.S. House of Representatives in 1922, the NAACP spent more than $10,000 lobbying Congress. This exhausted the antilynching fund.[12] Additionally, since the proposed legislation represented the culmination of eleven years of lobbying, few in the civil rights group were willing to invest scarce resources into the Bullock case, which most felt had only limited appeal beyond the borders of North Carolina. However, with the passage of the Dyer Anti-Lynching Bill by the U.S. House of Representatives, the Bullock case gained new importance. The fight to pass the Dyer Bill convinced NAACP officials that Southern resistance would increase once the bill reached the Senate. Faced with this challenge, the NAACP sought to continue its successful lobbying campaign. Still, few funds were available, and it appeared the campaign would stall. News from Buffalo, New York, encouraged the NAACP to chart a new course.

Dyer anti-lynching poster, circa 1922. The Dyer anti-lynching bill, introduced on April 11, 1921, defined lynching as the murder of any person by a mob of three or more persons. Law enforcement officials who failed to protect a prisoner in their charge could be sentenced up to five years in jail and fined five thousand dollars. Although Southerners vigorously opposed the bill, it passed the House of Representatives by a vote of 231 to 119. However, the resistance in the House alerted the NAACP that the fight would be much tougher in the Senate. This played a major role in the NAACP's decision to join the Bullock defense team (courtesy *Chicago Defender*).

With the arrest of Matthew Bullock, blacks in Buffalo rallied to his defense.[13] Harnessing this energy the NAACP's Buffalo chapter held a series of mass meetings that raised funds for Bullock's defense.[14] The chapter also hired an attorney and developed a plan to keep Bullock in New York should efforts fail in Canada. The plan called for Bullock's arrest by a sympathetic police officer upon deportation from Canada. Lawyers retained by the Buffalo chapter would then appeal to the governor of New York to block Bullock's extradition. If this failed, the attorney would prepare a writ of habeas corpus with the intention of gaining a hearing by a friendly Northern court that would presumably rule in their favor.[15]

The actions by the Buffalo chapter convinced national NAACP officials that Bullock's case not only held interest in North Carolina but also across the nation. By joining Bullock's defense team the cash-strapped NAACP could gain access to newspapers in America and Canada and thus could promote the Dyer Anti-Lynching Bill. Moreover, the existence of an active campaign to defer Bullock's legal expense freed the NAACP of any long-term financial commitments.[16]

Accordingly, on January 19, 1922, White arrived in Hamilton at the Buffalo chapter's expense.[17] After meeting with Howell, the secretary outlined the Buffalo chapter's plan to protect Bullock should Canada deport the fugitive.[18] More importantly he used his appearance to promote the Dyer Anti-Lynching Bill:

> Last year sixty-one lynchings occurred in the United States. Four of which were in North Carolina. Of that number, four were burned alive at the stake while the bodies of five others were burned after death. Two of the sixty-four victims were women.... There is pending before Congress at present a bill to make lynching a federal offense, since individual states have been unable to prevent lynchings or punish lynchers. This bill is being bitterly opposed by members of the Congress from Southern states. One of the leaders in the fight against the bill is the Congressman from North Carolina. It cannot be questioned that if Bullock is taken back to North Carolina, whether he is innocent or guilty of the crime charged against him he will probably be lynched.[19]

Two days later at a mass meeting in Buffalo, White promised to vigorously defend Bullock. Aroused by White, the crowd contributed $80 to Bullock's defense fund.[20] But none of the money would ever aid Bullock, since the Buffalo NAACP chapter benchmarked its use upon the fugitive's deportation from Canada and for White's trip to Buffalo.[21] However, to successfully resist Bullock's deportation, his defense team needed money. For that reason, Howell contacted the National Race Congress (NRC).

The National Race Congress owed its existence to a backlash against white dominance of the NAACP. From the founding of the NAACP, whites occupied all major top-level, non-salaried positions, such as president, chairman of the board, and treasurer, while lower-ranking officers and the executive secretary were black.[22] Consequently, to many blacks, the NAACP was little more than a social club for white liberals where African Americans held few important positions and had even less power. In 1912, dissidents formed the National Race Congress. Adopting the slogan "rights and privileges for the negro on the same basis as other Americans," the NRC embarked on an ambitious course as an all-black organization. Elected president of the new organization was William Henry Jernagin, the pastor of Washington, D.C.'s Mount Carmel Baptist Church. In accepting the NRC's presidency Jernagin declared:

> We refuse to follow hand picked leaders selected by others simply because they can be used like a rubber stamp. We want men who will stand up in a manly way and contest for the rights of our people and not simply do what the white man tells them to do.[23]

The NRC received a major boost in 1913, when a crisis arose in the Washington, D.C. chapter of the NAACP. Following allegations that the president of the chapter, Dr. J. Milton Waldron, had used his office to seek political favor from the Democratic Party, more than a hundred members of the chapter demanded his ouster.[24] However, Waldron denied the charges and refused to resign.[25] To resolve the dispute the chapter called on the NAACP's Executive Board. Although many members of the Executive Board wanted to remove Waldron, most felt this action would destroy the chapter.[26] Thus, the board

The Reverend W.H. Jernagin in 1921. Jernagin served as president of the National Race Congress. After leaving this post, he served as president of the National Fraternal Council of Negro Churches and as president of the National Baptist Convention (General Research and Reference Division, Schomburg Center for Research in Black Culture, New York Public Library, Astor, Lenox and Tilden Foundations).

ordered a new election to settle the dispute. This angered Waldron, leading him and his supporters to leave the NAACP and join the National Race Congress.[27]

Additional friction between the NRC and NAACP stemmed from the 1919 Pan-African Conference. After returning from the conference, Jernagin, W.E.B. Du Bois, and other notables were invited to address an overflow crowd at the Bethel Literary Society in Washington, D.C. After a short introduction Jernagin presented Du Bois to the crowd. However, when Du Bois gave his address he failed to mention that Jernagin had also attended the Pan-African Conference. This so incensed the NRC members who were in attendance that most walked out. Miss Nannie Burroughs, who was a leading NRC member, maintained that she had "made up (her) mind then, not to have anything more to do with the Pan-African Congress until it has as its chief promoter a man who has more respect for his fellows ... than was shown by Du Bois on that occasion."[28]

Despite hostility between the NRC and NAACP, changing political conditions created new challenges for both groups. In 1913, Woodrow Wilson entered the White House, becoming the first Southern Democratic president since 1867. Assisted by a cabinet dominated by Southerners, Wilson's first administration was flooded with anti-black legislation. The volume of legislation quickly surpassed the total output of the four preceding administrations combined. In response, the NRC called for the creation of a single governing body, presumably under its leadership, for all black civil rights organizations. With this structure in place, Jernagin argued that African Americans could form an effective barrier to racist legislation and violence across the South.[29] Although the NRC attracted the attention of Robert L. Vann, Nan H. Burroughs, and I.N. Ross, it failed to garner the support of the NAACP.[30] Instead, the NAACP made lynching its main target.

The lynching of 144 blacks between 1918 and 1919 and the outbreak of racial violence in cities ranging from East St. Louis to Washington, D.C. captured the attention of the nation. Thus, the NAACP's antilynching campaign garnered immediate support. In a bid to carve a role for itself, NRC officials called on every black organization that opposed lynching and endorsed the antilynching bill before Congress to send a delegation to the Congress's annual conference. However, since the NAACP had launched the antilynching bill and had garnered national attention without assistance from the NRC, NAACP officials found the proposal laughable.[31] Nonetheless, from across the nation hundreds attended the NRC's antilynching conference. Buoyed by this success and aware that the NRC could not sway the NAACP, Jernagin and other officials organized a riot defense fund that they hoped would rival the NAACP's antilynching fund. By the end of 1919, the fund contained $3,000. Still it paled in comparison to the NAACP's antilynching fund, which contained more than $10,000. And questions soon arose over the use of the NRC's defense fund.

NRC officials had failed to develop a coherent program for the use of the riot fund, which led to charges of embezzlement. In an article to the *Washington Bee*, J.C. Cunningham, possibly an alias for Calvin Chase, the paper's editor, charged Jernagin with misuse and challenged him to account for the money. "Too long our people have been browbeaten by these self-appointed leaders of the race, who are out and out for personal gain and this writer is going to open the eyes of people along that line."[32] Responding to the charges, J.R. Hawkins, the financial secretary of the NRC, claimed that the organization, in consultation with the Bar Association of Colored Lawyers, had used the money to pay attorney's fees.[33] This failed to end the controversy, and new charges soon arose.

When Royal Hughes, president of the Colored Bar Association, read Hawkins's rebuttal, he threatened to sue, because none of the members of his association had received any fees from the fund.[34]

Despite the new charges, NRC officials refused to respond, perhaps hoping the crisis would pass. This strategy merely compounded the problems, since failure to produce receipts seemed to confirm the charges made by Cunningham and Hughes and many abandoned the NRC.

With the loss of public confidence, NRC officials struggled mightily to save the organization. Just two years earlier, the NRC drew more than six hundred to its annual conference, and many predicted that it would surpass the NAACP as the dominant civil rights organization. Now as the riot fund controversy grew, the organization teetered on the brink of extinction. Out of this chaos a rallying point emerged, Matthew Bullock.[35] Accordingly, NRC officials agreed to pay the cost of Bullock's legal expenses.[36]

However, before the NRC could enter the case, important developments unfolded in Canada. On January 18, 1922, Canadian officials ordered Bullock's deportation. The ruling, however, carried little weight because Ottawa had issued a hold warrant.[37] This meant that local officials could not turn Bullock over to American officials without a release from senior Canadian authorities. Nonetheless, the ruling had some unintended consequences. Newspapers covering the case sympathized with Bullock, and editors from Buxton to York unleashed a steady stream of articles that attacked mob violence. Moreover, many suggested that even if North Carolina officials protected Bullock from lynching, the unwritten legal code of the South would ensure his death.[38] The Canadian government acknowledged this fact and called a cabinet meeting to discuss the case. The next day, January 26, 1922, Charles Stewart, the minister of the interior, released Bullock and announced that he could remain in Canada for three months because he had proven to be an exemplary citizen.[39]

Thinking that his son had weathered the worst part of the storm, four days later the Rev. William Bullock delivered a stirring sermon to a standing-room-only crowd at St. Paul's A.M.E. Church, where he told the story of how Daniel had been thrown into the lion's den so that the lions would devour him. Using his Christian faith as a backdrop, Bullock proclaimed that Daniel had escaped the lions because he believed in God. "So also, can I truthfully say that my son, Matthew, escaped from unjust punishment at the hands of prejudiced parties."[40] Yet, little did he know that his son's release was nothing more than a momentary pause in the unfolding drama between North Carolina and Canada.

6

The Old North State

The ruling by Canadian officials did little to dissuade North Carolina officials. On January 19, 1922, North Carolina prepared a writ of extradition that charged Bullock with attempted murder, conspiracy, and riot. To ensure that Canadian officials honored the notice, Cameron Morrison, the fifty-nine-year-old governor, forwarded the document to the United States State Department for execution.[1]

Like most Southern governors, Morrison's political roots lay in the Democratic Party. Born four years after the Civil War, Morrison spent his youth in Richmond County, a black belt county known for its high quality tobacco. His family's poor financial condition forced him to curtail his dream of a college education, and he worked a succession of jobs to support his family. In the late 1880s, he took a job as a clerk for the Richmond County Register of Deeds, and it appeared that his life would end uneventfully. However, dynamic political changes in North Carolina would change his life forever.

From the late 1870s throughout the 1880s, the price of cotton fell from a high of fifteen cents a pound to less than five cents a pound.[2] This led to farm foreclosures and the increased economic dependency of poor farmers on merchants and large planters.[3] By the early 1890s, the economic situation of poor white farmers had grown so desperate that many began to desert the Democratic Party. This led to the formation of a quasi-political organization called the Farmers Alliance. Within a few years, the Alliance was sponsoring its own group of candidates called Populists. However, other than causing a few distractions, the Populists failed to make any significant gains.[4] But like the old Chinese proverb that states "The enemy of my enemy is my friend," the Populists soon realized that the key to victory lay in forming a political alliance with the Republican Party, which contained a large number of blacks. This alliance, called fusion, led to smashing victories in 1894 and 1896.[5] For Morrison, the changing political situation created an ideal environment. In 1890, just before his twenty-first birthday, he joined the Republican Party and served as a delegate to the state convention.[6]

North Carolina governors Locke Craig (left), Cameron Morrison and T.W. Bickett in a photograph taken in the 1920s (courtesy North Carolina Office of Archives and History, Raleigh).

Despite this fact, in 1894 he abruptly left the Republican Party and became a Democrat. Shortly thereafter he became a Democratic candidate for the state senate.[7] Although he canvassed the state and received a number of votes, he lost the election. This setback bitterly disappointed Morrison, and he organized a group of red shirts and launched a campaign of terror, beating blacks and burning polling stations. In part due to his actions Democrats regained political control of Richmond County.[8]

With this success Morrison quickly made his way through the Democratic Party ranks, eventually winning the governor's office in 1918. Morrison's election produced a sense of hopelessness among African Americans. These fears were not unfounded, for Morrison believed that black progress "must be within the framework of the segregated society ordained by the white man."[9] Blacks were expected to know their place and to present no challenges to white hegemony. Thus, in Morrison's view, Bullock's attack on Raby Traylor represented a serious transgression that must be corrected.

However, for Bullock the threat presented by Morrison carried little weight. After all, Canadian justice, which had freed him, was present, but North

Carolina, which sought his capture, was miles away. Wearing a new suit purchased by his father, he walked down the stairs of the jail. After a brief prayer, Bullock traveled to J.D. Howell's home, where he confidently told his side of the story. The next day, on advice of his attorney, he secretly returned to the United States so he could enter Canada legally. Yet, the danger of kidnapping still lurked.[10] Therefore, shortly after his reentry into Canada, supporters whisked Bullock away to a safe house in Toronto. Over the next two weeks he remained hidden to all but his closest supporters.

When extradition papers failed to arrive in the days following his release, Bullock grew confident that North Carolina had given up the quest to extradite him. He became anxious to go back to work. "I owe it to myself and my friends who were keeping me to get back to work."[11] Consequently, he headed back to Hamilton where he went back to his job.

Meanwhile, in North Carolina problems with the petition delayed the request for extradition. The Webster-Ashburton Treaty called for the return of fugitives upon the receipt of evidence of criminality as accorded by the laws of the place of arrest.[12] In preparing the extradition petition, North Carolina made two mistakes. First, many of the charges were nonextraditable offenses, and Canadian courts frequently rejected the concept of double criminality.[13] Second, North Carolina officials failed to produce evidence of the crime.

John Anderson, fugitive Missouri slave. During Anderson's 1862 extradition case, Canadian courts admitted a deposition into his extradition hearing (courtesy Northamptonshire, UK, Record Office).

On February 9, 1922, upon advice from the State Department, Morrison amended the extradition request, reducing the charges to assault with intent to kill. Moreover, to ensure compliance, Morrison attached two affidavits. A week later, the American Consul Jose de Olivares presented the petition to Canadian Judge Colin Snider and requested Bullock's arrest.[14]

Two days later as Bullock stepped off a streetcar, police arrested the fugitive and brought him before Snider. However, since Treleaven was out of town, the judge postponed formal proceedings until February 24, 1922. He also requested that North Carolina send at least one witness who could present testimony as to Bullock's guilt.[15] Still, Snider's request seemed odd considering the fact that in the majority of extradition cases between the United States and Canada, written evidence alone was sufficient for extradition.

Perhaps no case better illustrates this point than the 1862 case of John Anderson. In 1853, Anderson, a runaway slave from Missouri, killed a white man as he made his way to Canada.[16] Over the next few years, he lived quietly, until a friend alerted authorities. In the days leading up to his trial, witnesses from Missouri arrived in Canada. But, since they had not seen the crime, the crux of the case rested on the testimony of a slave named Phil who had seen the murder. Canadian law granted freedom to all slaves who entered its domain, and it was apparent Phil could not enter Canada. Hence, Missouri officials submitted a deposition in his stead.[17] Although many questions surrounded the deposition — such as whether Phil's testimony was coerced — Anderson's attorney failed to object. Thus, the judge admitted the deposition and as a result ordered Anderson's extradition.[18]*

Yet, regardless of the precedent set by Anderson's case, namely, the introduction of depositions as evidence, Snider charted a new course. Despite this shift, North Carolina officials were confident in their ability to return Bullock to North Carolina. As luck would have it, several years earlier North Carolina had faced a similar situation when it attempted to extract Monroe Rogers from Massachusetts. After attempting to burn a neighbor's home, Monroe Rogers fled to Brockton, Massachusetts, where he was captured several months later.[19] The arrest, however, could not have occurred in a more supportive location. Less than ten miles from Boston, the citizens of Brockton were well known for taking unpopular causes. During the early 1800s, when most of America was experiencing a backlash against foreigners, Brockton's city fathers welcomed hundreds of East European Jews. In the early 1900s, the city continued this tradition by taking in African Americans seeking to escape racism sweeping across the nation.

In light of this fact, it was little surprise that Brockton launched a concerted effort to stop Rogers' extradition. Included in this effort was perhaps the most prominent African American in the nation, William Monroe Trotter. A fiery opponent of Jim Crow, Trotter stood in protest of those who believed blacks to be socially inferior to whites. He also opposed all compromises on civil rights. This placed him in direct opposition to Booker T. Washington, who favored a program of duty, agricultural pursuit, and self-determination rather than seeking full citizenship. When Washington arrived in Boston for a speaking engagement, Trotter and his supporters threw stink bombs that emptied the building and sparked a series of fights. Trotter was thrown in jail.

*Upon appeal, British officials released Anderson on a technicality.

However, when Trotter received news of Monroe Rogers's arrest, he hatched a plan to prevent the fugitive's extradition. A series of articles placed in his newspaper, *The Guardian*, aroused public sentiment by highlighting recent lynchings in North Carolina and the 1898 Wilmington race riot.[20] Moreover, since eight people had been lynched during Governor Charles B. Aycock's first two years in office, the paper also lampooned the governor as a lyncher. He also claimed Rogers would be lynched if he returned to North Carolina.[21]

Influenced by Trotter, W.H. Scott, head of the Massachusetts Racial Protective Association, organized a committee to pay for Rogers's defense and hired Clement G. Morgan as legal counsel. Next, he sent a letter to the *Boston Traveler*: "We shall not allow Monroe Rogers to go back to that hell where men are transformed into demons."[22] Uncertain of the letter's impact, several days later Scott tied Rogers's defense to black dissatisfaction with discrimination. "The plan to extradite Rogers is a deep-laid plan to annihilate the race. It is not Rogers alone whose safety we seek, it is the salvation of the race. This is a test case."[23] As a last line of defense Scott sent letters to governors across the North requesting that they ignore extradition papers from North Carolina until the case was settled.

Munroe Rogers, circa 1902. After extradition from Massachusetts, Rogers returned to North Carolina, where he served ten years at Central Prison. After his release Rogers lived for a short time in Durham and then disappeared (photograph from a picture taken by the *Boston Guardian*).

Over the course of the next week Scott's letter campaign caught the eye of the Massachusetts attorney general, Herbert Parker. As a result, when Durham officials arrived in Boston, the attorney general refused to release the fugitive. Using a legal technicality, he declared the extradition papers incomplete.[24] Federal law required that states seeking to extradite a prisoner needed to present a copy of the indictment or affidavit as well as a copy of the warrant. Since North Carolina only submitted a copy of the warrant and a statement from Governor Aycock, Massachusetts officials refused to accept the extradition petition.

On the heels of this victory Scott convinced Massachusetts

Governor Winthrop M. Crane to hold a hearing to determine if Rogers would be released or extradited should North Carolina amend its application. The significance of this development cannot be overlooked, for it provided Rogers's supporters with a forum to highlight race and economic conditions facing African Americans in North Carolina. Consequently, when the hearing opened, Rogers's attorney maintained, presumably because Rogers was black, "that there was no security for Rogers against lynching and no show for him before the North Carolina courts."[25] The hearing, however, did not help Rogers. Two days earlier North Carolina had corrected its extradition application. Massachusetts had no legal ground to retain Rogers. Nonetheless, Massachusetts held Rogers until Governor Aycock sent a letter that guaranteed Rogers's safety from lynching upon his return to North Carolina.[26]

Furious at the humiliation, Aycock urged the North Carolina legislature to speed up the trials of men charged with a crime. He felt this would allow the state to execute criminals in a timely manner and reduce extralegal violence. Moreover, it would prevent antilynching activists and states such as Massachusetts from charging that North Carolina was a hotbed for mob violence. The legislature, however, had little interest in the governor's proposal and soundly defeated the legislation. Nonetheless, the Rogers case convinced North Carolina officials that the key to success in extradition cases lay in persistence and patience. Since Matthew Bullock had been on the run for almost a year, the state had demonstrated its patience. Now it was time for persistence to carry the day.

Second Arrest

Reaction to Bullock's second arrest was markedly different in Canada and North Carolina. When J.D. Howell learned of the arrest, he declared, "Bullock was foolish to come back to Hamilton."[27] Nonetheless, he informed supporters and contacted the NAACP. The next day NRC officials telegraphed that they would continue to pay Bullock's attorneys.[28]

Meanwhile, in North Carolina, officials anxiously awaited the return of Bullock. In an attempt to influence Canadians and Northerners to drop their opposition to Bullock's extradition, Governor Morrison conducted an interview with the *New York Times*:

> Lynchings are never winked at by the authorities and are always prevented where the authorities have any knowledge of the approach of danger and an opportunity to prevent it. What has come to be called a lynching in the South is nothing but ordinary killings in other sectors of the country.[29]

Unfortunately, when Morrison's comments appeared in the paper, they not only sparked controversy but also led to a growing condemnation of the

North Carolina governor. Given that Plummer Bullock's lynching had stemmed from a minor altercation over some rotten apples, Morrison's suggestion that most victims of lynchings were criminals failed to resonate in the North. Moreover, Canadian and black newspapers soon picked up the interview, rallying others to Bullock's defense.[30]

Additionally, in the period between Matthew Bullock's flight and his capture, North Carolina experienced two lynchings. On August 14, 1921, in response to the purported rape of a farmer's wife in Jones County, vigilantes lynched Jerome Whitfield, a twenty-five-year-old African American.[31] One month later a mob in Chatham County hung Ernest Daniels for entering the bedroom of a white teenager.[32] In neither of these cases did local officials conduct a vigorous investigation and members of the mobs, though perhaps widely known, went unpunished.* Undoubtedly, this added credence to the claims of those who maintained that Bullock would be lynched if he returned to North Carolina.

As support for Bullock grew, Treleaven launched an investigation to determine what type of evidence North Carolina had collected in the case. To obtain

---

*On August 14, 1921, rural Jones County was aroused by the report of a sexual assault on a young white woman. According to the woman, as she walked down an isolated country road with her baby, she saw Jerome Whitfield walking in the opposite direction.[33] This did not cause any alarm since Whitfield worked as a sharecropper on her husband's farm. But as Whitfield passed he grabbed her baby and threw the infant to the ground. Then he dragged the woman into a ditch where he raped her.[34] After the attack the woman, holding her frightened baby, ran home and reported the assault. Whether the victim's husband reported the attack to authorities is unknown. However, from published reports it appears that he bypassed this formality. Instead he called on his neighbors to administer frontier justice. Within an hour a posse formed and a search was launched.[35] As several dozen men watched Whitfield's home, others numbering in the hundreds scoured nearby woods and fields. After several hours the mob found their quarry hiding in some bushes, about seven miles from the site of the attack. At gunpoint they forced him into a car and rushed him back to the victim's home.[36] When she saw Whitfield the farmer's wife exclaimed, "He is the man."[37] At this several men hit Whitfield with the butts of their guns. Others spit on him. After that they threw a rope over a limb of a tree, and placed a hangman's knot around his neck. Then they hosted their unfortunate quarry off the ground.[38] The next day the county coroner announced that Whitfield's death had come at the hands of persons unknown. However, due to the tacit support, or even possible involvement of police, local authorities did not investigate Whitfield's murder as many undoubtedly felt he was guilty of the crime of which he was charged. A little more than a month after Whitfield's death, North Carolina faced another lynching. Shortly before midnight on September 16, 1921, Gertrude Stone, a sixteen-year-old white teenager, awakened to find a man standing over her bed.[39] Peering into the darkness, she assumed the figure was her brother and called his name.[40] This frightened the intruder, and the stranger ran away. The next morning authorities using bloodhounds tracked the man to a nearby cabin, the home of Earnest Daniels. After questioning and quite possibly a beating, officers claimed that Daniels confessed to breaking into Stone's home.[41] At this, officers placed Daniels in the Chatham County jail. However, Daniels's stay in the jail would last less than ten hours. Just after midnight several dozen men surrounded the jail.[42] After two unsuccessful attempts the mob broke into the jail and "supposedly" overpowered the jailer. Then at gunpoint they seized Daniels. Several miles away they placed a rope around his neck and hoisted his badly battered body off the ground. Then while he slowly strangled the mob randomly fired shots into the doomed man.[43] At daybreak county officials held a jury of inquest, which adjourned after viewing the body. No further attempts were made to investigate the crime. From published reports it appears that Daniels's lynching had little to do with the crime in which he was charged and more to do with sending a message to would-be criminals. According to local newspapers, in the days before the lynching several violent crimes had been committed. The lynching was viewed as a climax to this anger.[44]

this evidence, he asked the NAACP's Walter White to use the organization's contacts in North Carolina to secure the necessary documentation. However, instead of retrieving the court records, White threatened to withdraw from the case. "Since the National Race Congress is handling the case, we will be glad to turn it over to them."[45] Meanwhile NRC officials, aware of the significance of the case, defiantly advised White that they wanted no duplicity on the part of the NAACP. Nonetheless, Howell could ill afford to lose the support of either organization, and he pretended he was ignorant as to the NRC's role or how they had gotten involved in the case while he secretly maintained contact with the NRC. Moreover, considering the fact that the NAACP's investment in the case was minimal and

Attorney Freeman Ferrier Treleaven, circa 1925 (courtesy Local History and Archives, Hamilton, Ontario, Public Library).

the potential returns great, White's protestations were nothing more than a ploy to rid the NAACP of a troubling rival.[46]

Nonetheless, the reality of the Dyer Anti-Lynching Bill, scheduled for a Senate vote at the end of February, led White to reconsider his stance, and he contacted R. McCants Andrews, a Durham attorney, who collected the court records from North Carolina.[47] Subsequent review of the documents failed to produce an affidavit of the crime. In fact, the total scope of North Carolina's evidence consisted of a two-page summary that outlined the sentences of the black participants of the Norlina riot.

On February 24, 1922, Snider summoned Bullock for his second hearing. Although a massive snowstorm blanketed Hamilton the night before, blacks and newspaper reporters packed the courtroom.[48] North Carolina officials, however, failed to attend the hearing, and De Olivares requested a second delay. S.F. Washington, who served as Bullock's co-counsel, vigorously objected because he felt North Carolina would fabricate evidence. To ease these fears, Snider ruled that Bullock's attorneys had the right to review all evidence submitted by North Carolina before the proceedings. Since no one was killed, the main thing that had to be proven was intent, of which the affidavits only told half the truth. Therefore, Snider reasserted his earlier decision that Bullock's counsel should have the full opportunity to cross-examine witnesses from North Carolina. "While it is my duty and my desire to order the giving up of this prisoner if a case of attempted murder is made out against him ... I also owe a duty to the prisoner, and that is to see that a case is made. Cross-examination of state witnesses is absolutely necessary."[49] Snider then granted a second delay; however, he ominously declared that this would be the last delay in the case.[50]

Over the next few days, the U.S. State Department, confused by Snider's ruling, sought counsel as to its legitimacy. De Olivares hired Hamilton attorney C.W. Bell to conduct a review of the decision. Bell's review indicated that Snider was within his rights. Article X of the Webster-Ashburton Treaty specified that extradition must be based upon the evidence of criminality according to the laws of the place where the fugitive or persons so charged shall be found.[51] Moreover, Bell maintained that the Canadian Extradition Act made witness testimony mandatory. While written evidence was allowable, courts were under no obligation to accept it. Although Bell's interpretation was extreme, the State Department accepted it.[52]

Meanwhile, in Canada many officials began to question Snider's ruling. Foremost in this charge were police. Before the Bullock case, Canadian police in the border areas routinely picked up American suspects and summarily turned them over to American authorities, without hearings, while U.S. officials responded in like fashion.[53] Snider's ruling threatened to destroy this collaboration. Aware of the long-term ramifications, S.J. Dickson, chief of the Toronto Police Force, wrote to Albert J. Caudron, superintendent of criminal investigation for the Royal Canadian Mounted Police, the following:

> I am not interested in what takes place in Hamilton. I am interested in the effect the procedures with regard to the negro Bullock is going to have upon the extradition of criminals who go to the United States to escape the laws of the country.... I know nothing about the case other than what has appeared in the press, but it does seem to me that the effect of all the nonsense concerning this negro will be that the police authorities acting in the interest of the people of Canada will have a very hard time to have criminals returned to Canada in the future if the procedure advocated at Hamilton is followed. As you know, we have always had the greatest cooperation with them in the passing back and forth of criminals wanted by the respective countries. Therefore I submit that it is high time that some official action should be taken to check the activities of those who are apparently trying to put stumbling blocks in the way of the police.[54]

Nonetheless, the slow movement of the Canadian government prevented intervention by the Canadian Department of Justice until after the case's end.

For Cameron Morrison, Snider's ruling and its subsequent acceptance by the United States State Department represented a major disappointment. From the start of the case, the governor had taken a low-key approach, corresponding with U.S. State Department officials and correcting problems in North Carolina's extradition petition. The reasons for the governor's actions are not difficult to fathom. It is plausible that Morrison thought that in the absence of aggressive action by North Carolina, the U.S. State Department would adopt the case. For Canadian officials this would present problems, since American officials could easily interpret the failure to extradite Bullock as an affront to the United States. Never had it occurred to Morrison that Canadians would resist Bullock's deportation and that his defense would become a cause célèbre across the both nations. This threatened to cast a shadow over North Carolina, destroying many of the recent gains made by the state.

At the start of the twentieth century North Carolina was one of the nation's most backward states. "Her people were among the most disease-ridden in the nation, her children among the most unschooled, her farmers among the most inefficient."[55] The development of the textile industry offered North Carolina a chance to improve its lot. Between 1900 and 1910 the value of the state's textile output increased from $95,000,000 to $217,000,000.[56] "To exponents of the New South every new mill established in the state was a symbol of progress; industrialization, they held, was the panacea for just about all of North Carolina's woes."[57]

Nonetheless, by 1915, the state's inefficient road system threatened to slow further growth. To address this problem, on February 17, 1921, the legislature passed the Highway Act. This law authorized bond issues of $50,000,000 to build and construct the highway system.[58] For investors, North Carolina's financial situation presented some challenges. Several years before Morrison became governor, North Carolina defaulted on bonds totaling ten million dollars.[59] In response, the Council for Foreign Shareholders in London sent out a notice advising against the purchase of North Carolina bonds.[60] Additionally, New York State laws prohibited the risk of savings bank money in the bonds of a state that had defaulted on the payment of its public debt preceding its application for new loans.[61]

In mid–July 1921 North Carolina opened bids on $5,000,000 of road bonds. Despite advertising the sale in newspapers and financial journals across the nation, only $17,700 worth of the bonds were sold.[62] To obtain the funds necessary to launch highway construction, in late September the state treasurer negotiated a loan of $5,000,000 from a New York syndicate headed by the First National Bank and Banker's Trust. However, due to past financial problems, the rate of interest on the loans was extremely high at six percent.[63]

Nonetheless, the loans did not improve the slow sale of North Carolina bonds. In late 1921, Governor Morrison and the state treasurer traveled to New York to meet with bankers. These meetings resulted in the sale of $4,500,000 worth of bonds. The sale, however, only represented ten percent of the bonds authorized by the legislature. To sell the remaining bonds and lower the rates of interest, in January 1922 Morrison again entered into negotiations with the New York bankers. At this stage Matthew Bullock stormed to the front pages of American newspapers. Because the NAACP had its headquarters in New York and quite possibly because many New York bankers were acquainted with the case, the governor undoubtedly lost his enthusiasm for bringing Bullock back to North Carolina. On February 24, 1922, he wired Fletcher:

> North Carolina will not make an appearance through attorney in any Canadian court. It will not send witnesses to have a trial before any court there. If there is any error in form or regularity of application for the extradition of this fugitive from justice, I will be glad to have it corrected as far as correction can be made in truth. If Canada will not honor our requisition in the regular way and you cannot through diplomatic channels convince them they should do, I hope you will not hereafter request North Carolina or any other self-respecting state of the union in any way honor a request from Canada.[64]

With Morrison's refusal, the only thing that stood in the way of Bullock's release was two affidavits. On March 3, 1922, Bullock entered the courtroom for the last time. When De Olivares attempted to present the affidavits and warrants from North Carolina, Snider refused this evidence. "I asked for oral evidence, and I cannot accept these documents."[65] Turning to Bullock, he dismissed the charges.

However, the release of Bullock failed to end the controversy surrounding Snider's decision. Many in Canada, from local police departments to the Canadian Department of Justice, felt the ruling would harm U.S./Canadian relations.[66] Accordingly, Snider drafted a long letter defending his actions in which he maintained that he did not make a single ruling adverse to the United States. In fact, he argued that he yielded several times to American officials when he issued a warrant for Bullock without the proper documentation and when he remanded the fugitive for a second seven-day period. However, Snider maintained that it was evident that North Carolina had no depositions. Thus, it was essential that Morrison produce a witness to identify Bullock and present an account of the crime.[67] Snider also pointed to misuse of terms as a factor for his decision. Throughout much of America, affidavits were known as depositions or vice versa. Doubtlessly, Snider was aware of these details as extradition cases quite frequently came before Canadian Courts. Perhaps in sympathy for Bullock, Snider refused to recognize minor language barriers and thus excluded such evidence. Nonetheless, with the release of Matthew Bullock the final phase of the drama started its slow march to conclusion.

7

One Million Klansmen

On the steps of the Hamilton Courthouse, Matthew Bullock wrapped himself in a British flag.[1] The symbolism of the moment — a North Carolina fugitive clothed in the Union Jack — proclaimed the moral superiority of the Canadian justice system while disparaging the Southern legal system. However, in North Carolina reaction was vastly different. When Cameron Morrison received news of Bullock's release, he attempted to bully Henry Fletcher, the undersecretary of state, by heading to the U.S. State Department accompanied by North Carolina Senators Furnifold Simmons and Lee Overman.[2] When this had no impact, Morrison angrily scoffed:

> The release of Matthew Bullock by the Canadian authorities establishes a precedent which promises to hinder and thwart the administration of Justice in this country.... It simply means that a criminal in the United States can assure himself of absolute safety if it is possible for him to evade arrest long enough to get across the border. Before you finally consent to the interpretation of the treaty with Great Britain which embraced Canada, as made by Canadian authorities I wish you consider the serious consequences to the administration of justice in this country. There is no legislation, national or state, with which witnesses can be forced to go to a foreign county and testify.[3]

In spite of the defeat, Morrison did not abandon the effort to bring Bullock back. In a letter to Furnifold Simmons, the governor threatened to hire detectives and dispatch them to the Canadian border where they could track Bullock's movements. If Bullock crossed the border, the detectives would seize the fugitive and deliver him to North Carolina.[4]

Conscious of this threat, Bullock moved to Toronto and got a job as a porter at Union Station. It lasted a little less than four weeks. On March 17, 1922, Arthur Talmage Abernethy, leader of the Ku Klux Klan, speaking to a crowd in Hickory, pledged to kidnap Bullock and return him to North Carolina. "One million members of the Ku Klux Klan from Maine to Florida are pledged to bring the Norlina negro from Canada to North Carolina for trial ...

On the steps of the Hamilton Courthouse, circa 1922. After winning the right to stay in Canada, Matthew Bullock posed proudly with his father and attorneys for the *Toronto Sun*. Pictured clockwise from the front center are Matthew Bullock, the Rev. William Bullock; the Rev. J.D. Howell; S.D. Washington; and S. Treleaven (courtesy Sun Media Corporation).

and this will happen in ninety days."[5] Since Abernethy was one of the most influential Klan leaders in the United States, such a threat could not be taken lightly. After graduating from Rutherford College, Abernethy made a name for himself by writing editorials for newspapers in Pennsylvania and New York.[6] However, what Abernethy was best known for was his collection of widely read novels and provocative books such as *The Jew a Negro: Being a Study of the Jewish Ancestry from an Impartial Standpoint*, in which he sought to prove through ethnology and biblical scripture that Jews are the kinsmen as well as the descendants of negroes, whom he considered to be little better than beasts.[7]

Later when Abernethy returned to North Carolina, he joined the Klan and became pastor of Asheville's First Christian Church. As a minister and Klansman, he sought to use pressure tactics to influence local officials to do the Klan's will. Perhaps no case better illustrates this point than that of Helen Garlington and Etyln Maurice. When Abernethy heard a rumor that the two white women were involved romantically with African American men, he organized a purity campaign that led authorities to sentence the women to one year in prison for adultery.[8]

Still Abernethy and his followers were little more than a microcosm of Klan activity sweeping the nation. Operating as if it were more of a fraternal organization, the Klan of the 1920s rose to prominence by opposing blacks, whom many whites felt had been corrupted by wartime experiences. With such an agenda, the Klan spread to Mobile, Birmingham, Atlanta, and Montgomery. However, the Klan remained little more than a regional phenomenon until two Atlanta publicists, Edward Clarke and Bessie Tyler, recognized the organization's financial potential. In return for two dollars and fifty cents for each new recruit, Clarke and Tyler launched a campaign that highlighted prejudice against immigrants, Jews, Catholics, suspected radicals, prostitutes, wife beaters, and those who were deemed to be morally corrupt. This allowed the Klan to grow from a small Southern organization to a national powerhouse as strong chapters were established in the Midwest, West, and Southwest. This growth allowed the Klan to gain several seats in the U.S. House of Representatives and to control the state governments in Tennessee, Indiana, Oklahoma, and Oregon.

The Klan, however, was still the Klan, and violence formed a big part of the organization's culture. In an exposé published over a three-week period in 1921, the *New York World* chronologically listed more than 152 acts of violence committed by members of the invisible empire, including lynchings, murders, floggings, and kidnappings.[9] This led to an investigation by the U.S. Congress that did little except to provide free publicity. As a result Klan membership doubled, and recruiters of the invisible empire marched across the border into Canada.

As in the United States the postwar period in Canada ushered in a period of intense nativism. This led to increasing fear among whites that they were being overrun by Jews, Catholics, and immigrants. As a result Klan organizers found receptive audiences in Canada. Chapters were organized in Alberta, Manitoba, Saskatchewan, British Columbia, and Ontario. It is for that reason that when Abernethy declared that the invisible empire would kidnap Bullock, there was great concern that Canadian Klansmen would attempt to carry out this command.

However, when Bullock heard of Abernethy's threat he maintained that the Klan's threat did not bother him one bit. "They'll have a long way to come to get me heah [*sic*].... It looks to me this was intended to scare me and start me running.... But if I run it won't be in the direction of the United States and fo [*sic*] present I don't intend to leave Toronto."[10] Nonetheless, the Klan threat caused serious concerns for Bullock's supporters.[11] At the insistence of J.D. Howell, Bullock disappeared. Several weeks later Howell proclaimed that Bullock safely arrived on another continent.[12]

Yet the central question still remains: Whatever happened to Matthew Bullock? In his article *With Intent to Kill Matthew Bullock: When Hamilton Defied Rednecks and White Hoods*, Robin Rowland maintained that after his release in 1922 Bullock sailed to England, and disappeared. Others maintain that Bullock lived most of his life in England and returned to the United States in mid–1960s and died in Washington, D.C., while many in Canada claim that Bullock never left the Dominion. After the trial he moved to Windsor, where he reestablished his life using an alias. In preparing this manuscript, the author painstakingly researched each assumption; however, like the lost continent of Atlantis, Matthew Bullock was never found.

8

Law and Order Must Prevail: North Carolina Efforts to Punish Lynch Mob Members 1919–1923

The Matthew Bullock case forced North Carolina political leaders to take a new approach to end mob violence, one of actively prosecuting members of lynch mobs. Although the state convicted its first mob participant in 1906, the position generally taken by governors until the early 1920s was one of indifference.* In short, the governors refused to enforce North Carolina's antilynching laws since such a stance would imply displeasure with the state's Jim Crow society. However, by the 1920s, several factors, such as northern investment, technological enhancements that improved newspaper coverage of mob violence, and the movement of hundreds of black farm laborers from the state coalesced to pressure state leaders to curb mob violence.

In light of these facts, in the early 1920s North Carolina officials announced a new policy to halt lynching. At the first sign of mob violence the governor would send troops to threatened points on his own initiative. Prior to this change, governors waited for requests from local authorities before taking action. Such a system meant that troops often arrived too late. In addition, state leaders authorized troops to use real bullets to guard suspects from mob violence. This provision was significant since before 1917, officials were reluctant to authorize troops to fire upon local citizens. Accordingly, troops were given blank cartridges or ordered to fire over the heads of mobs.[1] With this being the case, mobs often "treated the presence of troops as a solemn joke."[2] However, this would all change in 1920.

In 1906, North Carolina successfully prosecuted George Hall and sentenced him to fifteen years in prison for leading the mob that lynched John Gillespie, Nease Gillespie, and Jack Dillingham.

In the summer of 1920, after the brutal rape of an Alamance County house-wife, officials arrested a young African American named George Troxler and placed him in the county jail.[3] As in many such cases, news of the assault and arrest fueled the growth of an angry mob of over 1,500.[4]

For Governor Thomas Bickett, the threat of violence was particularly trou-bling. Elected to the governor's office in 1917, Bickett gained a reputation as a reformer by securing passage of legislation that improved the treatment of the mentally ill, and by reducing the amount of interest landlords could charge for extending supplies or credit under the crop lien system. Yet, in regards to lynch-ing, he had perhaps the most unique perspective of any governor. As a former attorney general, he had led efforts to prosecute lynch mob participants. How-ever, during Bickett's three years as governor, North Carolina experienced five lynchings. This made his administration one of the most violent eras in the state's history. Perhaps stunned by this dubious distinction, the governor ordered a company of the Durham National Guard to proceed to Alamance County. "Protect those prisoners at all hazards and notify the people that I have ordered you and your machine gunners to shoot straight if an attempt on the life of the prisoners is made."[5]

The presence of the troops did not deter the mob. Around 8:00 P.M., while several members of the mob staged a protest another group attempted to sneak into the rear of the building. However, before they reached the jail, they were spotted by soldiers and retreated into a nearby cornfield. After this failed attempt, the men tried to approach the jail from the side.[6] Again, the soldiers issued a warning. This time a voice replied "phaw [sic] I am not afraid of blank cartridges."[7] Then a shot rang out and the soldiers opened fire. At the end of the barrage one of the members of the mob, Jim Ray, lay dead and another man, Willie Phillips, lay mortally wounded.[8]

Yet, even this did not end the threat to the jail. The sound of gunfire attracted hundreds of onlookers. When they learned of Ray's death, several hotheads threatened to dynamite the jail. This time the governor ordered North Carolina's adjutant general, John Van B. Metts, and another company of troops to Alamance County. While these reinforcements gathered, a hard rain fell and the crowd around the jail dispersed.[9]

Still this did not bring calm to Graham. Shortly after the shooting sixty citizens signed a petition that asked the governor to prosecute the soldiers for murdering an innocent man.[10] In addition, the Alamance County attorney held a formal inquest.

Due to this pressure, Governor Bickett formed a commission to conduct an investigation into the troop's conduct. "In view of the action of the civil authorities ... I deem it due the soldiers on duty and the citizenship of the entire state to have a careful investigation made of ... the conduct of the troops on the night of July 19th."[11]

Two weeks after the shooting, the commission held a formal hearing to investigate the soldiers' conduct. The first person called to testify was John Thompson, a member of the company guarding the jail. Thompson maintained that when the order was issued for his company to go to Graham, he was already in the town visiting his sister. However, since he did not have his uniform, he could not participate in the operation, so he mingled with the mob gathered around the jail. In this manner, he overheard men, including Jim Ray and Willie Phillip, planning an attack on the jail later that night.[12] Following Thompson, the state called Captain Marion Butler, the commander of the soldiers. Butler said that shortly after his soldiers deployed, a group of masked men approached through a cornfield.[13] When the men got close enough, someone fired a shot. In response, the machine gun stationed at the rear of the jail opened fire. While this was going on, Butler said, he tried to contact the jailer and the sheriff. However, it took him more than two hours before he found either man. Even then the sheriff refused to visit the jail until the next day.[14]

The sheriff's actions seemed to confirm what many members of the commission felt — namely, that local officials were directly involved in the attack or provided tacit support to those who attacked the jail. Perhaps it was for that reason that two weeks later the commission submitted a report to Governor Bickett that exonerated the troops. Reading from a prepared statement, the chair of the commission maintained, "The conduct of the officers and men of the machine gun company from the time they reached Graham until they were relieved was in every respect most exemplary and soldierlike."[15]

Even more surprising, one month later officials released George Troxler. In court it was revealed that the main evidence against Troxler were bloodhounds that tied his scent to the crime. However, according to the judge, "The bloodhound test was not sufficient evidence on which to base a conviction in the absence of probable cause. The bloodhound test could only be used to corroborate other evidence."[16]

For Bickett, the ruling by the commission and the decision rendered by court proved the wisdom of his decision to send troops to Graham. More importantly, he was convinced that the decision had shown people across the state and the nation that North Carolina was committed to ending mob violence even if it meant firing on local citizens.

Yet, even the threat of being fired on by law enforcement officers did not break the hold of Judge Lynch. Only six days after the state released Jim Troxler, Alamance County was rocked by another outbreak of mob violence. This violence stemmed from reports that a young black man had attempted to rape a five-year-old child. Angered by this report, a posse of twenty-five citizens that included the president of Elon College, William Allen Harper, tracked down the suspect and transported him to the Alamance County Jail in Graham.[17] Since court was already in session, it was decided that the suspect identified as John Jeffress would face a judge and jury later in the day.

After several hours of preparation, court officials announced that they were ready for the case and the sheriff and six of his deputies were sent to the jail to escort the prisoner to the courthouse. Unfortunately, before they could reach the building vigilantes seized the suspect and murdered him in a hail of gunfire.[18]

Stunned by this act, the attorney general of North Carolina held a hearing to identify the men responsible for the murder. The first person called to testify was the sheriff. According to the sheriff, "Resistance to the mob would have been futile since it was made up of between twenty-five and fifty determined men."[19] Moreover, the sheriff maintained that there were at least 150 additional men nearby whose sympathies were with the mob. Since this was the second act of mob violence involving the lawman in less than two months, it was clear that the sheriff and his deputies were either involved in planning Jeffress's seizure, or they sympathized with the mob's action since there was not a shot fired, not even a gun drawn during the scuffle between the mob and the lawmen.[20] Nonetheless, state officials made no attempt to investigate the possible involvement of authorities in Jeffress's death. Instead, after several hours of testimony, state officials closed the investigation. There are several factors that led to this decision. For one, Governor Bickett realized that by opening a full-scale investigation the state would run the risk of reigniting tensions in Alamance County, which were just starting to subside. Second, an investigation might damage his political support statewide. This was extremely important since there were rumors that Bickett planned to seek election to the U.S. Congress after his term as governor ended. However, this setback did not end the effort to punish those responsible for mob violence in North Carolina.

Three months after Jeffress's death, a violent attack in Goldsboro presented North Carolina with another opportunity to punish mob participants. This time the state sentenced H.B. Futrelle to four years in jail.[21] The origins of the case stemmed from the murder of a well-known local merchant named Herman Jones.[22]* The day after the murder, officials arrested several black men and charged them with the crime. However, when the suspects were placed in the Goldsboro jail, a lawless element formed and there was real fear that local

*According to Jones's wife several black men shot her husband in order to cover a botched robbery. On the day before the murder several of the suspects visited Jones's store and purchased gasoline. When Jones made change he displayed a large amount of cash that his wife thought may have played a role in her husband's death. However, a more likely scenario came from Paul Williams, one of the men suspected in Jones's death. While in Central Prison Williams maintained that he had shot Jones over a disputed liquor sale. Officers arrested five African American men-Harry Caldwell, Frank Williams, Jesse Foster, George Pearsall and Jim Hill-for the murder of Herman Jones. In a trial held the day after the jail incident, a Wayne County Court sentenced Harry Caldwell and Jesse Foster to death and gave the other suspects sentences of twenty years each.

troublemakers would attempt to lynch the suspects.[23]* For that reason, the sheriff transferred the men to Raleigh. Unfortunately, officials failed to move the trial. This meant that the same hotheads would await the suspects when they returned to Goldsboro to stand trial.

Taking this into account, the sheriff devised a plan to deceive anyone planning to harm the suspects. On the day before the trial he placed the prisoners aboard a train and headed toward Goldsboro. When they reached a point a few miles from town, the sheriff transferred the men to a car. Somehow, news of the plan leaked and a score of angry men headed to ambush the men. However, before the mob could take its vengeance the sheriff rushed the prisoners to a nearby swamp, where they hid in a ditch.[24] A few minutes later the highway was filled with cars and angry men searching for the prisoners.

When they were unable to find the suspects, the mob headed back to Goldsboro and stormed the jail. As they breached the door, a bullet struck one of the men, Herbert Futrelle. Apparently, this unnerved the rest of the mob, and they abandoned the effort to enter the jail. Even so, the violence angered state leaders who were at this time trying to improve North Carolina's image abroad. For that reason, two months later North Carolina officials charged Futrelle with inciting a riot. Then they sentenced him to four years in prison for his role in storming the jail.[25] Yet the conviction merely marked a minor victory for the opponents of lynching in the seesaw battle with the proponents of Judge Lynch.

*Several years earlier Goldsboro had been the site of Jim Richards lynching.

9

The Needleman Case

Mob action against blacks was not the only violence faced by North Carolinians. During the first three decades of the twentieth century a growing wave of anti–Jewish sentiment spread across America. Much of this resentment sprang from the murder of Mary Phagan. In sensational tabloid accounts, Leo Frank, a Jewish factory manager, was accused of bizarre sexual crimes and of the murder of Mary Phagan, a thirteen-year-old white girl employed at his factory. After a highly charged trial, Georgia officials sentenced Frank to death for the crime. Since serious questions of his guilt remained, the governor of Georgia commuted Frank's sentence to life in prison. However, Frank never served the term, as a mob calling itself the Knights of Mary Phagan broke into the prison and lynched him. Ironically, evidence actually pointed to Jim Conley, the factory's black janitor who the prosecution claimed only helped Frank dispose of Phagan's body. Nonetheless, the Frank case played a major role in the formation of the new Klan in 1915, which at its inception was decidedly anti–Semitic.

In addition to the Frank case, other anti–Jewish sentiment was spurred by Henry Ford in his newspaper *The Dearborn Independent*. The *Independent*, which ran from 1920 to 1927, published a host of anti–Jewish articles and editorials such as the *Protocols of the Learned Elders of Zion*, which claimed that atheism in Europe was a Jewish plot. In 1920, *The Dearborn Independent* released the four-volume bound set titled the *International Jews, the World's Foremost Problem*, which claimed that a Jewish conspiracy planned to gain global hegemony by manipulating world economics.

For North Carolina, anti–Jewish sentiment manifested itself in one of the most celebrated case of mob violence in North Carolina history, the flogging of Joseph Needleman, a twenty-year-old Jewish salesman. This case stemmed from the alleged rape of a nineteen-year-old white woman named Effie Griffin.[1] According to Griffin, she had gone on a date with Needleman, during which Needleman drove his car into a secluded side road and raped her at gunpoint.[2]

After the assault Griffin claimed that Needleman threatened to kill her if she told anyone.[3] Nonetheless, several days later, Griffin told her mother who in turn had an arrest warrant sworn out for Needleman.

Yet, there were several troubling questions about the account given by Griffin. According to Needleman, on the day of the attack he and Griffin planned to see a movie in Washington, North Carolina. On the way to the movie, they stopped for a soda and then drove to a secluded spot where they had a consensual encounter.[4] Needleman's version of the events appears to be substantiated by Griffin's actions after the attack. According to the owner of the store where Griffin worked, two days after the assault Needleman came into the store, and he spent time chatting with Griffin. "Together they dressed a show window and seemed to be very friendly."[5] Several days later, Needleman again visited Griffin. During none of these visits did Griffin report the incidents nor did she exhibit any apprehension when Needleman's appeared.[6]

At any rate, one week later authorities arrested Needleman in nearby Edenton and took him to the Martin County jail in Williamston where he would be held until his hearing. However, the next day Martin County officials canceled the hearing when Griffin claimed she was sick and could not attend.[7] Ironically, on the same day, Griffin although supposedly ill, recovered enough to get married.[8]

Meanwhile as news of Needleman's arrest spread, a host of curious townsmen from Williamston and the surrounding area traveled in and out of the jail to hurl insults and to see the man that had raped one of their girls. As a result of this traffic, several townsmen concerned for Needleman's safety asked Sheriff Robertson to provide a guard for the jail.[9] However, Robertson arrogantly refused this request. Then he made it easier should anyone decide to attack Needleman by leaving the jail unguarded for the night.[10]

To no one's surprise, shortly after midnight several dozen men broke into the unguarded jail. With a sledgehammer the men started to pound the locks on Needleman's cell. Startled by the noise Needleman jumped from his bed and turned on a light. To his surprise he saw several men cutting the lock on his cell. When he shouted, "Paul Sparrow, what in the hell are you doing here?"[11] one of the men replied, "We are going to take you where your father's money will do no good."[12] With that, the men burst into his cell and roughly handled the salesman. Then they threw him into the back seat of a car and sped away. As they traveled down main street one of the men shouted "We have come after your sexual organs.... Which do you prefer to give up, them or your head?"[13] Since he thought the men planned to murder him, Needleman told them to do as they pleased.[14]

When they reached Skewarkee Church on the outskirts of town, they forced Needleman to enter some woods. However, at this point several of the vigilantes began to have second thoughts. When the leader of the mob asked several men to castrate Needleman, they all replied that they could not.[15] As a result, the man forced Needleman to the ground and ripped the salesman's underwear away. Then he pulled out a knife and began to hack at Needleman's testicles. As Needleman screamed in pain the man made two small incisions, forced his fingers inside the slits, and ripped out Needleman's testicles.[16] Then he ominously threatened that if Needleman reported the crime, "or got on the stand and swore against an American girl he was dead."[17] After that the mob left.

Unfortunately, Needleman's torment had not ended. Bleeding profusely and near death, he walked to several nearby homes for help. However, each of the homeowners refused to aid the stricken man, and he staggered nearly a mile and a half to the Britt Hotel in Williamston before he received help. Still, due to the severity of his wounds most felt that Needleman would not live through the day. They summoned the sheriff so that he could take a report before Needleman succumbed. However, when the sheriff arrived, Needleman said that he did not know who was behind the assault.[18] But he reversed his course later when Dr. Warren arrived by whispering the names of his attackers to the doctor.[19]

The next day when news of the attack reached Governor Angus McLean, he issued a reward of $400, the maximum allowed by North Carolina law.[20] Then he sent a telegram to Solicitor Dornell Gilliam:

> I have issued proclamation and offered reward of four hundred dollars for each person apprehended and found guilty of the unlawful taking of prisoners from the jail in Martin County or mutilating him after he was taken from jail. I call your attention to public law eighteen hundred and ninety-three, chapter four hundred and sixty one, which enable you to exercise special powers. Hope you will urge County Commissioners of Martin County to offer rewards similar to those offered by me. If you deem it proper you can have Justice of the Peace issue warrant and designate special officers to apprehend guilty parties. I heartily commend your prompt and vigorous action in trying to bring to justice all parties that are responsible for this terrible crime against the laws of our state. If I can aid you in any way please advise.[21]

In any case, the motivation for the governor's prompt action had little to do with Needleman and more to do with Northern investment. As a prominent businessman, Governor McLean certainly knew that failure to punish those responsible for the attack on Needleman would bring unwanted scrutiny by investors and industrialists interested in relocating to the state.[22]* Conse-

---

*McLean served as governor of North Carolina from 1925 to 1929. Prior to assuming the governor's office he was a successful businessman. As a businessman he held extensive holdings in real estate, banking, railroad, and in the textile sector. In the early 1890s he entered politics by serving as the chair of the Roberson County Democratic Committee. He later became state chair of Woodrow Wilson's 1912 and 1916 campaigns. Perhaps due to this connection, in 1920 Wilson appointed him as assistant secretary of the Treasury. In 1924 he gained the state party nomination for the governor's office and was easily elected.

quently, shortly after the attack, Gilliam arrived in Williamston and opened the investigation into the assault of Needleman. After meeting with Dr. Warren and reading Needleman's statement, Gilliam issued arrest warrants for John Griffin and John Gurkin, the brother and brother-in-law of Effie Griffin.[23] Then he ordered police to apprehend twenty-one-year-old Ferrnie W. Sparrow Jr., the husband of Effie Griffin.[24] Over the next week, Gilliam ordered the

arrest of twenty additional suspects. Among the men arrested were Ferrnie W. Sparrow Sr., Effie Griffin's father-in-law, and Edward Stone, Griffin's stepfather and pastor of Skewarkee Primitive Baptist Church.[25] After the arrests Governor McLean ordered a special term of criminal court. Then he assigned the case to one of the state's leading judges, N.A. Sinclair.

At the time of the Needleman case, Sinclair had been on the bench little more than three years. However, during that time he had gained a reputation for handling difficult cases. For example, in 1922 he presided over the case of three Klansmen charged with flogging two white women in Roberson County. Though the jury found the men innocent, Sinclair stunned the crowd when he sentenced H.F. Taliferro, who represented the Klansmen, to ninety days in jail and a $750 fine for interfering with a witness.[26] In another case, Sinclair removed the superintendent of the state tuberculosis hospital for violating state law.[27]

With Sinclair on the case, the Grand Jury of Martin County returned true bills of indictment against Fernie W. Sparrow Sr., Fernie W. Sparrow Jr., Claro Heath, Julian Bullock, Henry Dennis Griffin, Ray Gray, Edward Stone, and Johnny Gurkins, charging the men with mutilation and jail breaking.[28] The state charged the remaining

Joseph Needleman on the day of his mutilation trial in Williamston (courtesy *The News & Observer* of Raleigh, North Carolina).

Above: Skewarkee Primitive Baptist Church, site of the Needleman attack. Photograph by the author, September 2007. *Below:* The Martin County Courthouse. Photograph by the author, March 2008.

Solicitor Dom Gilliam (left) and Judge N.A. Sinclair, outside of the Martin County Courthouse, circa 1925 (courtesy *The News & Observer* of Raleigh, North Carolina).

suspects as accessories to the crime. However, when the indictments were handed down, one of the conspirators, Tom Lilley, was notably absent. Several days before the hearing, Lilley placed the barrel of his .22-caliber rifle between his eyes and tried to commit suicide.[29] Though he survived, Lilley was critically wounded and was unable to attend the trial. The indictments, however, did not remove the original charges that Needleman faced. On the same day that the state indicted members of the mob, the grand jury found enough probable cause to charge Needleman with rape.[30]

The next day the state opened the trial of the vigilantes by calling one of the defendants, twenty-six-year-old John Gurkin. According to Gurkin, on the night before the attack on Needleman, Edward Stone and Denis Griffin came to his home and asked him to join them in roughing up the salesman.[31] The next day Gurkin said he and Edward Stone, accompanied by J.T. Smithwick, drove to Skewarkee Church where they met a group of about twenty-five men that included Ferrnie W. Sparrow Jr., Dennis Griffin, and Ferrnie W. Sparrow Sr. After the men assembled, they took the tags off their cars and headed to the sheriff's house. When they were unable to get the jailhouse key from the sheriff, they drove to the Martin County Jail and broke into Needleman's cell.[32] After that they threw the salesman into the backseat and headed to Skewarkee Church.

Upon reaching the church, Gurkin maintained that Ferrnie Sparrow Jr., Dennis Griffin, and Ferrnie Sparrow Sr. snatched the salesman out of the car and led him to some woods. At this point there was some debate as to who would castrate Needleman, and Dennis Griffin replied, "Dammed, if I can't do it," pulled out his pocketknife, and castrated Needleman.[33]

The next witness called by the prosecution was Joseph Needleman. Helped by two attendants, Needleman hobbled to the witness stand. After stating his name, Needleman said that he had moved to North Carolina about one year earlier and opened a business in Kinston with his brother. It was through this business that he met Ferrnie Sparrow Jr., whom he called Paul. When the business failed, Needleman took a job as a salesman with the Lorillard Tobacco Company.[34] It was through this job that he met with Effie Griffin.

According to Needleman, after he was placed in the Martin County Jail, he was awakened by a strange noise. When he turned on the light, he saw several men standing around his cell, one of whom he recognized. After stating this, Needleman rose from his chair, extended his arm, and pointed at Dennis Griffin, "And that man is sitting right there, he's the guy."[35] After this outburst, Needleman described how Fernie Sparrow Jr. and two other men held him down while Griffin castrated him. At this juncture the defense attempted to discredit Needleman by asking him how he could suddenly remember the participants of the attack, when several hours after the attack he had told the sheriff that he did not recognize anyone. Needleman replied that he lied to the sheriff since he feared that Robertson was involved in the attack.[36]

The next day the defense opened its rebuttal by calling Ferrnie Sparrow Sr. In a rambling testimony, Sparrow claimed he was at home at the time of the attack. According to Sparrow, he closed his store around 12:00 A.M. and then drove home.[37] To corroborate his alibi, Sparrow's wife testified that she had worked in the store with her husband. Following Sparrow's wife, William Croom, a Kinston police officer, testified that he saw Sparrow between 10:00 P.M. and 12:00 A.M. He also claimed that Sparrow's car was home at 1:00 A.M.[38] Two other Kinston police officers gave virtually the same testimony. However, upon cross-examination, the state seriously weakened the officer's creditability when it was revealed that Sparrow's nephew was chief of police in Kinston and that the officers owed their jobs to him.[39]

The defense then called Julian Bullock and Dennis Griffin. According to Bullock, he left his barbershop at 1:00 A.M. Then he and Dennis Griffin went to Griffin's father-in-law's house where he stayed until 3:00 A.M.[40] Griffin's story corroborated much of Bullock's story although there were several minor differences. For one, he admitted to knowing about the plot to seize Needleman. According to Griffin, he was asked by Edward Stone and John Gurkin to come to Williamston on Friday night to plan the attack, but he refused.[41] Cross-examination by the state's attorney raised serious questions about the integrity of Griffin's testimony when it was revealed that he had come to Williamston on the day of the attack to attend the preliminary hearing for Needleman. As a result, Griffin changed his story. Griffin now maintained that when the hearing was canceled he met John Gurkin and Tommy Lilley at a hardware store, where they told him of the plan to get Needleman out of jail.[42] However, when Griffin saw that his response did not satisfy the solicitor, he added that on the Sunday following the attack he had gone to Edward Stone's house. While there, Griffin claimed that he overheard Ferrnie Sparrow Jr. boast about holding Needleman while the mob castrated him. Then he added, "If I quivered when Needleman pointed at me yesterday I did not know it, yet such an accusation against anyone guilty or innocent would make him shudder."[43] That was why Griffin said he lost his nerve when Needleman identified him as the man who performed the castration.

The last defendant called to the witness stand by the defense was Claro Heath. Heath claimed he went to a movie with his girlfriend. After the movie he met Ferrnie Sparrow Jr. in Kinston. Then to the amazement of the jury, he claimed the two went to a clothing store in order to buy a suit for Sparrow's wedding the next day. Then he added "I was not at the church, the sheriff's, nor the jail at Williamston in the early morning of March 29th."[44] After Heath's testimony the defense rested its case and the lawyers gave closing arguments.

Vernon Cowper, who represented Claro Heath, declared that his client had provided a powerful alibi and that Heath was innocent. He also declared that "in trying all of the cases at one time the state seeks to bundle all of the defendants into the vortex of stripe and bonds without regard to the separate stories of the man."[45] Following Cowper, Harry Stubbs, who represented Henry Griffin and Julian Bullock, compared the trial with the crucifixion. "Give us Barabarus, the crowd before Pilate cried ... the state in a like manner today is seeking the crucifixion of Griffin, being willing to release Barabarus in order to get Griffin.[46] Then he declared that Needleman's "identification" of Griffin was insufficient and that Griffin should not be convicted of it.[47]

However, the most dramatic closing argument happened next when Solicitor Gilliam spoke. First he provided a summary of the testimony provided by Needleman. Then he attacked the alibi given by Ferrnie Sparrow Sr. by asking the jurors if they would not know how a man looked who had held them while they were being tortured.[48] Finally, in an obvious reference to the remaining mob members, Gilliam closed by declaring that "any man who is mean enough to stand by and see a crime like that committed is mean enough to commit it if he had the nerve."[49]

After Gilliam finished, Judge Sinclair instructed the jury to convict anyone who encouraged, counseled, or advised the perpetuators of the crime as an accessory.[50] Four hours later, the jury returned verdicts of guilty with malice against Julian Bullock, Dennis Griffin, Ferrnie W. Sparrow Sr. and a verdict of guilty without malice against Claro Heath.[51] Then the solicitor sent another shockwave across the courtroom when he announced that the state did not have enough evidence to prosecute Needleman for rape. All charges against Needleman were dropped.[52]

The next day Judge Sinclair sentenced Dennis Griffin to thirty years in the state penitentiary. Then he sentenced Ferrnie Sparrow Sr., Ferrnie Sparrow Jr., and Julian Bullock to prison terms ranging from six to ten years. Co-conspirators Claro Heath, Edward Stone, Johnny Gurkin, Alfred Griffin, Albert Gurkin, and Ray Gray received prison terms ranging from one to three years. For the remaining members of the mob, Sinclair imposed a fine of $500 each. Then to show he meant business, he held the men in custody until the fines were paid.[53] In passing sentence on the prisoners, Sinclair said:

> I think this trial is a demonstration of the fact that the people of North Carolina can trust the courts.... The old sentiment that because some woman has been wronged you must revert to barbarism and become savages, taking the law into your own hands and redressing such wrongs, is a reflection upon civilization. Men who ought to know better, from time to time attempt to justify and excuse such conduct is absolute poison running through the state and the men who express such sentiments are bad citizens and a positive menace to the government of the state. That spirit must be stamped out in North Carolina.[54]

The Needleman case, however, refused to go away. Two weeks after Sinclair closed the trial, Dennis Griffin's attorney filed an appeal and secured his release on the grounds that improper evidence was used in his conviction. The appeal also claimed that Griffin's thirty-year sentence was cruel and unusual punishment.[55] Griffin's freedom, however, was short-lived. One month after his release, the North Carolina Supreme Court upheld his conviction, and Griffin returned to Central Prison. Then in November 1926, Ferrnie Sparrow Jr. attempted to get a pardon.[56] This effort was unsuccessful. Several months later Julian Bullock escaped from Caledonia State Prison Farm and disappeared.[57] However, by far the biggest surprise came in July 1927, when Joseph Needleman filed a $100,000 lawsuit against Sheriff Thad Robertson, Deputy Luther Peele, and the men charged with attacking him.[58]

In filing the lawsuit, Needleman faced many obstacles. For one, the suit was filed more than a year after the crime. North Carolina law required persons seeking compensatory damages for assault to file suit within one year from the date of assault. Needleman's suit was filed more than two years after the assault.[59] In addition, during the trial, Needleman signed an agreement with several of the codefendants in which the men agreed to plead guilty as accessories, and in return Needleman agreed not to bring civil suits to recover damages.[60] However, it was soon discovered that Needleman had overcome these obstacles by filing suit in federal court. This meant that federal law would supersede state law. Undoubtedly, the prospect of a lawsuit unnerved Sheriff Robertson, Effie Griffin, and the members of the mob. Consequently, in June 1929 the defendants concluded an out-of-court settlement with Needleman.[61]

With the settlement of the civil suit, the last chapter in the Needleman case came to a close. However, the results of the case were far-reaching, since it marked the first time in the state's history that an entire lynch mob was successfully prosecuted. Still, the propensity for mob violence still remained. For example, in September of 1925, less than six months after the Needleman case, the rape of a woman in Asheville led to the formation of a mob determined to avenge the crime.[62] When the sheriff learned that the mob planned to storm the jail, he secretly slipped the suspect, Alvin Mansel, into the backseat of a car and rushed the prisoner to Charlotte.[63] Meanwhile, in Asheville the situation continued to spiral out of control. By 10:00 P.M., more than five hundred men surrounded the jail.[64] To calm the horde and reduce violence, officials announced that Mansel had been transferred to another city. Few, however, believed this announcement, and they demanded admittance to the jail.

Since officials feared that the men would riot, they announced that they would allow thirteen representatives of the mob to enter the jail and confirm that Mansel was not in Asheville.[65] As a result, the mob picked its representatives and the jailer opened the gates. However, no sooner than the main gate was cracked, the entire mob surged inside and the officers retreated.[66] This led the vigilantes to ransack every cell. When they did not find Mansel, several men smashed a heavy iron door guarding the coalhouse. Then they shoveled through the coal to make certain the suspect was not hidden beneath.[67]

Several minutes later someone shouted, "Here he is," and members of the mob converged on the courtyard in front of the jail. Once there they attacked Elbert Wood, a black prisoner, until he was rescued by a handful of deputies.[68] However, this did not dissuade the mob. After attacking the Buncombe County jail, several dozen men, thinking Mansel was hidden nearby, traveled to Henderson. Arriving in the town, the men surrounded the jail. There they forced the jailer to allow them to search the building. When they did not find Mansel, the mob dispersed.[69]

The next day, Governor McLean sent a detachment of the National Guard to Asheville. Then he ordered the solicitor to conduct an investigation. Consequently, several days later officials arrested thirty men and charged them with breaking into the jail. After a two-month delay, the state sentenced fourteen of the suspects to prison terms ranging from six months to five years in prison. In an interview given shortly after the trial the judge declared, "God save the state that has to depend upon mobs for their protection, the law will attend to that."[70]

Unfortunately, many across the state did not take the judge's statement to heart. After all, there was widespread belief that lynching and the threat of mob violence was useful for keeping certain elements of society under control. This was especially true in the eastern part of North Carolina where, in many counties, blacks outnumbered whites. For that reason, many whites interpreted the judge's statement to mean that North Carolina was determined to punish the perpetrators of mob violence who attacked symbols of state authority such as a county jail or those that destroyed public property. Thus, lynching in North Carolina moved to a new phase — one in which mobs practiced their deadly craft in the seclusion of North Carolina's backwoods.

10

"You Don't Know What the Law Will Do to You?" A Move Toward Legal Lynching

The introduction of new antilynching measures in the wake of the Bullock case allowed North Carolina to cast itself as a symbol of the new South in which lynching and mob violence were no longer tolerated. To support this view, several scholars and former North Carolina state government officials published a series of articles and books that championed the end of mob violence in the state. One of the most important figures in this effort was William H. Richardson, the former private secretary for Governor Cameron Morrison.

In 1924, Richardson published "No More Lynchings! How North Carolina Has Solved the Problem,"[1] According to Richardson:

> North Carolina, through the use of troops at the first sign of mob violence, has in a measure at least met the challenge (of mob violence) that has been flung at the South since the negro was freed from slavery; and in its successful battle against mob rule it has not only set an example for Southern states but Northern States as well.

However, when the Needleman case and the Asheville incident shattered the state's reputation, Richardson responded with a second article in April 1926. This article, titled "North Carolina Crushes Mob Rule," was published in the influential *Dearborn Independent*, which was owned by Henry Ford. In this article, Richardson praised the state for its stance in the Needleman and Asheville cases. Moreover, in a concession to Northern industrialists who were concerned about mob violence, Richardson boldly stated that one of the major reasons that the state acted so swiftly and decisively was economic:[2]

> It requires no stretch of the imagination to visualize the succession of striking victories for law and order recently won in North Carolina. This state, when it awoke to a realization of its economic possibilities after years of torpidity, set

in motion programs that attracted nation-wide attention.... In the suppression
and punishment of mob rule lies North Carolina's greatest achievement.[3]

Unfortunately, Richardson only chronicled a brief truce in the war against
lynching. Less than twelve months after the release of the second article, the
lynching of Tom Bradshaw in Nash County brought the truce to an abrupt
halt. However, unlike the earlier Needleman and Asheville cases, this time
North Carolina did nothing to punish those responsible for the crime.

As stated by published reports, shortly before dawn on August 3, 1927, an
intruder slipped through an open window of a Nash County home and kidnapped a twelve-year-old girl.[4] To keep the girl from crying out, the man
wrapped her head in a sheet. Then he carried her to a wooded area and sexually assaulted the girl. Within the hour, a posse formed and bloodhounds were
sent to scour the surrounding woods.[5] After several hours of searching authorities arrested a young black man named Tom Bradshaw who fit the description
of the rapist. However, before they could transport the suspect to the Nash
County Jail, he escaped.[6] For the remainder of the day officials searched until
they located Bradshaw in a sawmill. Again, the suspect escaped.

The next day the posse found Bradshaw in a small clump of bushes. After
running from dogs and armed men for nearly two days, the suspect was barely
able to walk.[7] However, instead of arresting the fugitive, the posse unleashed
a hail of bullets and Bradshaw fell dead.[8]

Since Bradshaw was supposedly running from authorities when he was
shot, his death was ruled a justifiable homicide, and North Carolina officials
refused to investigate. But there were several troubling issues surrounding Bradshaw's death, and it appears that his murder was merely a clever way to administer state-sanctioned mob justice. For one, according to published reports,
after his arrest Bradshaw asked for permission to pray. Kneeling beside a car
Bradshaw jumped to his feet and escaped.[9] This seems unlikely since armed men
surrounded the car. For that reason, it appears that Bradshaw's initial escape
was set up by the mob to justify the suspect's murder. However, when an
unarmed man got between Bradshaw and the other members of the posse, the
plan was thwarted. By the time the posse cornered Bradshaw the third time, he
had lost his pants and he was unable to run. As a result, capturing Bradshaw
should have been easy. Instead, the mob administered its own brand of justice.

The Bradshaw case was not the only case in which questionable tactics
were used by officials to ensure that the public's appetite for swift retribution
was carried out. A second case stemmed from the brutal rape of a young white
woman in Moore County. According to published reports, on August 4, 1922,
A.E. Ketchen, his wife, and one-year-old son, who were traveling from Miami
to Connecticut, stopped just outside of Aberdeen to spend the night. Just what
made the Ketchens stop at this point is unclear, however considering that they

camped in an abandoned building, it appears that they were hobos who were hitchhiking to Connecticut.[10] Whatever the case may be, shortly after midnight three darkened figures entered the building. Without warning one of the men fired a shot that critically injured A.E. Ketchen as he slept.[11] Frightened by the commotion, Ketchen's wife grabbed her baby and fled through a window. Screaming hysterically, she ran to a nearby house. When no one came to the door, she inexplicably went back to the warehouse. However, no sooner had she reentered the building, then one of the men threw her to the ground and ravished the woman. Then he took her wristwatch, and a small amount of cash.[12] With that the robbers fled, and Ketchen ran to a nearby home where she reported the crime.

Within minutes a posse set out in pursuit. After tracking the villains to a swamp, the trail went cold near some train tracks. This led officials to conclude that the men had fled on a passing freight train, and they contacted police in Aberdeen, the next town in the train's path.[13] Hence, when the train pulled into Aberdeen, officers arrested three black men riding in a coal car, sixteen-year-old John Lee, thirty-six-year-old Angus Murphy, and twenty-year-old Jasper Thomas.[14] In the men's possession officers found a pistol, a small amount of cash, and, most damning, Ketchen's watch. However, before the police could remove the men from the rail yard, a crowd of angry men gathered to seek vengeance. Only the timely arrival of the Moore County sheriff, S.A. Blue, who convinced the mob that the suspects should be taken before Ketchen for identification, prevented violence.[15] Then he loaded the suspects in his car and headed to Southern Pines while members of the mob piled into their cars and followed. When they reached Southern Pines, Ketchen positively identified the suspects as the men who had raped her.[16]

At this point, the sheriff outwitted the mob. Immediately after Ketchen identified the suspects, Blue, instead of marching the men into a holding cell, placed the suspects in a Packard touring car. Then before the mob knew what was happening, the sheriff sped off at top speed. Soon ten cars loaded with vigilantes set out to overtake him. To confuse the men Blue first headed South toward Pinehurst, then reversed course and headed toward Southern Pines. Afterward he headed north toward the safety of Raleigh's Central Prison, seventy-five miles away.[17]

Two hours later the sheriff pulled through the gates of Central Prison, and the prisoners were turned over to the warden. Twenty minutes later a dozen cars carrying the mob reached the prison. When they found out that the sheriff had deposited the suspects in the prison, one of the men said, "Boys, I'll be damned if something hasn't got to be done about this thing."[18] There was fear that the men would storm the prison. Consequently, Governor Cameron Morrison dispatched a company of National Guardsmen to protect the prison and the night passed without incident.[19]

The next day the Raleigh chapter of the Ku Klux Klan, which counted among its number several members of Cameron Morrison's cabinet, sent a telegram to the Raleigh *News & Observer*.[20] "We wish to commend the sheriff for the way in which he handled this matter and also our governor for his part."[21] However, more importantly, the Klan issued a call for what many called a legal lynching. "We urge a special term of court and a speedy execution."[22] With the Klan's mandate coloring public opinion, Governor Morrison ordered county officials to hold a trial for the men less than three weeks after the rape of Ketchen. Then to ensure that he got the outcome that he wanted, he hand-picked a judge, hired a compliant defense attorney, and placed the suspects before a biased Moore County jury.

Since there was no place in Carthage large enough to hold a case of such importance, Moore County officials moved the trial to a tobacco warehouse, which would be protected by a company of National Guardsmen. Yet, this did not dissuade hundreds of spectators who drove to Carthage to see if there would be a lynching as a rumor claimed.[23]

Although no lynching took place, the spectators were not disappointed as the trial provided plenty of excitement. The first witness called to the stand was Mrs. A.E. Ketchen. In a lengthy testimony she maintained that after the suspects shot her husband, one of the men raped her while another held a flashlight. Then she saw a third man emerge from the shadows before the gang departed.[24] However, in a stunning admission, Ketchen said that it was so dark in the warehouse, she could not make out the features of the men. The only way she could identify her attackers was to hear them talk. But Ketchen said she felt certain that from his appearance, the rapist was Jasper Thomas.[25] This led to several concerns, such as, if she could not recognize the men in court, how was she able to identify them when they were brought to her the day after the attack?[26] Moreover, if only one man raped Ketchen, which suspect was guilty of the crime? These questions the defense attorney failed to raise. The trial continued.

John Lee took the stand next and turned state's evidence. According to Lee, Angus Murphy, Jasper Thomas, and he were walking toward Pinehurst when they came upon the Ketchens in a warehouse near Southern Pines.[27]* After looking through a window, Murphy suggested they go inside to see what they could get. But since he did not think going into the warehouse was a good idea, Lee claimed that he left and walked on toward Pinehurst. He had not gone far when two shots rang out. Then he headed back to the warehouse to see what

---

*According to Lee, he had recently left Greensboro and had drifted into the area thinking he could find work there. When he arrived in Southern Pines, he was hungry and out of money until he ran into the other two suspects. According to Lee, he thought the men were going to see some girls. However, as they passed an abandoned warehouse, his companions discovered the Ketchens and decided to rob the family.

had happened. When he reached the building, Lee claimed that he saw a woman with a baby climbing through a window. Then in direct contradiction to Ketchen, Lee said that Angus Murphy raped the woman while Thomas held a flashlight.[28] Afterwards, in an attempt to distance himself from the other men, Lee said that he had warned Murphy not to rape the woman, but Murphy threatened to shoot him if he did not keep quiet. It was for that reason, he claimed, that he walked outside while his traveling companions raped and robbed the Ketchens. After the attack, the three men ran through some nearby woods and jumped aboard a freight train. It was at this point, Lee said, that Murphy gave him eighty-five cents as his take in the robbery.[29]

However, the story told by Lee differed greatly from a statement Murphy gave later in the day. Murphy claimed that on the day of the attack, he and Jasper Thomas slipped aboard a freight train that was heading to Raleigh. When the train slowed to pass the small town of Vass, a man entered the freight car and offered to sell them a wristwatch and a pistol. Since the man was hungry and had no money, Murphy said that they gave the man two dollars for the watch and a dollar and a half for the pistol. Shortly afterward, John Lee boarded the train and they all agreed to be traveling companions.[30] Later when Jasper Thomas took the stand, he told a story that corroborated the account given by Murphy. However, the defining moment came next when the state called a surprise witness, the conductor of the freight train. In agreement with Lee, the conductor said that he saw three men board the train as it passed Southern Pines. These were the same men that police arrested in Aberdeen.[31]* At this point, the judge stopped the proceedings, and instead of waiting for closing arguments delivered a charge to the jury. If you "believe the testimony of the two negroes on their own behalf ... set them free, but if (you) believe the testimony of the state ... find them both guilty of rape."[32] Eight minutes later the jury found Angus Murphy and Jasper Thomas guilty of rape. With the verdicts Judge Long sentenced Angus Murphy and Jasper Thomas to death. Then he sent John Lee to prison for twelve years.[33]†

For North Carolina, the trial represented somewhat of a milestone since it showed the state's willingness to use its power to perform a task traditionally reserved for lynch mobs.[34] In other words, state officials chose to use the power of the courts to conduct a legal lynching. The trial also was useful in convincing critics in the North that unlike the mob-crazed image put forth by newspapers, North Carolinians were actually law-abiding citizens who gave

*Surprisingly the conductor's name was not brought to the prosecution until court adjourned for lunch. However, since the people of Moore County by and large had made up their minds, not even the suspect's lawyer bothered to question the entrance of this surprise witness.

†Lee's stay in prison was much shorter than expected. After spending a year in custody, he was released. He was readmitted to prison less than a year later when he was charged with murder in a case from Mocksville, North Carolina.

blacks, even those charged with a terrible crime, a chance to have their day in court.

This policy, however, would be put to the test less than one year later in Spruce Pine, North Carolina. On the morning of September 27, 1923, Viola Thomas, a sixty-year-old white woman, reported that she had been raped by a black man along the side of an isolated road near her home. As usual in such cases, a posse formed and set off in search of the attacker. However, since the

Above: Spruce Pine, circa 1923. Spruce Pine was founded in 1907 when the Clinchfield Railroad made its way down the North Toe River from Erwin, Tennessee (courtesy North Carolina Collection, University of North Carolina Library at Chapel Hill). *Below:* Spruce Pine mob, 1923. After driving blacks from Spruce Pine members of the mob posed for this picture. Undoubtedly this further infuriated state officials who launched plans to arrest members of the mob (courtesy *The News & Observer* of Raleigh, North Carolina).

Some of the soldiers sent to Spruce Pine by Governor Morrison to restore order pose for this picture (courtesy North Carolina Collection, University of North Carolina Library at Chapel Hill).

Spruce Pine posse, Circa 1923. Members of the Spruce Pine posse searching for Goss (courtesy North Carolina Collection, University of North Carolina Library at Chapel Hill).

assailant was black, many in mob reasoned that it would be best to search black communities. For that reason, the mob headed to Dogwood Mountain, where a sizeable community of African Americans lived. At gunpoint the vigilantes rounded up everyone in the community and placed them on a freight train headed out of town. Then they invaded a camp occupied by black road workers. Again, they forced the workers to leave Spruce Pine.[35] Next, the mob marched to the state prison for black convicts and ordered the warden to move the prisoners out of the area by noon or suffer an assault upon the camp.

When news of the ultimatum reached Governor Morrison, it created a great deal of apprehension since he feared that it would, like the Bullock case, bring unwanted attention from the national media. This he feared in turn could jeopardize the sale of road bonds and threaten infrastructure improvement in North Carolina. It is for that reason Governor Morrison sent two companies of the National Guard to Spruce Pine. Then perhaps in order to satisfy Northern investors, he "declared himself ready to maintain the right of all citizens white or black at any cost.[36] Yet, the governor's declaration did not ease the concern of many outside of North Carolina. Foremost in this group was the NAACP. Shortly after most blacks were forced to leave Spruce Pine, the NAACP sent Morrison a telegram:

> Press dispatches report that an armed mob of two hundred citizens of Spruce
> Pine, North Carolina are today rounding up all male negroes in Spruce Pine

and vicinity and deported them on freight trains because of an alleged attack by a negro on an aged white woman. The National Association for Advancement of Colored People requests of you information regarding the correctness of this report and is also asking that you as governor of the state use all power at your command to protect the civil and constitutional rights of colored citizens who are being driven from their homes and jobs regardless of their innocence or guilt.[37]

Since the NAACP had played a major role in the Bullock case, the telegram provoked the ire of Cameron Morrison. Angrily the governor replied, "My action in [the] matter referred to by you are being given to the Associated Press as quickly as can be done."[38] Moreover, he maintained that he would make no private reports to the NAACP. "You can get [your] information through the news sources as the rest of the public acquire it."[39]

Nonetheless, while Morrison quarreled with the NAACP, another chapter was unfolding in the North Carolina mountains. Several days after the rape of Viola Thomas, authorities came to the conclusion that the attacker was John Goss, a trustee who had recently escaped from the prison in Spruce Pine. Notices were sent to all of the towns that surrounded Spruce Pine and authorities set off in pursuit. After tracking the suspect for several miles, they lost Goss's trail. However, since few blacks lived in the mountains, authorities assumed that the suspect would head east. With this in mind the sheriff contacted officials in nearby Burke County.

The next day Burke County officials noticed a man fitting Goss's description crawling from under a house.[40] After surrounding the house, officers took the man, identified as Goss, into custody.[41] Then they hustled the man off to the state penitentiary in Raleigh for safekeeping.[42]

With the suspect in custody, Morrison, in apparent reference to Goss's status as a trustee, announced that he would seek legal authority to abolish the trustee system in North Carolina's prison system.[43] "If they are qualified to enjoy freedom and unrestricted association outside the camp, then they ought to be pardoned."[44] Unfortunately, the governor's statement did nothing to calm the situation in Spruce Pine. Several days later, a new crisis arose when two men started a drive to remove the mayor of Spruce Pine, who they blamed for bringing troops to the town. In a widely circulated petition the men alleged that the mayor was improperly elected, since the citizens of Spruce Pine had not voted for him.[45] When the mayor's response failed to satisfy the men, they whipped several hundred people into a mob-like frenzy. Only the presence of troops prevented violence.[46]

In the midst of this crisis an organizer of the Klan arrived, closely followed by the annual tri-county fair, which was sure to attract large crowds. For that reason, town officials enacted two ordinances, one that prohibited the sale of guns and ammunition and another that required all stores and restau-

rants within the town limits to close at 10:00 P.M., while the fair was in session.
The town also required all employees of the fair, many of whom were foreign
or black, to remain on the fairgrounds during evening hours.[47]

In the meantime North Carolina officials tried to convince black road
workers to return to Spruce Pine by pointing to the presence of the troops,
which would ensure their safety. Even so, most workers were hesitant about
returning to the town. Accordingly, owners of the companies constructing the
road into Spruce Pine began to look at white convicts as suitable replacements.
This, however, created a firestorm in the Morrison administration as many felt
that road work was unsuitable for whites. In an interview given to the Raleigh
News & Observer, State Highway Commissioner Frank Page maintained that
white convicts had low work efficiency and would only be used as a last resort.[48]
Nonetheless, state officials had little to worry about since shortly after Page's
interview many of the deported workers returned.[49]

While officials debated the use of white workers, Governor Morrison continued to ponder ways to restore order in Spruce Pine. Unlike other hot spots
Spruce Pine was unique since the presence of troops and the threat of prosecution did little to lower tensions. Moreover, the town's history of resistance
toward foreigners and blacks convinced Morrison that the crisis could only be
solved by using the same formula that he had used in Moore County, namely,
a quick trial that could have only one outcome, the swift execution of Goss.
Accordingly, Morrison announced that North Carolina would hold a special
term of Superior Court to put Goss on trial for his life.[50] Moreover, to ensure
that the trial ended in a death sentence, Morrison handpicked T.B. Finley to
preside over the case.

With a judge in place, North Carolina officials set a date for the trial and
Goss was loaded on a train headed to Mitchell County to stand trial. At Hickory, the officials transferred the suspect to a truck. Then a company of soldiers
escorted him to the Mitchell County Courthouse.[51] Yet, this did little to dim
interest in the case, since on the day of the trial a crowd of several thousand
onlookers came to Bakersville. Few made it into the courthouse since troops
restricted access. In addition, since officials expected graphic testimony, Judge
Thomas B. Finley ordered all women and children to leave the courtroom.[52]
Then Finley assigned S.J. Black, a slow-witted country lawyer, to represent
Goss.

After hastily gathering a grand jury, officials pushed through a bill of
indictment that charged Goss with rape.[53] Following this decision the sheriff
rounded up a trial jury, and the case against Goss commenced. First up to testify for the state was Jimmy Holloway, the superintendent of the state prison
at Spruce Pine. After identifying the suspect, Holloway confirmed that Goss
had escaped while serving as part of a road construction crew. Next the state
called Viola Thomas. In a rousing testimony she maintained that Goss forced

her to have sex against her will.[54] When Goss's attorney attempted to cast reasonable doubt by asking Thomas if she was certain Goss was the attacker, she forcefully replied that she was positive that he was the man. With the conclusion of this exchange, Thomas ended her testimony and the final witness, Melvina Silver, took the stand.

In a short, poignant testimony, Silver said that several hours before the rape Goss entered her yard and cut the bell from her cow's neck. When he knocked on her door and asked for some water, she outwitted Goss by giving him a glass and pointing to a nearby spring. While he was at the well she dashed out of the back door and ran to a neighbor's home.[55] When she finished her testimony the state concluded its case, and after five minutes of deliberation the jury returned a verdict of guilty. Shortly afterward Judge Finley announced that it was "the judgment of the court that the defendant, John Goss (colored) be put to death by electrocution."[56]

With Goss's fate sealed, authorities transported the condemned man back to the state prison in Raleigh. Then they scheduled the execution for November 30, 1923. However, there would be no execution that day since Cameron Morrison was out of the state. Morrison had ordered that no execution could take place when he was out of the state. At any rate, after a delay of several days Goss was executed with little fanfare on December 7, 1923. The next morning newspapers across the state announced the convict's death. The Raleigh News & Observer reported:

> John Goss met death with a stolid face when they led him into the execution chamber yesterday morning to pay with his life for a criminal attack on an aged white woman in Mitchell County late in September after he had escaped from a convict camp where he was serving the last month of a sentence for a similar crime committed in Wilmington 15 years ago.... Goss looked the part of the picture that "mean nigger" conjures up. Short, squat, thick bodied, and with the face of a gorilla. Even the eyes were muddy with a diffusion of the color of his skin. He held them steadfastly open as death came steadily toward him and when he was dead, he stared with solid indifference toward the ceiling. Four shocks were required to take the life out of him. The steady pumping of his heart against the black thick breast was perceptible after the first. The second had weakened it but slightly, and the third a little more. After the fourth the stethoscope could find no trace of life in the black carcass and he was dumped into a basket to be sent to one of the medical schools of the state.[57]

However, none of the articles were more in tune with Morrison's quick trial and execution plan than the Asheville Citizen:

> On Goss' arrest, the people of Mitchell quieted themselves and the law proceeded to establish another record for speedy trial and prompt punishment. It is such triumphs of law over tendencies to lawlessness and such records for dispatch in court procedure in aggravated criminal cases that have done so much to give North Carolina a good name as a law-abiding state.[58]

Yet, while many state officials hailed Morrison's quick trial and execution plan as a cure for lynching, others, most notably in the mountains, were determined to use the cover of the law to conduct police-sanctioned lynching. Perhaps the most notable of these incidents was the murder of Broadus Miller. On June 21, 1927, the family of fifteen-year-old Gladys Kincaid, worried that she had not returned from work, set out to find the teenager. Walking the road usually traveled by the girl, her brother heard a groan in a small clump of trees. When he went to investigate he discovered his mortally wounded sister.[59] The girl was rushed to a local hospital, however doctors held out little hope that she would recover.[60]

While Kincaid lingered near death, authorities launched an investigation to find her attacker. Although they found few clues at the scene of the crime, they soon discovered that a yellow raincoat the girl had been wearing was missing. With this information, the sheriff learned from people living near the crime scene that a tall "yellow" negro had passed through the neighborhood on the day of the crime with a raincoat.[61] The next day, the sheriff found the raincoat, covered in blood, in the home of a black man named Will Berry. After questioning Berry, officials learned that the raincoat belonged to Broadus Miller, a black construction worker who boarded at the house.[62]

On the heels of this information authorities launched a search to find the attacker. However, just as the search was getting underway, news spread that Mary Kincaid had succumbed to her injuries. In response to this information, a mob estimated to number two thousand grabbed their guns and set out to find Miller. Included in this thong was the local company of the National Guard.[63] In addition to these efforts, Governor McLean offered a reward of $500 and declared Miller an outlaw. The last development was significant since it meant that Miller could be killed on sight if he in any way resisted arrest.[64]

Over the next few days the search for Miller picked up its pace. Every freight train passing through the area was checked and rechecked. Additionally, a picture supposedly of the suspect was distributed across western North Carolina.* As a result, authorities arrested scores of black men. In one of the more interesting cases, authorities in Chatham County arrested Gene Martin as he worked in a coal mine.† For safekeeping officials transported the suspect to Newton until Burke County officials could confirm his identity. Newton, however, lay less than an hour from Morganton and as soon as it was discovered that a suspect was in the jail, a crowd formed and there was fear that the

---

*There was quite a bit of confusion over the identity of the individual on the picture. Miller's wife, perhaps to protect her spouse, maintained that the photograph was that of her husband. Others familiar with Miller, however, maintained that the photograph was not Broadus Miller. "Report Morganton Outlaw, Gene Martin, Held In Jail At Newton," Gastonia Daily Gazette, June 30, 1927.
†Several months earlier Martin had escaped from a Buncombe County chain gang.

men would attempt to lynch the suspect. Due to these threats authorities transferred Martin to Gastonia and placed armed guards outside of his cell.

While this sideshow was going on, the hunt for Broadus Miller continued. However, after a week of searching many members of the posse had lost their enthusiasm for the chase and returned home. By the start of the second week only a few hundred remained, and there was a great deal of concern that the murderer would escape.

Almost a week later, things changed. On July 3, 1927 authorities in nearby McDowell County reported that someone had broken into a restaurant in the small crossroads of Ashford. Since authorities felt that Miller was responsible for the break-in, a posse formed and set out to apprehend the thief. Included in this group was Commodore Burleson, an ex–Morganton policeman turned bounty hunter, and three other Morganton men who had driven over to join the search.[65]

Shortly after entering the woods Burleson and his party identified tracks that he felt belonged to Miller — one foot covered with a rag with two toes through.[66] Less than a mile away the men noticed Miller sitting on a boulder. However, according to Burleson when Miller saw his party he grabbed his shotgun and ordered the men to halt.[67] At this point Burleson claimed he pulled his pistol, slowly backed away, and crouched behind a stump while his companions circled behind the fugitive. No sooner had he gotten behind the stump, Burleson claimed, then Miller opened fire. In response Burleson fired his revolver six times. On the sixth shot he hit Miller in the heart and the fugitive fell dead.[68]

After Miller's death, Burleson and his companions took Miller's corpse to the Burke County Courthouse. As news of the fugitive's death spread there was fear that outraged citizens would storm the building. For that reason, officials moved Miller's body to a slab on the steps of the jail.[69] A passageway was roped off and deputies stationed around the body. Over the next few hours an almost carnival-like atmosphere developed as five thousand people viewed the body while a photographer did big business selling pictures of the corpse.[70] After this macabre display Sam J. Ervin Jr., the attorney for the sheriff, shipped Miller's body to an unknown location for burial.[71]*

The burial of Miller's body did not end the controversy surrounding the fugitive. Several days after Miller's death, H.W. Gragg claimed that the fugitive was not shot in a gun battle, but was fired upon while asleep.[72] According to Gragg, he and eight other men, including a deputy sheriff, were within 150 yards of the place Miller was found. He claimed "that the men did not hear any shotgun fired, and that they were on the scene with a few moments."[73] Gragg also claimed that Miller did not have a shotgun and it would have been

*Ervin later became a U.S. senator.

impossible for Miller to carry a gun. According to Gragg, on the trail that the
fugitive traveled they found thickets where Miller had to crawl a considerable
distance on his hands and knees. There was never any sign of any gun on this
trail.[74] Perhaps most damning, Gragg claimed that he could produce affidavits
to substantiate his claim.[75]

The next day Gragg's claim hit local newspapers and created an uproar.
Commodore Burleson responded by stating that Gragg's story was without
merit and he challenged others to produce their evidence.[76] Additionally, Fons
Duckworth, chair of the Burke County Road Commission and one of the first
to reach the scene after the shooting, maintained that there was absolutely no
doubt in his mind that Miller had a gun.[77] However, this failed to quell the
debate. As a result, several days later, Burleson filed a suit against Gragg and
C.L. Dula for slander.[78] However, the case would never reach court as the next
day H.W. Gragg offered an apology:

> The statements in the newspaper regarding the killing of the outlaw Broadus
> Miller by Commodore Burleson, credited to me, were not made by me, but were
> made by a party of seven men who aided in the chase of the outlaw.... I want to
> correct the statement and let people know that I knew nothing at all about the
> manner in which Mr. Burleson killed the negro outlaw. It made no difference
> to me how he was killed just so he was dead. If I have innocently been the cause
> of any reflection on Mr. Burleson's character or integrity I hereby offer my
> apologies.[79]

One month later H.W. Gragg and C.L. Dula settled out of court by paying the costs of court and giving one cent to Burleson.[80] Still, the settlement of
the lawsuit did not remove the lingering question of whether Broadus Miller
was lynched. Evidence collected after his death seems to point to this conclusion. For one, if Miller were running for his life, why would he give away his
location by asking his pursuers to halt? Then after issuing the challenge, why
would the fugitive allow his pursuers time to crouch behind a stump before
firing? Yet, these questions assume Miller had a gun. While it is unclear if Miller
had a weapon, reports issued at the start of the manhunt seem to suggest that
he was unarmed. Although members of the posse maintained that Miller later
obtained a shotgun by breaking into a home, authorities were unable to verify that he committed this crime. Finally, if Miller did indeed have a shotgun
why did Burleson and his companions, who were armed with pistols, fail to
summon more heavily armed members of the posse, who were only 150 yards
away? Such questions, unfortunately, will never be answered due to the passage
of time and will always cloud the death of Broadus Miller.

Despite questions surrounding Miller's death, incidents in which police
used their authority to carry out what amounted to state-sponsored lynchings
were nothing new. In November 1906, almost twenty years before Broadus
Miller's death, North Carolina experienced a similar murder. The victim in

this case was a young black man named Will Harris. There can be little doubt that Harris was a despicable character; he had served several prison terms for armed robbery, arson, and assault. Moreover, prison officials wanted him for escaping from the chain gang.[81] Due to this factor, Harris fled to Asheville. Two weeks later he purchased a high-powered rifle and ammunition. The next day, driven in part by a drunken stupor, he exploded into a violent rage and killed two police officers.[82] Then as he made his way from the scene Harris began firing at anything that moved. In the ensuing melee he left in his wake three more dead citizens and another wounded police officer.[83]

Needless to say, public reaction to this violence was swift as a huge posse formed and set out to after Harris. Two days later, the posse cornered Harris in a small clump of trees about ten miles from town. When the posse moved in to arrest the fugitive, he opened fire wounding two men.[84] From this point there is some debate about Harris's actions. Many maintain that after firing several shots Harris ran out of ammunition. Then he threw up his hands and tried to surrender. However, the posse would have none of it and they opened fire and riddled his body with bullets. Another version of the story claims that after Harris opened the gunfight he suffered several bullet wounds that incapacitated him. After he had fallen, members of the posse closed to point-blank range and poured shot after shot into his body.[85]

Whatever the case, after Harris's death officials brought his corpse back to Asheville. The next day at the coroner's inquest the jury thanked the members of the posse and announced that "Will Harris alias Rufe Lindsey came to his death at the hands of public-spirited citizens who were at the time in the fearless and unselfish discharge of a public duty (and) are entitled to the commendation and thanks of the whole community."[86]

11

Lynching in North Carolina 1930–1935

With the onset of the Great Depression economic conditions throughout North Carolina went from bad to worse. Nowhere were conditions poorer than in eastern North Carolina, where the price of tobacco fell from 26¢ per pound in 1926 to 12¢ per pound in 1932.[1] This economic downturn led to a financial crisis for many farmers who were unable to make mortgage or crop lien payments. This in turn forced banks to initiate a record number of foreclosures. As a result, the number of white tenant farmers in the state swelled from 65,542 in 1920 to 93,173 by 1935.[2] In an attempt to improve conditions for farmers, the federal government created the Agricultural Adjustment Administration. This agency enacted policies that limited production. It also implemented crop contracts. However, these policies did little to help many farmers, since limiting production simply reduced the opportunities available for poor white as well as black farmers. In response to these changes hundreds of poor white farmers moved to the Piedmont section of North Carolina to obtain textile jobs, while hundreds of black sharecroppers slipped into the ranks of farm laborers. In this sordid environment the specter of Judge Lynch was never far from the surface. For example, in September of 1929, labor unrest in Gaston County led to the lynching of white labor organizer Ella Mae Wiggins. Although North Carolina officials quickly identified her attackers, a Grand Jury refused to indict the suspects.[3]

The ruling, however, caused national and international outrage. In response, Governor O. Max Gardner ordered a special hearing for the men charged in the attack. However, when the defense argued that the men should not be found guilty because the dead woman was a communist, the jury agreed, and returned a verdict of not guilty.[4]

Less than a year after Wiggins's death another serious case of mob violence arose in southeastern North Carolina. On the evening of January 18, 1930

Stephen English, a young farmer, returned home to find his twenty-year-old wife dead at the hands of an unknown assailant. Authorities hurried to the scene and searched for the killer. However, neither they nor their bloodhounds were able to pick up the trail of the killer. Nonetheless, several hours later authorities got their first break in the case. A motorist reported to police that he had given a ride to a "negro" from the vicinity of the crime to Wilmington.[5]

Since police suspected the man might have knowledge of the woman's murder, they arrested the hitchhiker. The next day, Wilmington authorities announced that the suspect, identified as Dave Locke, had confessed to the crime.[6] In the confession authorities alleged that Locke went to the English house to ask for food. When the young woman turned to look in the cupboard, Locke seized her. Then he grabbed a fire iron and stuck the fatal blow. To corroborate this theory Wilmington authorities claimed that Locke had some buttons in his pants pocket when they arrested him. According to Locke, he tore these buttons off his pants while picking cotton. However, Wilmington police concluded that the buttons were most likely torn off during a struggle with English.[7]

The next day the sheriff to Duplin County transported Locke back to the Kenansville jail. Unfortunately, tempers in nearby Wallace had reached the boiling point and rumors began to swirl that a mob was forming to lynch Locke.[8] Aware of these rumors, shortly before sundown the sheriff slipped Locke from his cell and rushed him to Raleigh's Central Prison. In the meantime, a mob of more than hundred men gathered in Wallace and headed for Kenansville. However, when they reached the town, they learned of Locke's transfer to Raleigh and most went home. Nonetheless, fifteen determined souls headed for the jail. Storming up the steps the men demanded to see the sheriff. When they found out he was away, they could only be persuaded to leave by allowing them to search the jail and confirm Locke was not there.

The effort by the mob did not end the controversy surrounding Locke. On the day before the mob marched into Kenansville, Locke recanted his confession. According to Locke, Wilmington police officers had beaten him and coerced his confession. Moreover, as luck would have it, events in Wallace would soon confirm his innocence. Throughout Wallace veiled whispers circulated that Stephen English had killed his wife. Almost two weeks after the murder, the rumors appeared to be confirmed when, nineteen-year-old Raeford Albertson told one of English's neighbors that he had seen English murder his wife. Stunned by the allegation, the neighbor contacted Duplin County authorities who in turn arrested English.[9]

At this point, the evidence against English continued to mount. At a preliminary hearing, Raeford Albertson testified that English was in a relationship with another woman. Albertson alleged that to maintain this relationship, English offered him an automobile to kill his wife.[10] However, on the day that he was supposed to commit the deed, Albertson lost his nerve. For that reason, English entered the house and murdered his own wife. As a result of this testimony, authorities released Dave Locke and another black man that they had charged with the crime named Dave Brockington.

Two months later, North Carolina officials sentenced English to twenty years in prison for his wife's death. While the case ended in English's conviction, it also revealed that despite the recent conviction of mob members in Williamston and Asheville, many parts of North Carolina remained prone to mob violence. Only the courage and quick thinking of the Duplin County sheriff prevented an attempt by vigilantes to kill Locke. Unfortunately, such determination did not extend to scores of law officers across the state. Such would be the case less than six months later when North Carolina suffered one of its most noted acts of mob violence — the lynching of Oliver Moore.

On July 18, 1930, Edgecombe County officials received a report that Oliver Moore, a twenty-nine-year-old field hand, had raped two young white girls, Ethel and Lucille Morgan, ages five and seven.[11] Quickly gathering a posse, officials set out to find Moore. However, Moore eluded the posse and escaped. Several weeks later, the Edgecombe County sheriff received word that Moore had fled to Norfolk, Virginia. He contacted Virginia officials and offered them a reward of $100 for the capture of the suspect.[12] Yet, there was little need for the reward. After several weeks in Virginia, Moore secretly made his way back to Edgecombe County. Unfortunately, word of his return leaked, and Moore was apprehended in a closet in his brother's house.[13]

In the meantime, while officials prepared for Moore's preliminary hearing, another drama was taking place in the home of the young rape victims. Reports published after the rape indicated that both of the victims had contracted gonorrhea three days after the attack.[14] This claim would prove to be extremely important, since if Moore had gonorrhea, it would corroborate the children's claim of rape. As a result, the next day at Moore's first hearing, the judge ordered Dr. Curtis Norfleet to examine Moore and determine if he had gonorrhea. Norfleet procrastinated and this examination was not done.[15]

At any rate, after the hearing, Moore was taken to the Edgecombe County Jail where he was placed under the guard of Deputy R.O. Watson, who was serving as the acting jailer. According to Watson, shortly after midnight he heard someone knock on the door. Thinking it was the Tarboro police bringing in a suspect for lockup, he opened the door. Before he could react, several armed men stormed into the jail. At gunpoint, they seized Moore and dragged him to a waiting car. About six miles from town, they found a sturdy tree near the highway and secured a plow line under Moore's arms. Then the mob hoisted him above the road and tore his body apart with bullets and buckshot.[16]

In the hours after the lynching, "whole families came together, mothers and fathers bringing even their youngest children. It was the show of the countryside ... a very popular show. Men joked loudly at the sight of the bleeding body ... girls giggled as flies fed on the blood that dripped from the negro's nose."[17]

In addition to the usual cast viewing the mob's handiwork, the onlookers also included several African Americans, one of which gave a report to the Baltimore Afro-American:

> We got out and walked down the road and we found a bunch of white women and children. There was no sign of terror in their faces. There was nothing but giggles and laughter as the blood dripped from the nose and from the blood-riddled victim.... I wanted to get a picture but before I got close enough Moore was cut down from the tree. I looked at the man's body and there appeared to be about 100 holes in it, all around up as far as the neck. He had on a pair of pants, no shirt, no shoes. One of his legs looked like someone had cut him on it. I heard a man say (after they had cut him down).... Don't move him you don't know what the law will do to you.[18]

The lynching of Moore caught Governor Gardner by surprise. Vacationing in Hendersonville when he received news of the violence, he offered a reward of $400 for the identity of the members of the lynch mob.[19] Then he contacted Solicitor Don Gilliam and ordered him to launch an investigation of the crime. However, unlike the zeal he displayed during the investigation and prosecution of the Needleman case,

Gilliam was less than enthusiastic. "Of course I think he is the man that attacked those children.... I don't know how I am going to find out the name of a single member of the mob."[20] Nonetheless, shortly after he opened the investigation Gilliam ordered that a pathological examination be taken from Moore's body before burial in order to confirm guilt.[21]

However, other than ordering the pathological exam, Gilliam did little. After several months, the state quietly ended the investigation, though troubling questions remained. For example, the nature of the crime suggested that Sheriff Bardin should have transferred Moore to another county jail for safekeeping. Bardin, however, maintained that during the preliminary hearing he had walked Moore to and from the jail with no problem.[22] For that reason, he felt that there would not be any attempts to seize Moore. Another concern stemmed from the decision to assign Deputy R.O. Watson to guard the jail when H.C. Brown, the regular jailer, lived across the street from the facility.[23] On the night the mob stormed the jail, Brown claimed he was awakened by the mob. Looking out of his front window, "he saw about 14 cars parked in front of the jail."[24] He also saw a crowd of men forcing the jail's door open. Despite this fact, he made no effort to reinforce Watson or sound the alarm. The final question centers on the role of the Tarboro Police Department. On the night the mob seized Moore, three police officers were on duty. Each of these officers

The 1930 lynching of Oliver Moore (courtesy *The News & Observer* of Raleigh, North Carolina).

claimed that they heard "nothing and knew nothing of the mob's activities until after the mob had left town."[25]

The actions of Sheriff Bardin and the local police were little more than a microcosm of the resentment most whites in Tarboro harbored toward Moore. For example, several days after Moore's death a county official stated, "I hate this thing occurred on account of the criticism it has brought. There is no question of Moore's guilt and personally I am glad it happened."[26] A reporter from a local newspaper reported, "In principle, I am against lynching but this crime was so horrible I think it was all right. There's no doubt about Moore's guilt."[27]

Yet, there was doubt about Moore's guilt. During the preliminary hearing, the judge refused to allow Moore to speak and no attorney would take the suspect's case.[28] After Moore's death, tests taken from his corpse failed to confirm that he had gonorrhea. Speaking to reporters shortly after the crime, the physician hired by the state said, "There will always be an element of doubt in the minds as to Moore's guilt. This is the first virulent case of gonorrhea (referring to the young victims) I have ever seen develop in three days."[29]

Despite these doubts, many whites used the case to highlight the specter of the black menace to white women. An editorial written by the *Rocky Mount Telegram* best summed these feelings:

> The increasing number of criminal assaults upon white women in the Southern States, the accounts of which frequently are exaggerated, add nothing to the effort to bring about harmonious interracial feeling ... because of the inability of officers to cope with the situations arising in their territories; because of the seeming indifference among the leading class of negro citizens; because of the regular recurrence of crimes of such revolting nature that no man may pass them unnoticed we feel keenly the necessity for careful consideration.... To discuss the matter frankly we hold the negro to blame for the repeated unfavorable publicity he receives.... No people can endure criminal assaults of the nature we constantly have called to our attention. Three cases of the nature to which we refer, have been brought forcibly to our attention within the last two weeks. One of them is so terribly obnoxious that we have a feeling of nausea whenever we consider it.... We have looked in vain for negro leaders in the state to make even the slightest gesture of protest. The responsibility rests with the negro.[30]

A week after this editorial appeared in the *Telegram*, an unidentified black reader responded:

> The negroes of Rocky Mount, the state and the nation think with equal horror and incredibility as the white man upon the recent crime of which Oliver Moore was accused, and for which he was lynched. I say accused for he was actually proved neither guilty nor innocent.... First leading negroes cannot publicly denounce criminal attacks on white women, nor on any women unless it be known they were positively committed and by whom. One wouldn't know where nor how to begin denouncing. Secondly, attacks on white women are not always at the bottom of lynching. A negro was recently lynched in a Southern State for being accused of shooting a white man. Thirdly, a negro leader would wonder how publicly denouncing attacks on white women could possibly be a remedy for the lynching disease. For in all probability, Oliver Moore, if guilty or not, in his depraved mind never heard of negro leaders much less of their denouncing anything.[31]

The content of this letter captured much of the resentment African Americans harbored at the lynching of Moore. Indeed shortly after the lynching, the National Negro Business League urged Governor Gardner to "curb the forces of lawlessness and to bring to justice the perpetrators of Moore's murder."[32] In addition, the NAACP launched an investigation to determine the identity of the members of the mob.

Leading the NAACP's investigation was C.F. Rich, an African American attorney from Rocky Mount. Two months after the lynching, Rich wrote that he had proof as to the identity of several of the mob members.[33] "Gentlemen I have definite proof as to some of the lynchers of the late lynching in Edgecombe County."[34] According to Rich, several African Americans were in the jail on the night of the lynching. One of these men claimed that he recognized three of the attackers. However, since the men were prominent citizens, the witnesses were reluctant to come forward. Therefore Rich, in his letter to the NAACP, implored the organization to send an official as soon as possible to meet with the witnesses to verify his statement. In addition, he urged the NAACP to use its influence to convince Governor Gardner to arrest at least one of the men. That way, Rich reasoned, law enforcement officials could interrogate the man and obtain the names of the remaining mob members.[35] However, when Rich's letter reached the NAACP, the organization was heavily involved in the protest to prevent John Parker from gaining a seat on the Supreme Court, and it took several weeks to send Robert Banal to interview the witness. By the time he arrived things had changed considerably, as fear of reprisal caused the witness to retract his story.[36]

Yet, even this setback did not end the effort to bring Moore's killers to justice. Several days after the murder, H.K. Williams, the director of the Home Detective Company in Greensboro, sent a letter to the governor offering the services of his company to identify the leaders of the mob:

> Doubtless the efficient Solicitor and Sheriff have devoted their untiring and best efforts to bring to justice these lynchers, however quite naturally they are handicapped due to being so well known and the usual reticence of residents to confide in them, as known officers, and due further to the nature of the case.... I have been sufficiently interested in this matter to make a preliminary investigation, without obligation to anyone, and I am absolutely convinced that persistent effort upon the part of competent investigators working under cover, would positively fasten this crime on the instigators and perpetrators thereof. Such operations should be of a diversified type, possibly necessitating the assignment of a colored investigator.... If you are interested in our proposition I suggest you telegraph us and the writer will come to your office immediately.[37]

Unfortunately, Gardner turned down Williams's offer and the murder of Oliver Moore slipped into oblivion.[38]

Less than two years after Moore's death another act of mob violence sprang from Pender County — the lynching of Dock Rogers. Late on Saturday August 26, 1933, Rogers went to the home of Tom Piner to purchase some whiskey.[39] After Rogers paid for the whiskey, Piner claimed that he did not have anything to put the liquor in and Rogers left. The next day Rogers returned to Piner's home, and this time he asked for his money back. Piner, however, refused to give him his money and an argument broke out. When Rogers refused to leave,

Piner's son-in-law picked up a chair and hit Rogers over the head.[40] Instead of nursing his wounds, Rogers went home, grabbed his gun and fired into Piner's home, wounding Piner's wife.[41] Then he returned home.

Unfortunately, thirty minutes later a mob surrounded Rogers's house. With their shotguns ready they ordered Rogers to come out. When he refused to comply, one of these men attempted to storm the door. Rogers shot the man.[42] This infuriated the mob and several men decided to burn Rogers out. After stealing a jar from a nearby home, the men siphoned gas from a car.[43] Then they dashed the gas on the home and started a fire.[44] Within minutes fire covered most of the structure and it appeared that Rogers would perish in the flames. Just before the flames consumed the home, Rogers made a bid to escape. However, before he could reach the safety of a nearby cornfield he was sighted and severely wounded. Following this incident Sheriff J.T. Brown hired a truck and threw the badly wounded Rogers aboard. Then he headed to Burgaw.

On the way to the jail the truck unexpectedly pulled to the side of the road and several cars and a group of men surrounded the truck. With guns in their hands the men unleashed several volleys into his body.[45] Then they bashed Rogers's brains out and dragged the body behind a truck until it was battered beyond recognition.[46]

The next day Governor Ehringhaus offered a $200 reward for information about the murder.[47] Then he contacted Woodus Kellum, the local solicitor, and asked him to conduct a vigorous investigation into Rogers's murder.[48] One week later, Kellum opened the investigation by holding a hearing in Burgaw in which he called fifty men suspected of participating in the crime to testify.[49] Perhaps the most important witness was Sheriff J.T. Brown. After a brief opening exchange, Kellum got Brown to admit that he was at Rogers's house before it was burned. Then he got Brown to admit that he was present at the lynching of Rogers.[50]

According to Brown, he went to Rogers's house after he received a call about the shooting at Piner's home. When the solicitor asked the sheriff if he had asked Rogers to surrender, the sheriff replied that he had not.[51] Brown maintained that "he was figuring some way to crawl up to the edge of the house to see what he could see."[52] However, when he got close to the house, the house was set on fire and Rogers was wounded as he tried to escape. Afterward Brown said he hired a truck to transport Rogers to the Pender County Jail.

When Rogers was placed on the truck, Brown maintained that he returned to his car and followed the truck to town. Then two cars passed and slowed down to separate him from the truck.[53] Several miles down the road he saw the truck pulled to the side of the road with a flat tire. However, more ominously, he saw a crowd of men standing near the truck. For that reason, Brown claimed, he parked 75 yards away.[54] When the solicitor asked why he did not just park across the highway from the truck or immediately in front of the vehicle, Brown replied that he just did not think that anyone would attempt to lynch Rogers.[55]

After concluding this line of questioning Kellum asked the sheriff if he did not recognize any of the members of the lynch mob. Brown maintained that it was too dark for him to recognize anyone.[56] Nevertheless, when Brown was asked if he had made an effort to arrest the men who were present, Brown claimed that he had made no effort: "I got to the place I didn't know what to do at that point when I asked the question and no one answered."[57]

Then perhaps one of the most damning exchanges occurred when Kellum asked the sheriff if he had launched an investigation to locate the killers. Again, Brown offered an excuse: "I have summoned witnesses but then I could not find out anything."[58] After Brown's testimony, the solicitor called several other suspects including A.C. Blake, justice of the peace. However, the story that each of the men told merely corroborated the version of events described by Brown. Two months after concluding the first hearing, Kellum held a second inquest. This time he called six witnesses. However, like the first hearing, his session did not produce any new evidence, nor did it lead to any arrests.[59] After this failure, Kellum wrote to Ehringhaus:

> The only aid that I know that can be rendered is for someone to go into the community and become part and parcel of the community, thereby gaining the confidence of the perpetrators of this wrong and obtain information of those who know. Such cannot be accomplished in a few days, nor in my opinion, in a few weeks. If you can provide the expense, I shall be glad to cooperate in suggesting the person or adapting any suggestion you may have as to who shall do this work.[60]

Instead of offering assistance or recommending someone who could conduct an investigation, Ehringhaus waited more than three months before he responded to Kellum.

In this response, Ehringhaus attempted to remove the state from the case by maintaining that the primary

North Carolina Governor John Ehringhaus, circa 1933 (courtesy North Carolina Collection, University of North Carolina Library at Chapel Hill).

responsibility for the case "rested upon the constitutional officer charged with the duty of prosecuting."[61] That was why the governor maintained he had allowed Kellum to move at his own pace. Then, in somewhat of a disingenuous manner, he offered assistance from the state. However, no assistance ever arrived and the investigation into Rogers's death closed with little fanfare.

The Sweat Ward Case

Two years after Pender County assassins killed Rogers, North Carolina lynch mobs struck again, this time in the north central part of the state, in Franklin County. On July 30, 1935, Sweat Ward, a thirty-year-old African American, attacked Charles G. Stokes, a white farmer, with a rock. As Stokes lay unconscious on the ground, Ward grabbed an axe and cut off Stoke's head.[62] Then he calmly took a sheet from his home, wrapped the head, and placed it by his side. Later when authorities arrived, they were surprised to find Ward sitting in a chair holding Stokes's severed head.[63]

Since Franklin County officials feared that the attack would raise tensions, they decided to move Ward to another county. After placing the suspect into a car, officials headed to nearby Nashville, North Carolina. However, about five miles outside of Louisburg an armed mob seized Ward. At gunpoint they placed a rope around his neck and hung him from a nearby tree.[64] Several days after the lynching the Raleigh chapter of the NAACP sent a letter to Governor Erhinghaus:

> About two years ago, a similar occurrence took place in this state. There was [sic] attempt made to investigate with the usual result in such matters— nothing. This time the case seems to be a clear one. There will be no excuse that North Carolina can make that will eradicate this latest disgrace. You are called upon to exert your good office and your influence in seeing these offenders against the laws of nature and men are brought to justice.[65]

In response to this plea North Carolina officials launched a halfhearted attempt to find Ward's killers by holding a hearing to investigate the murder. However, the hearing failed to identify any of the culprits or generate any additional information. For that reason, the NAACP's Walter White sent a letter to Ehringhaus in which he claimed that Ward was insane. According to this account, about three weeks before his death, Ward returned home to attend his mother's funeral. He was unable to handle his mother's death and he started acting strange. There was even talk of sending him to the state hospital.[66] Then several days after his mother's funeral, Ward in his distraught condition took some cocaine and became violently insane.[67] After that he went on a rampage, striking a man with a Coke bottle and attacking a relative with an iron poker.[68] Next, he attacked Stokes.[69] Though his actions proved that he was insane, White

Above and below: The lynching of Govan "Sweat" Ward. After suspending Ward by his arms with a plough line the mob unleashed a deadly blast. In the photograph above, taken minutes after the lynching, a crowd of curious onlookers and undoubtedly many members of the mob view Ward's lifeless body. Careful analysis of this picture clearly shows several bullet holes in Ward's shirt (courtesy *The News & Observer* of Raleigh, North Carolina).

nonetheless maintained that city leaders and local law enforcement officials were among the first to call for Ward's lynching.[70] Therefore he called for the state to punish the perpetrators of the crime. White's letter, however, garnered little attention from state officials.

Nonetheless, pressure was building in Washington to enact federal legislation to punish the perpetrators of mob violence. In January 1934, Senators Edward Costigan from Colorado and Robert Wagner of New York, stunned by lynchings in California and Maryland, introduced legislation to end mob violence. The proposed bill set strict penalties for state and local law enforcement officials who through negligence or collusion caused the lynching of persons in their custody. The legislation also called for persons charged with aiding or abetting lynch mobs to face trial at the hands of local juries. Thus, state officials would have the ability to act on their own. If no state response occurred, the federal government would have the ability to step in. The language used in the proposed legislation was very important since it attempted to remove many of the earlier objections Southerners found in the Dyer Bill, namely, the claim that the bill would usurp state power.

As the bill made its way through senatorial committees, a series of horrific lynchings, such as those of Claude Neal in Marianna, Florida; George Armwood in Maryland; and Reuben Stacy in Fort Lauderdale, Florida, appeared to increase support for the legislation. In addition, Walter White and the NAACP launched a public relations campaign to build support for the legislation. In part due to this campaign, White garnered endorsements from the American Civil Liberties Union, the National Council of Jewish Women, the *Richmond News Leader*, the *Chattanooga Times*, the *Greensboro News & Record*, and the National Urban League, as well as endorsements from several state legislatures.[71]

Yet, these endorsements meant little in the Senate. When the Costigan bill reached the Senate floor, opposition immediately arose from Southern and Western Senators. The leader of this opposition was Josiah W. Bailey of North Carolina. Born in 1873, Bailey was a significant figure in North Carolina history. After graduating from Wake Forest College in 1893, he succeeded his father as editor of the *Biblical Recorder*. In 1930, after a successful career as an editor and attorney he entered the U.S. Senate as a representative from North Carolina.[72] Once in the Senate, Bailey gained a reputation as a very pious, deeply religious man, so much so that his colleagues gave him the nickname "Holy Joe."[73] Yet, Bailey was hard to figure out. Although many considered him a moderate member of the Democratic Party, he nonetheless opposed Roosevelt's New Deal. Further, he helped compose what later became known as the Conservative Manifesto.[74] Thus, when the Costigan Anti-Lynching bill reached the Senate, Bailey warned that it would not pass. Then he threatened to launch a filibuster: "We'll speak night and day if necessary to prevent its passage."[75]

In an attempt to prevent the filibuster, Walter White, with the assistance of Eleanor Roosevelt, scheduled a meeting with Franklin Roosevelt. However, Roosevelt refused to use his influence to aid the antilynching bill effort. "The Southerners by reason of seniority rule in Congress, are chairman or occupy strategic places in most of the House and Senate Committees. If I come out for the anti-lynching bill now, they will block every bill I ask Congress.... I just can't take that risk."[76] Less than a month later, the bill was dropped.

For White and the NAACP, Congress's failure to pass the Costigan bill represented a serious setback. Twice the NAACP had spent a significant amount of its annual resources to lobby for the passage of antilynching legislation. Both times the NAACP failed to achieve victory. As a result, White lashed out by sending a series of critical letters to the most vocal opponents of the legislation. One of the strongest letters was sent to Senator Josiah Bailey. In this letter, sent shortly after Sweat Ward's death, White pointed out that contrary to the Senator's belief, local law enforcement officials were unable or unwilling to protect a prisoner with whose safety they were charged. White also charged in his letter that despite numerous witnesses, North Carolina had failed to prosecute anyone for the crime. Then he asked Bailey if he was willing to reconsider the recent statements he had made on the Senate floor, that in punishing lynchers Southerners "need no incentive to do our duty."[77] Annoyed by the letter, Bailey responded that he did not want to be bothered by White or the NAACP. Then he advised White to go out and make an honest living instead of attending to other people's business.

Nonetheless, White made one last attempt to get Congress to pass anti-lynching legislation. In 1936, the NAACP leader convinced Congressman Joseph A. Gavagan, who represented Harlem, to introduce legislation in the House of Representatives that outlawed lynching. The bill that Gavagan announced placed a fine on the county in which a lynching occurred. It also placed a fine and a prison sentence on officials whose negligence allowed a lynching to take place.[78] While Congress debated the legislation, news reached the House of a heinous act of mob violence from Duck Hill, Mississippi, in which two black murder suspects were taken from officials, tortured, and burned to death. As a result, proponents garnered enough support to pass the bill. However, only 17 of the 123 Southern Representatives voted for the bill.[79] When the bill reached the Senate, it was combined with another antilynching proposal known as the Wagner-Van Nuys Bill. However, like earlier antilynching measures the bill had little chance of becoming law. In the Senate, Southern opponents staged a twenty-seven-hour filibuster, while Roosevelt, afraid of losing Southern support, made no effort to promote the bill. As a result, the bill was dropped with little fanfare.

12

A Matter for the Judiciary

Despite the NAACP's failure to secure the passage of an antilynching bill, the Wagner-Van Nuys Bill loss nonetheless marked the demarcation point between the past and profound social, political and economic changes that occurred between 1940 and 1956. Several factors led to these changes. First, as a result of participation in World War II, many African Americans were no longer willing to accept second-class citizenship. At the same time the battle against the racial beliefs of Adolph Hitler's Germany prompted many whites to accept racial equality. Enhancing these views were a series of writings such as Gunnar Myrdal's *An American Dilemma: The Negro Problem and Modern Democracy* (1944) and John Hope Franklin's *From Slavery to Freedom* (1947), which increased understanding of the black experience.[1] Perhaps influenced by these writings, many restaurants and hotels across the North began to grant black customers the same privileges as whites.

Following closely on these changes were rulings by the Supreme Court that struck down segregation in graduate and professional schools, restrictive property covenants, segregation in interstate bus travel and discrimination in the federal service. In addition, the period saw the NAACP launch a careful planned campaign against Southern Jim Crow laws. This campaign culminated in the landmark *Brown v. Board of Education of Topeka* that decreed that separate educational facilities were inherently unequal, thus unconstitutional. While these changes were taking place, the Cold War started to creep into American race relations. As the champion of the free world, the United States cast itself as a bastion of freedom and democracy. However, the poor treatment of African Americans placed America in an awkward position. Consequently, across the nation the period was marked by improved police protection and increased action to prosecute those who committed acts of mob violence and lynching. For example, in 1946 the U.S. Justice Department successfully prosecuted for the first time a member of a lynch mob when it sent a Florida policeman to one year in the penitentiary for the murder of a black laborer.[2]

Influenced by this transformation Southern states began to pass local antilynching laws. By 1939 the number of lynchings nationwide dropped to a low of two.

In North Carolina the period 1935–1950 also saw numerous changes. In 1937 North Carolina created a Department of Justice in order to "catch super crooks, recodify laws and compile statistics on crime."[3] To provide the new Justice Department with an investigative arm, the state created the State Bureau of Investigation. The mission of the new bureau was to prevent crime and to procure the speedy apprehension and identification of criminals. In addition, to these changes the state authorized the State Bureau of Investigation upon the "request of the Governor to investigate and prepare evidence in the event of any lynching or mob violence in the State."[4] The impact of these developments were significant since it meant that investigations of cases of mob violence would no longer be in the hands of local authorities or ad-hoc committees assigned by the governor — instead, such cases could be handled by professionals who had little interest in protecting lynch mob participants.

These changes, however, did not totally remove the propensity for mob violence in many parts of North Carolina. For example, in February of 1939, a mob in Goldsboro seized two black men who were being held in the local jail for beating up the mayor, and flogged both men.[5] Several months before America entered World War II another incident flared in the small town of Roxboro. On August 15, 1941, Cy Winstead, a twenty-two-year-old African American was arrested for assaulting the sister of his white employer.[6] As news of the assault spread, an angry mob gathered around the jail. The situation grew worse when someone tossed a rope into a tree on the courthouse lawn and there was fear that Winstead would be lynched.[7] After all, Roxboro had been the scene of a lynching twenty years earlier. Yet, on this day blacks in the town were determined that history not repeat itself. At the height of this tension several dozen black Civilian Conservation Corps (CCC) recruits armed themselves with sticks and marched toward the courthouse. However, before they reached the courthouse, gunfire rang out and the men scattered.[8]

With the CCC recruits out of the way the mob turned its attention to the jail. Around 10:00 P.M., several men broke into a nearby bottling plant and hauled away several hundred empty bottles. Then they launched a barrage against the jail. Another group of men charged the jail. However, when the men got near the door the sheriff fired several canisters of tear gas.[9] Then while the mob reeled from the tear gas, a handful of state troopers and police officers from nearby Durham arrived to help protect the jail.[10] Unfortunately, this did not dissuade the mob and for hours on end the small band of police officers and sheriff deputies held the jail while the mob fired a barrage of gunshots and bottles.[11]

At 5:00 A.M. the next morning things calmed down enough for officers to bundle Winstead into a patrol car and race him to Raleigh's Central Prison for safekeeping. Nonetheless, apprehension remained high and rumors began to circulate of an impending race riot. The next day Governor Melville Broughton, in office less than a year, ordered the State Patrol and National Guard to Roxboro to restore order. "There is still a lot of feeling in Roxboro and I have instructed the patrol to continue to aid the Roxboro officers the rest of the day and tonight."[12] The governor also ordered the State Bureau of Investigation (SBI) to conduct an investigation. In a tribute to its efficiency the SBI arrested five men and charged them with the attack on the jail. Six months later the state sentenced the men to prison terms ranging from 12 to 18 months.[13]

As a final outcome, the SBI investigation led to a reduction of the charges brought against Cy Winstead. According to the SBI report it appears that Winstead and the young woman were involved in a consensual relationship. Consequently, when the case reached the courts the judge allowed Winstead to plead guilty to a charge of assault on a female and he was sentenced to a prison term of two to five years.[14]

The most serious incident of the era was the lynching of a twenty-three-year-old black man named Robert Melker in Cherryville. The incident that led to Melker's death began on April 13, 1941, when a car occupied by four young white men passed Melker and his wife as they walked along side a highway. As the car passed, one of the men yelled at the couple and Melker replied.[15] Unfortunately, this angered the men and they stopped the car and began to throw rocks at the Melkers until the couple retreated into their home. At this point Melker's mother grabbed a shotgun and fired at the attackers, sending the men scurrying for safety.[16] However, this did not end the day's drama. As soon as the white men reached their homes, they grabbed their shotguns. Then they returned to the Melker's home and called for Melker to come out. When he refused, one of the men shouted, "We'll kill every G_ _ d Nigger in here if we have to."[17] At this point Melker opened the door and the men unleashed their fury by firing several shotgun blasts into his body.[18]

The next day Gaston County authorities arrested four men — Haywood Dellinger, twenty-six; Graham Dellinger, twenty-three; Fred Hudson, twenty-five; and Robert Sellers, twenty-eight — and charged them with Melker's death.[19] However, more importantly officials announced that two of the men, Haywood Dellinger and Robert Sellers, had confessed.[20] Yet, despite this evidence many feared that the men still might go unpunished, since North Carolina had never convicted a white man for lynching an African American. But on this occasion these fears were unwarranted. Ten days after Melker's death all of the suspects submitted guilty pleas when the solicitor agreed to reduce the charges to second-degree murder.[21] One week later the authorities sentenced Haywood Dellinger, Robert Sellers and Fred Hudson to prison terms of eighteen to twenty-five years and Graham Dellinger, who drove the get away car, to a term of fourteen years.[22]

Yet, the sentences did not provide closure for the Melker case. Three months after Melker's death Tuskegee Institute listed his murder as a lynching. This unleashed a firestorm across North Carolina. Heading this chorus were Gaston County business leaders, who felt that a lynching would undermine their efforts to attract industry. For that reason, in July 1941, Brice T. Dickerson, who served as executive secretary of the Gastonia Chamber of Commerce, sent a letter to Tuskegee protesting the college's decision to classify Melker's death as a lynching. According to Dickerson, "Melker was killed as a result of a spontaneous argument with these men."[23] When Dickerson's protest failed to persuade Tuskegee to reclassify Melker's death, newspapers across North Carolina rallied to the cause by publishing editorials that questioned Tuskegee's methodology. These editorials also charged that the leaders of Tuskegee were under the influence of antilynching radicals such as Jessie Daniels Ames and Walter White, who presented the worst possible picture to promote their radical causes.[24] However, in the end these arguments, like Dickerson's, failed to persuade Tuskegee to reclassify Melker's death.

Despite this controversy, the Melker case marked a turning point in North Carolina. For the first time in state history white men charged with participating in the lynching of a black man were convicted and sentenced to prison. Such action undoubtedly sent a message to others that North Carolina was serious about ending the reign of Judge Lynch.

The Case Godwin Bush

Six years after Melker's death another case of mob violence arose in Northampton County. On May 29, 1947, seventeen-year-old Margaret Allen Bryant reported that she had been attacked by a black assailant in the small town of Rich Square. According to Bryant, a black man jumped from the shadows of an alley and attempted to grab her.[25] Terrified, Bryant claimed she screamed and the man ran away. News of the attack was enough to stir up a frenzy in Rich Square, and police accompanied by a large number of armed volunteers set out to find the assailant. After several hours they found the assailant, identified as Godwin Bush, and charged him with attempted rape. Then they took him to the county jail in the nearby town of Jackson.[26] Unfortunately, the arrest was like a match to a powder keg, providing the spark needed to ignite pent-up racial tensions.

Several weeks earlier police had arrested two black men, twenty-four-year-old Willie Cherry and twenty-one-year-old James Dick Boone, for the burglary and rape of a white Rich Square housewife.[27] As indicated in published reports, on the night of April 25, 1947, someone cut a screen and climbed through a window into the home of Mrs. Jane Tarrant.[28] After getting into the house the intruder robbed Tarrant of $15.11 and raped her at knifepoint.[29]

The next day Rich Square police chief Frank Outland arrested Willie Cherry and charged him with the crime. Moreover, Outland claimed that he had evidence to connect Cherry to the crime, such as the $15.11 in the same denomination of bills that Tarrant reported missing. He also maintained that he had found a coat with two missing buttons that matched buttons found on the floor of Tarrant's kitchen.[30] However, this did not mark the end of Outland's good fortune. After interrogating the suspect, Outland claimed that Cherry confessed to the crime and implicated Richard "Dick" Boone as an accomplice.[31] As a result, Outland also arrested Boone and placed him in the county jail.

Margaret Allen Bryant, circa 1947 (courtesy *The News & Observer* of Raleigh, North Carolina).

Word of Cherry's arrest stirred feelings in Rich Square and Northampton County to a fever pitch, and several lynch-minded citizens plotted his death. The night after Cherry was placed in the Jackson Jail, a crowd of vigilantes surrounded the jail.[32] However, the vigilantes soon dispersed when it was revealed that Cherry had been moved earlier in the day to nearby Nashville. Needless to say tensions remained high in Rich Square and lynching spirit prevailed in the community. And so it was two weeks later when authorities arrested Godwin Bush.

Less than six hours after Bush was placed in the Northampton County Jail, vigilantes surrounded the building. With guns drawn they forced their way into the building and seized Bush. Then they headed off into the Northampton countryside.[33] The next day, when he received news of the jail break, Northampton County sheriff A.C. Stephenson said, "Today I am afraid that a lynching has taken place."[34] Then Stephenson formed a posse and combed the deep woods that surrounded Jackson for Bush's body.[35] However, the search failed to locate the prisoner's body.

In Raleigh, news of the attack led Governor Gregg Cherry to take immediate action. The day after the jailbreak the governor ordered the State Bureau of Investigation (SBI) to look into the crime.[36] Then he declared, "I will not condone lynchings or this kind of play as long as I am governor."[37] A few days later, SBI agents got their first big break when they spoke with Rosa Howard,

Left: Godwin Bush, circa 1947. *Right:* Northampton County jailer E.D. Edwards, circa 1947. *Below:* Godwin Bush and the warden of Central Prison, circa 1947 (all photographs courtesy *The News & Observer* of Raleigh, North Carolina).

a black woman who lived across the street from the jail. According to Howard, around 2:00 A.M. on May 23, 1947, she saw two cars parked on the street beside the jail.[38] Then she heard someone running and a gunshot.[39] When she looked out a window to see what had happened, she saw a man pick something up and then drive away.[40]

Agents later corroborated Howard's statement when they found a bullet embedded in a shed across from the jail and a footprint in the mud, apparently made by someone running.[41] Yet this did not answer the central question — where was Godwin Bush? Moreover, as the SBI continued to probe into Bush's disappearance, rumors began to spread that blacks, who made up more than seventy percent of Northampton County's population, planned to burn Rich Square in retaliation for Bush's lynching. As a result, many white families either left or sent their children to neighboring villages.

In addition to this precaution, local authorities convinced the governor to assign several dozen state police to patrol the streets of Rich Square.[42] However, when the rumored attack failed to materialize, newspapers across the nation began to publish unflattering articles about the people of Rich Square and Margaret Allen Bryant. In response, Police Chief Frank Outland sent a letter to the *Jackson News*:

> I am not in favor of lynching and have never forgotten my duty to a prisoner but I can certainly appreciate the world's most law abiding, when they are maligned as a group for the mistakes of a few. Another factor not taken into consideration is the fact that 19 sex crimes including one of the most brutal and premeditated rapes and 15 instances of peeping tom have occurred in the Rich Square area in the past three months— an average of over one per week. The better class negro citizens of our area, which includes the great majority have asked me to help them and have offered their help to stop this wave of sex crimes, before some innocent people really get hurt.... Some of the crime may be due to the negro men who mixed with white women in Europe while they were members of the armed forces, some of it no doubt due to the spreading of vicious and lewd pictures of white women by the lowest dregs of society.... Since this wave of notoriety has been heaped on the shoulders of the local citizenry numerous insulting letters from New York and New Jersey have been mailed to the principles in the Bush case. The young lady involved in the case has been called by mail libelous and vile things by cranks from all over the country.... The people of this section are mad as hornets.... Unless we can get to the bottom of this series of crimes there is serious danger of violence that will hurt innocent people.[43]

In the midst of the newspaper barrage, the investigation into Bush's disappearance got its biggest lead when William Johnson, the minister of Rich Square's AME Church, contacted officials and advised them that Bush was alive. However, Johnson maintained that Bush feared an attack would be made on his life and would only surrender to FBI agents.[44] The next day FBI agents went to a prearranged location and met Bush.[45] Then with their quarry in tow they headed to Raleigh's Central Prison, where agents interrogated the fugitive. From this interview the first details of Bush's escape and life in hiding began to emerge.

According to Bush two masked men took him from the jail and forced him into a parked car. In their haste the men placed him next to the door in the backseat. However, as they prepared to drive away one of the men said, "Let him sit in the middle."[46] When one of the men opened the door to make the change, Bush jumped out and ran for his life. As he ran one of the vigilantes fired, but fortunately he missed. Then he sprinted into some nearby woods.[47] For the next two days he wandered through the woods, "sleeping an hour here and an hour there." All the time, he said, "he feared a posse would get him."[48] After two days of hiding he sneaked to the home of a black farmer, who contacted his father. His father, in turn, contacted Johnson who arranged Bush's surrender. However, to the officers perhaps the most important information provided by Bush was the identity of one of his abductors. According to Bush, one of the men that took him from the jail was a man who took up tickets at the negro entrance to the Rich Square Theater.[49]

This information led agents to arrest Joe Lee Cunningham, who worked at the Myers Theater in Rich Square.[50] To prevent news of the arrest from reaching Northampton officials, agents took Cunningham to a hotel in nearby Weldon, North Carolina, where he was interrogated by agents and subsequently confessed to being a member of the mob that kidnapped Bush. According to Cunningham, on the night Bush was placed in the Jackson Jail, he received a call around 12:15 A.M.: "We have got Nigger trouble down here and need you — come on down,"[51] In response he claimed he hurriedly dressed and got his .22 pistol and went to downtown Rich Square. Arriving downtown, Cunningham claimed that he and Glenn Collier, Robert Vann, W.C. Cooper, Gilbert Bryant, Lynwood Bryant and Russell Bryant went to a barbershop and got some towels to use as masks.[52] Then they drove to Jackson. When they arrived at the jail Cunningham claimed he grabbed Bush and put him in a car. However, as they started to drive away Bush opened the door and made a dash for some nearby woods. After that all of the men jumped in their cars and hurried home.[53]

In the meantime in Jackson, the sheriff of Northampton County, unaware of Cunningham's confession and somewhat sympathetic to members of the mob, announced, "I shouldn't wonder if they never find out who took the negro.[54] Local citizens advanced the theory that Bush had been permitted to escape, since he was the first known person in the state to escape from a lynch mob. To support this theory they maintained that the bullet fired at Bush was found in the eaves of a shed about nine feet from the ground, meaning that whoever had fired the bullet had aimed it above Bush's head. For that reason, most citizens of Rich Square and neighboring Jackson sympathized with the sheriff in that they hoped that those that were responsible for the abduction would not be found.[55]

Despite this fact, the pace of the investigation was rapidly accelerating. The day after Cunningham's arrest, FBI agents obtained a .32-caliber pistol from the owner of a Rich Square restaurant. According to Cunningham, on the night of the attack on the jail Bob Vann used a .32-caliber pistol that he supposedly got from the owner of the restaurant. The pistol was sent to the FBI lab for ballistics testing to see if bullets fired from the gun matched those found in the shed.[56] One day later, agents arrested the six men identified by Cunningham and charged the men with conspiracy, jail breaking and assault. Yet, ominously, FBI officials announced that there was no violation of federal law. As a result, all information that they collected was handed over to local officials in Northampton County, who undoubtedly were sympathetic to the mob.[57]

For Governor Cherry the arrests were a welcome development, since it confirmed the state's and his personal commitment to end mob violence. In an interview given shortly after the arrests Cherry said, "I am glad they're making progress and I hope they'll get enough evidence to sustain convictions."[58] However, for many white residents in Rich Square, news of the arrests fell like an anvil. While most refused to comment to outsiders, they nonetheless gathered on the streets to discuss the arrests. Moreover, many of the citizens "showed signs of nervousness and wore nervous expression on their face."[59]

Other citizens, however, angered by the arrests, were determined to show that blacks were the root cause of the problems. In an interview given to the *Murfreesboro News*, the wife of Police Chief Outland said:

> The real heroes in the Rich Square mob case are the members of the white mob.... Until the negroes are educated to the fact that they were brought here as servants and are not to be placed on a basis of equality with whites (meaning interracial dating), I fear we shall have trouble in this country. The meanest men would be a jury, which would convict and separate these young men from their families and loved ones from trying to protect Rich Square from one of the worst tragedies we have ever had.[60]

However, perhaps the most outrageous attempt to prove black wrongdoing was a woman who reported an attempted sexual assault the day after Outland's article appeared in the newspaper.[61] According to the victim, Ellen Davis Byrd, a seventeen-year-old housewife, she was at home with her mother-in-law around 10:30 P.M. when she heard a knock at the back door. Thinking it was her husband returning from the store, she opened the door, and a black man grabbed her.[62] However, before the man could accomplish his purpose Byrd claimed that she screamed, then fainted. In the midst of this commotion her assailant fled.[63] The woman's accusation was more than enough to arouse neighbors, and a posse formed and begin searching for the suspect. Officials feared the outbreak of violence and the sheriff threw the posse off of the trail of the suspects. Then he doubled back and arrested three black men — James Bowser, Mack Ayers and Johnny Goode — who lived about two miles from the victim.[64]

As if these arrests did not color public fear of black rapists enough, three weeks later jury selection began in the Cherry case. Although blacks made up two-thirds of Northampton County's population and many were registered to vote, the solicitor excluded all blacks on the grounds that they could not make an unbiased decision in a case involving another member of the race.[65] Such reasoning seems illogical considering that whites had sat on juries judging other whites for centuries. Nonetheless, Bush's defense attorney made no objection and officials quickly seated an all-white jury.

The next day Cherry's trial opened before a packed courtroom. First to approach the judge was E.N. Riddle, Cherry's lawyer, who moved that the trial be transferred to another location due to pretrial publicity. However, this motion was denied since the judge maintained that "publicity had been statewide and even nationwide."[66] Then the judge called the first witness to the stand, the victim of the attack, Jane Tarrant. According to Tarrant she was awakened around 11:00 P.M. on April 25, 1947, by a metallic sound. Hearing this noise she walked to the stairs and called her husband's name. When she did not receive an answer, she assumed that her husband was injured and she ran downstairs and called his name again. As she entered the living room someone grabbed her throat.[67]

After struggling for a few minutes she broke away and ran into the kitchen. But the man grabbed her again. This time, the attacker threatened her with a pocketknife and forced her upstairs, where she was sexually assaulted. Then the intruder plundered through her bureau, took $15.11 and ran out the back door. After the man left, Tarrant said she looked out of the back window and saw a man ride away on a bicycle.[68] Due to the darkened conditions she was unable to identify her attacker, but she was sure she knew his voice. The next day while sitting in a neighbor's home, out of sight of a man working there, she identified Cherry's voice.[69] Despite the troubling questions surrounding voice identification, Cherry's attorney did not challenge this aspect of Tarrant's testimony. Instead he asked Tarrant if she had detected any alcohol on the breath of her attacker.[70] She replied yes.

Next to take the stand was Police Chief Frank Outland. According to Outland, Cherry confessed to him the day after the arrest. Cherry told him that he and James "Dick" Boone planned to rape and rob Tarrant. After meeting Boone in the Bluebird Cafe, the two men drank beer and whiskey and then went to Tarrant's home. When they reached the home Cherry cut a screen and climbed through the window with Boone's help. Once inside he took a bottle of brandy from a closet.[71] Outland maintained that the partly filled bottle of brandy was found at Cherry's home when he was arrested.

Despite the damning nature of Outland's testimony, there remained many questions. For one, even if Cherry were guilty, it is hard to fathom that he would confess to a crime that would lead to the death penalty. Second, if Cherry did indeed confess, why was Frank Outland the only person to hear the confession?* Despite this fact, the defense failed to question the "so-called" confession presented by Outland. Instead Cherry took the stand and presented testimony that attempted to place the blame for the crime on his drunkenness. Such testimony merely confirmed his guilt.[72] After several more hours of testimony the state closed its case. Twenty minutes later the jury found Cherry guilty of attempted rape and robbery. Then the judge sentenced Cherry to death.[73] Immediately after Cherry's sentence was announced, Northampton officials opened Richard Dick Boone's case. Instead of receiving the death penalty, Boone was given life in prison.[74]

Still, the cases of Cherry and Boone only represented a prelude to the main event, the trial of the men charged with Godwin Bush's kidnapping. On August 5, 1947, before a packed courtroom of more than 350 spectators, the Grand Jury opened a hearing to determine if a true bill of indictment would be returned against the men charged in Bush's kidnapping and against Bush for the attempted rape of Margaret Allen.[75] However, as in countless cases of mob violence, the Grand Jury refused to indict the men. The Grand Jury also refused to issue a bill of indictment against Godwin Bush.[76] In response Bush said, "I am glad it came out this way. It was all a mistake anyway."[77] Yet, for many in the court room the release of the seven accused mob members represented a significant victory of local vigilante justice over the forces of progress and change.

At this point the case took an unusual turn as shortly after the trial Governor Cherry held a press conference and condemned the crime. Then he stated, "The action of the grand jury a grave miscarriage of justice and a reflection on the State of North Carolina.... Undoubtedly a crime had been committed since one of the men had confessed."[78] Yet, the governor's actions had little to do with his personal beliefs and more to do with preserving North Carolina's image abroad. Undoubtedly, Cherry was familiar with the impact a recent case of mob violence had on Georgia. In this case almost one year earlier, reports from Georgia confirmed that a mob had lynched four young African Americans at an isolated spot known as Moore's Ford. The origins of this violence started with a fight. Several days before the lynching, authorities arrested Roger Malcom, a black farm worker, for stabbing Barney Hester, a white farmer.[79] What precipitated this argument has never been clearly determined. However, many scholars maintain that the both men were having a relationship with Dorothy Malcom, a black woman who lived on a farm owned by Hester's father. What-

*It appears that Outland had a habit of obtaining confessions from suspects in which he was the only witness. In addition to Cherry's confession, Outland claimed Godwin Bush confessed.

ever the case may be, after the fight, authorities transported Hester to the hospital and Roger Malcom to jail. Several days later, Loy Harrison, a white landowner, bailed Roger Malcom out of jail.[80]

After leaving the jail, Harrison, accompanied by Roger Malcom, Dorothy Malcom, George Dorsey — a World War II veteran who many whites considered was uppity — and Dorsey's wife Mae Dorsey, headed home.[81] On this trip, Harrison returned on a remote highway that was off the beaten path.[82] When they reached Moore's Ford Bridge they found the road blocked by a car. Before they could turn around, armed men rushed from nearby woods and seized both black men.[83] A short distance away, the mob tore their bodies apart with over 100 gunshots. Then the mob dragged the women from the car. As with the men, the women were subjected to a barrage of bullets and shotgun pellets.[84] After their deaths, several of the men took a knife and cut Dorothy Malcom's unborn baby from her womb. Then the mob calmly drove from the scene leaving the bodies beside the road.

Yet, while none of the members of the mob wore a mask, Harrison maintained that he did not recognize any of the vigilantes.[85] As a result, authorities did not prosecute anyone for the murders. The murders shocked the nation and letters of condemnation poured into the Georgia governor's office. Though the volume of letters did not bother state power brokers, their content did, as many suggested that they would encourage northern industry and business, which Georgia was trying to attract, to move elsewhere.[86] Governor Cherry was determined that North Carolina would not face the same national scrutiny and condemnation as Georgia. Moreover, he was fully aware that such condemnation was bad for business. The next day the governor ordered the solicitor to reopen the case.[87]

Several days later, officers rearrested the men and charged them with kidnapping Bush.[88] The decision to retry to the men, however, led the supporters of the men to write a series of scathing letters to the governor. An unsigned letter sent to the governor on August 9, 1947, maintained that if the seven white suspects were to be retried, "why isn't (referring to Bush) the negro to be retried also?"[89] Another letter was even more demanding: "Why not let sleeping dogs lie. The negro was not harmed even though that probably would have been best in the long run."[90] The letter went on to warn Cherry that if he continued to assume "the attitude of Northern do gooders you will so incite white prejudice against negroes in your state that lynchings will mushroom overnight."[91]

During the same period the governor also received hundreds of letters from supporters. One such letter came from L. Barnwell Washington, a North Carolina chaplain. "The stand you have taken with regards to the lynch mob that was organized in Jackson, North Carolina proves to the world that there are decent men and women in the State of North Carolina."[92] A letter from a black writer was even more supportive:

> Your action in attempting to obtain indictments against the men connected with the lynching of Godwin Bush ... will undoubtedly place you high on the list of great men in North Carolina.... As little as you might think of it you have become ... a symbol of freedom to hundreds of thousands of little people, otherwise hopeless individuals by your action.... Sir we, the negro population of America, thank almighty God for men like you.[93]

Despite the supportive letters, the results of the second Grand Jury hearing were much like the first. Since officials had no evidence other than the confession of one man, the judge dropped charges against six of the suspects. Ironically, officials used the confession of one man, namely, Chief Frank Outland, to convict Cherry.* However, the suspect who provided the confession along with the elderly jailer were charged with the crime and a preliminary hearing was set.[94]

To ensure that local supporters of the men would not impact the outcome of the hearing, officials moved the trial to nearby Warren County. The results, however, were the same, as a Warren County Grand Jury refused to indict the men.[95] Speaking to the press after the hearing, Governor Cherry remarked, "I have nothing to say at this time. It is a matter for the judiciary."[96]

Despite the failure to prosecute or convict the men, the governor's determination to find and prosecute the men responsible for Bush's kidnapping ensured that the court of Judge Lynch would become a thing of the past. Since the 1920s the governors of North Carolina had conducted campaigns with varying success to end mob violence. As a result, mob violence, while significant, nonetheless remained lower than surrounding states. However, as industrialization and Northern investment increased, eradicating mob violence became more than just lip service. Thus, from the early 1930s forward, ending mob violence and prosecuting those responsible for committing such crimes became a priority. Governor Cherry's decision to aggressively seek out and prosecute the men responsible for kidnapping Bush, even though not successful, showed that the state meant business. More importantly, the fact that North Carolina had experienced moderate success in prosecuting mob participants made mob violence somewhat problematic for those, including police officers, who undertook it.

The actions of North Carolina officials during the Bush affair also signaled another sinister change, a movement toward state-sanctioned executions, legal lynchings. During much of the time officials searched for Bush's kidnappers, local authorities were preoccupied with the case of Willie Cherry. Although much of the evidence used to convict Cherry was questionable, his trial was nothing more than a formality with a forgone conclusion. Unfortunately, the move toward legally sanctioned executions created a blood-soaked landscape

---

Although Tarrant provided testimony in court, authorities were unable to use much of her statement since she was unable to identify her attacker.

that only moderated slightly when federal legislation in 1972 ruled that the death penalty was unconstitutional when a jury had the right to impose this penalty at its discretion. In view of this decision the North Carolina Supreme Court ruled that the death penalty would be mandatory for several specified crimes. As a result the number of persons on death row rose to 120, the highest in the nation. In 1976, in the case of *Woodson v. North Carolina* the U.S. Supreme Court ruled in a 5 to 4 decision that North Carolina death penalty laws were unconstitutional. As a result of this ruling all of the people on death row were given new trials or had their sentences commuted to life terms. Unfortunately, in 1977 North Carolina revised its death penalty laws to conform to federal mandates and the process started again. However, the legal challenges had an impact as the number of executions in North Carolina slipped to their lowest point ever.

13

Summary

The image is fixed in the minds of most Americans — a man, usually black, hangs from a pole with a rope around his neck. Watching this spectacle, hundreds of onlookers displayed their pleasure by taking pieces of the victim's body for souvenirs and by posing for pictures in front of the dead body. Regrettably, throughout American history such spectacles were nothing new. In colonial America, mobs used extralegal violence to murder religious outcasts. In the Old West, citizens used lynching to punish so-called criminals, while in the South, whites used lynching as a means of overturning the social revolution that occurred at the end of the Civil War.

In North Carolina, this drama played out dozens of times leading to a multitude of deaths. Like most of the South, the violence in North Carolina originated centuries earlier with the importation of black slaves. To control slaves, whites developed a harsh and inhumane system. The mandates of this system meant that slaves were governed by legally sanctioned violence. As historian David Brion Davis writes, "Even the most kindly and humane masters knew that only the threat of violence could force gangs of field hands to work from dawn to dusk.... Frequent public floggings reminded every slave of the penalty for inefficient labor, disorderly conduct, or refusal to accept the authority of a superior."[1] Yet, ever fearful of insurrection, planters also kept a sharp eye for suspicious slave behavior. "When conditions warranted, vigilantes ... savagely suppressed both real and slave uprisings."[2] For example, in the wake of Nat Turner's revolt, North Carolina mobs killed more than forty innocent slaves and free blacks. Therefore, by the end of the antebellum period the practice of mob violence was firmly woven into North Carolina's white society.[3]

With such violence as a model, it is little wonder that after the Civil War, whites in North Carolina readily resumed this familiar form of terror. Nonetheless, the violence of this period would reveal something of North Carolina's inner soul, namely, a divided consciousness. On one hand, state officials passed laws and made noble efforts to end mob violence. On the other hand, local law enforcement and white citizens refused to comply with antilynching legislation. Such division made it difficult to enforce the state's lynching laws. This weakness turned out to be a boon for members of the Democratic Party, which was struggling to find a way to return to power.

During the legislative campaign of 1898, Democrats launched a white supremacy campaign. Declaring that only white men were fit to hold political office, Democrats charged members of the Republican Party of supporting "negro rule" in North Carolina. In addition, they launched a campaign of terror to keep blacks, the primary supporters of the Republicans, away from the polls. In the end, this campaign left in its wake the bodies of dozens of black men. Nonetheless, the campaign served its purpose by crushing the Republican Party and ending black suffrage.

However, in ending black suffrage, the Democrats unwittingly set in motion measures that would extinguish the flame of mob violence. In adopting laws that disenfranchised blacks, the Democrats raised fears among poor whites that they would also lose their right to vote. Consequently, to ensure poor "illiterate" whites that they would not be disenfranchised in the future, party bosses sponsored legislation to build schools. Then to ensure that poor whites remained firmly entrenched in the Democratic Party and did not leave party ranks as they did during the Populist movement, party bosses called for the expansion of the state's textile industry in order to provide jobs for poor whites.

To obtain the capital needed to expand these programs and improve the state's infrastructure, Democrats, who dominated North Carolina government, made several attempts to sell state-issued bonds. However, several years earlier, North Carolina defaulted on a series of bonds, which threatened the state's ability to raise the capital. As a result, state leaders turned to Northern financiers. However, Northern investment came with a cost — namely, increased scrutiny and a tacit demand for social stability. In such an environment the cruel and brutal practices of the past now became a liability as it threatened to unravel the state's ability to undertake economic improvement.

Yet, regardless of the cost many North Carolinians were determined to continue the age-old tradition. On a cold night in 1921, tradition would meet progress in perhaps the most famous act of mob violence in North Carolina history, the lynchings of Alfred Williams and Plummer Bullock and the subsequent extradition case of Matthew Bullock. For North Carolina this case not only brought unwanted national attention but also led to international condemnation. From England, the editors of the *Pall Mall Gazette* wrote, "All extradition law is based upon the assumption that the country in which the accused is handed over can guarantee a fair trial.... Assurances should certainly be required that the man will not be thrown to the mercy of white barbarism in the Southern States."[4] The *Toronto Globe* maintained, "Behind the legal situation there is the ugly fact that Bullock's brother did not stand trial, but was strung up outside of the jail that failed to shelter him from the mob."[5] Condemnations from the black press were even more critical. The *Chicago Defender* asserted, "A black man has no rights that a white man is bound to respect.... Jails are no shelter when a Southern mob desires to wreak vengeance for some alleged wrong."[6]

The furor caused by the Bullock case raised fears among state leaders that such criticisms would damage North Carolina's ability to attract Northern investment. As a result, North Carolina's state government altered its stance toward mob violence. This change required the governor to dispatch troops at the first sign of violence. It also called for state officials to aggressively prosecute individuals charged with mob violence. This course led to notable convictions in Asheville, Goldsboro and Williamston. This, however, did not totally stamp out mob violence in the Tar Heel State. For instance, in the period from 1926 to 1947 North Carolina experienced six lynchings and more than ten serious acts of mob violence. Moreover, in only one of these cases, the 1941 Roxboro riot, would the perpetrators of the crimes be convicted and sentenced to jail. Yet, the trail had been blazed — lynching would become passé. For one, most state officials realized that the economic progress started by the Democratic Party bosses continued to need outside investment. Mob violence was counterproductive to this goal.

Although at times North Carolina's Democratic leaders failed to prevent the outbreak of mob violence, they nonetheless were forced by their own fears, borne of losing the support of poor whites to whom they had promised so much. Thus they created a Department of Justice and an investigative arm, the State Bureau of Investigation. With these new agencies North Carolina had a body of trained professionals that did not owe their positions to local voters. As North Carolina made these changes, a quadruple lynching in Georgia rocked the nation and forced the federal government to finally take action to look into the nation's bloody pastime. The case also brought international and national condemnation to Georgia, a fate North Carolina officials were determined to avoid at all costs.

Consequently, one year later when vigilantes kidnapped Godwin Bush, North Carolina officials aggressively investigated the case using the new SBI and Justice Department. In short order, arrests were made and the case was sent to Grand Jury. When the Grand Jury refused to indict the suspects, a surprising development took place. Governor Cherry rejected the findings and empanelled a special Grand Jury to conduct a second investigation of the crimes. Although the special Grand Jury refused to indict the suspects, the stance taken by North Carolina allowed the state to escape the scrutiny and condemnation faced by states like Georgia. Such amenity allowed North Carolina, by 1960, to become the largest textile manufacturing state in the nation, creating hundreds of jobs for poor whites. This in turn played a major role in the urbanization of North Carolina and in the development of a society that no longer had a need for lynching and mob violence. However, for the victims of North Carolina lynch mobs, no explanation can adequately serve them justice. Thus, I honor their spirits and sincerely hope that their deaths not be in vain but will serve as a constant reminder of man's inhumanity to his fellow man.

Appendix I

Other Notable Lynchings

John Taylor *Guilford County. June 10, 1881*

On the night of June 10, 1881, a large body of armed men quietly rode into Greensboro. After securing the area around the jail, several men entered the lock-up and demanded John Taylor, a young African American.[1] When the jailer refused, several burly men broke into the cell and seized Taylor. Then they dragged him outside and disappeared into the darkness. The next morning the doomed man's body was found hanging by the neck from a small oak tree about seven miles from Reidsville.[2]

The events that led to this lynching stemmed from perhaps the most common cause for mob violence, rape of a white woman. On the night of June 3, 1881, the wife of Colonel James Irwin reported that one her husband's field hands, John Taylor, had assaulted her while her husband was away at a concert.[3] In short order, authorities arrested Taylor and his accomplice George Gunn in nearby Reidsville. The next day they took the men before a magistrate where the suspects supposedly confessed their guilt.[4] However, as often been said, it seems odd that the men would confess to such a crime considering the deadly response such actions would elicit.

Whatever the case, after recording the confession officers placed the suspects in the Wentworth town jail. But when rumors surfaced that a mob was forming, the sheriff secretly moved the prisoners to Danville, Virginia. After a day in that town he headed to Greensboro and deposited the prisoners in the Guilford County Jail.[5] Somehow despite all of the movement, news of the prisoners' location leaked and soon a rumor spread that a mob was forming to attack the jail in Greensboro. In response, Greensboro officials took the men into the country and remained there two days. When it appeared that the threat had passed, they brought the men back to the jail. Unfortunately, the news leaked, and several nights later the mob struck.

After the death of Taylor authorities made no attempt to identify or arrest the men responsible for his murder, as most citizens viewed the lynching as warranted. An article appearing in the *Greensboro North State* best summed up this feeling:

> Thus ended the life of a brute — he cannot be called a man — and it is hard to believe there was anything human in him. We have never heard of a more brutal crime than that committed by him. We are disposed to plead for the enforcement of the laws and their strict observance. The safety of society depends upon this conservative principle. This is a case, however, where we feel like shuttering our eyes and concluding that the swift punishment was well-deserved and was properly administered.[6]

Edmund Davis   *Union County. October 16, 1881*

At daybreak on Sunday, October 16, 1881, a party of men set out to apprehend Edmund Davis, a young black man. After several hours of searching the men found him in a cabin in Lancaster County, South Carolina. At gunpoint they forced him from his home and took him back to Union County, North Carolina, so the victim of his alleged crime could identify him. When the woman saw the suspect she was unable to identify him as her attacker. Yet, this mattered little since a neighbor claimed that a stick and a hammer found in the home belonged to Davis.[7]

In short order, the local justice of the peace ordered Davis held in the Union County Jail until he could stand trial. However, before they could complete the transfer, word reached officials that a mob planned to lynch the suspect. To prevent this from happening, that night Davis and his guards hid in some woods near the South Carolina line. Unfortunately, the next day, the vigilantes discovered Davis's hiding place and snatched him from his guards. Then in a show of bravado the men traveled through the community announcing that they would lynch Davis at 10:00 A.M. at the victim's home and hundreds of men, women and children descended upon the site.[8]

At the appointed hour, several masked men brought Davis from his hiding place. As described by local newspapers, "He seemed entirely indifferent to his fate." Then, according to local newspapers, he confessed to the crime and "without reserve said he was willing to be hanged."[9] While Davis may have indeed been guilty of the crime, it seems odd that someone would willingly agree to be hanged. It appears that this was more of a ploy that the mob used to justify its action. Whatever the case, shortly after the men brought Davis from his hiding place they placed a noose around his neck. Then several husky men yanked him off the ground. He hung for forty minutes before the crowd, satisfied that he was quite dead, dispersed.[10] Afterwards officials made no effort to arrest any of the men responsible for the murder. After all, the lynching served a useful purpose since it showed blacks that they would suffer a terrible fate should they in any way cross the line that protected white womanhood.

The crime for which Davis gave his life stemmed from the rape of a white woman. Two days before his death Mrs. E. Godfrey was awakened by the smothered cries of her thirty-one-year-old daughter, who slept in an adjoining room. She woke her houseboy and sent him to summon help.[11] However, when a neighbor arrived the intruder jumped from the bed and ran out the door into the darkness.[12] Yet, all was not lost, for on the floor near the bed lay a stick and a wagon hammer, which the neighbor immediately identified as one belonging to a black man named Edmund Davis.[13]

Charles Campbell   *Iredell County. October 16, 1883*

Monday, October 16, 1883, was a festive day in Statesville, North Carolina. The circus was in town and the streets were throbbing with life. In the spirit of the moment, many people drank too much whiskey. And as a result numerous drunken and boisterous men rode in and followed the circus procession through the streets.[14] However, the revelry would soon end. Around 1:00 P.M. Jacob Redman, a young white man, attacked Charles Campbell, a twenty-two-year-old black man, and knocked him down. Then he grabbed a stick and started to beat Campbell. In the ensuing melee Campbell pulled out a small handgun and fired two shots, mortally wounding Redman.[15]

After the shooting, Campbell attempted to flee but police easily captured him and placed him in the city jail. However, what most citizens did not know was that the violence of the day was not over. After the shooting a handful of angry citizens plotted Campbell's execution. Shortly after midnight the vigilantes tricked the jailer by pretending that they had brought a prisoner to the lock-up. When he "foolishly" opened the door, an armed mob of masked men ran inside. At gunpoint, they snatched Campbell. Instead of cowering in a corner he defiantly told the men, "God will settle with you for this."[16] Then the mob and their quarry disappeared into the darkness.

The next day authorities discovered Campbell's body hanging by the neck from a tree. When the coroner arrived he cut down the body and issued the verdict that Campbell's death resulted from hanging by an unknown mob.[17] The next day blacks in Statesville held a meeting in which they introduced a resolution calling on officers to "ferret out Campbell's lynchers."[18] Despite this resolution, officials placed Campbell's body in a plain wooden box and buried him at the foot of the tree on which he died. They made no further efforts to arrest the men responsible for the lynching.

Lawrence White   *Rowan County. November 15, 1883*

Throughout the records of North Carolina lynching history, there were several cases of black-on-black lynchings. One of the earliest cases of this unique brand of mob violence occurred on November 15, 1883, just outside of Salisbury. The trouble began when two black sharecroppers, Julius Frazier and Lawrence White, got into a fight.[19] When White broke away and attempted to flee, Frazier struck him with a hickory.[20] In the midst of this tussle White pulled out his pocketknife and slashed Frazier's jugular vein.[21]

After the murder, authorities arrested White and his brother and charged them with Frazier's death. They also arrested Frazier's brother for assaulting White.[22] Since it was late in the day, authorities locked all three prisoners in a lumber room at J.F. McLean's store until the next day, when they planned to transfer them to the jail in Salisbury. Moreover, since the offenses for which the men were charged were black-on-black crimes, authorities had little concern that someone would attempt to settle the score. Yet, that is exactly what happened. About thirty minutes before midnight a dozen or so armed black men rushed into the store and overpowered the guard.[23] They seized the prisoners and rode off into the darkness.

The next day they found White's body hanging from the limb of a tree.[24] The other two prisoners were nowhere to be found. Although a posse formed and searched for the missing prisoners, neither the inmates nor any members of the mob were ever found.

Lee Staten   *Union County. March 6, 1885*

Wednesday, March 6, 1885, was a day of great excitement in Monroe. Hundreds of citizens made their way to the outskirts of town to view the body of Lee Staten.[25] One month earlier police had charged Staten, a young black man, with the sexual assault of a nine-year-old white girl.[26] After conducting a cursory investigation, authorities arrested Staten and placed him in the local jail until they could schedule a date for him to see a judge. However, Staten would never keep this appointment. Several days before his trial, the child died, setting the stage for violence.

In the predawn hours of March 4, 1885, N.A. Horne, who served as acting jailer, heard a knock on the door of the detention center. Cautiously opening the door, he saw a body of men holding a man bound with cords.[27] One of the men told the jailer that the prisoner had committed murder. They had brought him to be locked up.[28] However, when the jailer turned to escort the prisoner into jail, the men dropped their ruse. With pistols aimed at the jailer, the mob seized Staten. About one mile away, the men hung the doomed man from a tall pine tree.[29] Although authorities formed a posse and set off after the mob, by the time they reached the site of the attack, Staten was dead and the mob had vanished.[30]

Harriet Finch, Jerry Finch, John Pattisall, Lee Tyson
Chatham County. September 30, 1885

Shortly after midnight on September 29, 1885, a band of masked men stormed the Pittsboro jail and seized four black prisoners, John Pattisall, Lee Tyson, Jerry Finch and Harriet Finch.[31] About one mile away the mob stopped under the branches of a large red oak tree. There they methodically tied four ropes to the limbs of the tree and slipped a noose over each prisoner's neck. "Several of the prisoners frantically declared their innocence and begged for mercy."[32] The mob responded by hanging Lee Tyson and Jerry Finch. All, however, did not go as planned. The limb used to hang Finch was too small and it bent. To solve this problem one of the gang members used a long fence rail to shore up the branch.[33] Then, like marionettes, the men bounced around, kicked and grabbed the ropes around their necks as they slowly strangled to death.[34] After several minutes the men's arms dropped by their sides, their eyes closed. They were dead. Yet, the mob was not ready for its entertainment to end. On a queue, one of the rabble-rousers hoisted John Pattisall into the air, breaking his neck.[35] Then the mob turned its attention to the last victim, thirty-two-year-old Harriet Finch. After binding her feet and hands several men seized the rope around her neck and she shot up into the air. As an encore to the show, for the next few minutes Finch's body jerked and moved like a ragdoll until she could move no more and her body stilled with death.[36] Then the mob dispersed, leaving their strange fruit hanging from the tree.

With daybreak, news of the hangings spread like wildfire and a mass of humanity descended upon the site to see the mob's handiwork.[37] After several hours of this circus-like atmosphere, authorities cut the bodies down. Then they declared, as in thousands of lynchings involving blacks, that the deceased had come to their deaths at the hands of persons unknown.[38]

Yet, just what were the facts surrounding the crimes with which the victims were charged? Almost two years earlier Thomas Gunter, a forty-seven-year-old white farmer, had discovered the bodies of his mother, eighty-nine-year-old Olive Gunter, and his sister, sixty-four-year-old Jane Gunter, in their home. Their heads had been bashed with an axe.[39] In addition, Gunter found his eight-year-old daughter, who had been spending the night with her grandmother, suffering multiple wounds to her head, barely clinging to life.[40]

Although authorities hoped that the child could identify the killers, they were sorely disappointed when she awakened, for she had no memory of the attack.[41] Without viable suspects when the jury of inquest met in March 1884, it declared, "Mrs. Olive Gunter and Miss Jane Gunter came to their deaths by blows from an axe, but part of the jury find that there is not sufficient evidence to designate any person or persons as the guilty part; the other part of the jury think that the circumstances point to Baxter (Thomas) Gunter as the murderer and warrant his arrest."[42] However, after the jury rendered its verdict the judge ruled that there was insufficient evidence to arrest Gunter.[43]

Almost eighteen months later a second axe massacre rocked Chatham

County. On July 5, 1885, Mary Neal, a black domestic who worked for Edward Finch, an elderly white farmer, and his sister Sally Finch, arrived at work and started her daily routine of milking the cows. As she worked she called for Ephraim Ellington, the Finch's live-in servant. However, when she got no answer she walked toward the home and called her employer.[44] When no one answered this time, she looked through a window and noticed something unusual: Miss Sally's door was ajar. Alarmed, Neal ran to the home of Finch's son Henry White and advised him that something was wrong.[45]

White, accompanied by Neal and his son Tommy, set out immediately for the home. Tommy ran ahead and entered the house. Within minutes, he ran outside and exclaimed, "They are all dead."[46] Perhaps stunned, or having some prior knowledge of what was inside, White refused to enter the home. Instead, he went to a neighbor's home and called James Poe and Nathan Gilmore.[47] When these two men entered the house, they discovered Edward Finch's body with a stab wound to the throat and an axe wound to his head. Someone had similarly butchered Miss Sally. On the floor lay the corpse of Ephraim Ellington with its head nearly severed from the body.[48] Scattered on the floor around the bodies were legal documents, clothes and the drawers of a dresser the killers had ransacked in their attempt to find money.

Upon arriving on the scene, authorities launched an investigation. On the outside of the home the sheriff discovered two sets of footprints believed to be those of the killers. Then, the sheriff crossed a ploughed field and came to a fence. Here he found perhaps the biggest clue, threads from some trousers caught on the rail fence.[49] On the other side of the fence authorities found a set of mule tracks that led to the cabin of Jerry Finch, a black sharecropper who leased from Edward Finch, and his wife Harriet.[50]

Upon searching the home, authorities found a pair of pants hanging on a fence with both legs wet, hanging out to dry. More importantly the threads found earlier appeared to match the fabric of the trousers.[51] They seized the pants and sent them to Raleigh for testing to determine if they had any signs of blood. Then authorities arrested Jerry Finch and Lee Tyson, who was visiting the Finches' home.

Upon questioning, both men denied any involvement in the murders. According to Jerry Finch, on the day before the murders, the Fourth of July, he and Tyson had gone to nearby Pittsboro to celebrate. About thirty minutes before midnight, they headed home when a thunderstorm forced them to seek shelter in a building housing a cotton gin.[52] For this reason, Finch claimed that he did not arrive home until shortly before dawn. However, the men's alibi mattered little since authorities had strong circumstantial evidence, pants that matched threads found in the fence, shoe prints around the cabin that matched those found outside the murder scene, and most importantly knowledge by the suspects that Edward Finch kept a large sum of money in his home.[53]

The findings by the Sheriff's Department created a near state of hysteria in Chatham County and wild rumors began to circulate. One of the more fantastic tales centered around a plot by blacks to storm the Pittsboro jail and free Jerry Finch and Lee Tyson. For instance, three days after the Finch murders, Jerry Faucett, a young black man, claimed that he had found a note that outlined detailed plans of blacks to storm the jail.[54] While such a plot seems ludicrous today, in 1885 it seemed plausible to whites. In response, the sheriff added extra guards around the jail. Then he arrested four black men mentioned in the note, forty-five-year-old William Bryan, sixty-six-year-old Pete Harris, forty-four-year-old William Harris, forty-year-old Erasmus Cotton, and thirty-eight-year-old Ephraim Neal.[55] Even Governor Scales was caught in the frenzy. After being told of the planned uprising he ordered a company of militia to stand ready for possible deployment to Pittsboro to restore order should the need arise.[56] Yet, all of these preparations were for naught as an investigation revealed that the note was a fraud, written by the man who supposedly found it to get back at the men for a "wrong they formerly did him."[57]*

Several months after this storm subsided the Chatham County coroner's jury returned a verdict in the Finch murders. All had come to their deaths due to blows inflicted by Jerry Finch, Harriet Finch and Lee Tyson.[59] Court dates for the suspects along with John Pattisall, a twenty-year-old who was charged with the Gunter murders, was scheduled for the next term of superior court.[60] However, the suspects would never make it to court, as the mob would take its deadly action less than a month later.

Despite this fact there remained considerable doubt about the guilt of the lynching victims. For one, although officials confiscated Finch's pants, experts in Raleigh maintained that the trousers, "had been thoroughly washed in boiling water and it could not be definitely stated that the stains (found on the pants) were made by human blood."[61] Second, although authorities claimed that the shoe prints found at the crime scene matched tracks outside of Finch's cabin, they failed to conduct any analysis on the shoes found in the Finches' cabin. Despite these questions, most white people in Chatham County were satisfied with the outcome, and they made no effort to investigate the lynchings.

Bud Mebane   *Alamance County. October 1, 1885*

On October 3 1885, a posse captured Bud Mebane, a young black man wanted for the rape and murder of Mrs. W. H. Walker.[62] After threatening to

---

*Several weeks after this panic a mob of masked men seized Mary Neil and Harriet Finch. They hung each woman by the neck with ropes. However, despite this frightening episode each woman maintained that they knew nothing about the Finch murders (Source: Patrick Huber, "Caught Up in the Violent Whirlwind of Lynching: The 1885 Quadruple Lynching in Chatham County, North Carolina," North Carolina Historical Review, vol. LXXV, no. 7, April 1998, p. 154)

lynch the suspect, the posse was convinced by authorities to take Mebane before the local magistrate so that he could be charged with the crime. However, news of the hearing attracted a large mob and there was fear someone would attempt to kill Mebane. As a result, after the arraignment the magistrate ordered officers to transport the suspect to Yanceyville.[63] Unfortunately, the sheriff failed to secure a sufficient guard for the trip, and he foolishly placed Mebane in a buggy with only two guards.

About two miles outside of town a mob of more than 150 men overwhelmed the officers guarding Mebane.[64] Then as they tortured the prisoner, he confessed to the crime. He also claimed that others were also involved in the murder. However, the mob would have none of it. Instead they placed a noose around his neck and tied the other end of the rope to the limb of an oak tree.[65] Then someone slapped the back of the horse pulling the wagon in which he stood, and Mebane shot into the sky.[66] As he swung, the mob fired more than one hundred shots into his body. Despite the brutality of the murder, authorities refused to investigate and the lynching joined hundreds of other unsolved cases across the South.

John Lee   *Union County. December 18, 1885*

Shortly after 9:00 P.M. on the evening of December 18, 1885, a mob numbering several hundred burst into the Richmond County Jail.[67] They demanded and obtained the keys from the jailer that opened the door leading to the cellblock. However, to open the cells they needed the keys that were in possession of Deputy Sheriff Patterson, who lived nearby in the Long Hotel. Several men went to get the key, but the deputy refused to open his door.[68]

Returning to the jail, the mob secured two axes and a sledgehammer. After a half-hour of hammering, they broke the lock and surged into the cell of a young black man named John Lee. Once inside several men battered him with gun butts and sticks. Then they seized him.[69] Two miles away they hung Lee beside the road,[70] and pinned a note on his body: "Merry Christmas and happy New Year. To this limb hangs the body of John Lee. Until the packing of juries ceases this process of justice will be sought."[71]

The next day authorities followed the usual course, held a coroner's inquest and announced that Lee had come to his death at the hands of parties unknown.[72] Then they closed the investigation, dug a grave and threw Lee's corpse into the ground.[73] The local newspaper, perhaps to justify the actions taken by the mob, printed an article that detailed Lee's criminal and violent past—claiming that he had previously cut the throat of his wife and had murdered a woman whose land he wanted to buy.

Yet, from evidence presented in newspaper accounts, it seems improbable that authorities could not identify the men responsible for Lee's murder.

For one, when the mob entered the jail many of the vigilantes spent more than an hour in the presence of the jailer. Yet the jailer, who lived in the community, claimed he could not identify any faces or voices.[74] Second, it also stands to reason that when the mob entered the Long Hotel, the owner or someone employed by the hotel met the mob at the door and granted them access to Deputy Patterson's room. However, the sheriff made no effort to interview these individuals.[75]

It also seems likely that local law officers were involved in the murder. For example, after mob members notified Deputy Patterson of their presence by knocking on his room door, he failed to sound the alarm. Moreover, considering that the mob spent an additional thirty minutes breaking into Lee's cell, Patterson had ample opportunity to gather a posse and perhaps prevent the lynching. Yet, he did nothing.

Perhaps for this reason, several days after the lynching Judge James McRae called into question the actions of the jailer and members of the Sheriff's Department:

We have heard it suggested that the lynching would not have taken place but for fear that Lee would have escaped before court, only last week two prisoners having made their escape by reason of negligence of mismanagement of the jailer who unfortunately is too fond of liquor for the good of himself or the public.[76]

Despite the judge's criticism, after a few days of excitement, life in Rockingham returned to normal as many whites in the town obviously believed that Lee got what he deserved. Three weeks earlier Lee had been accused of murdering Solomon Welch, a white man about twenty-five years old.[77]*

Eugene Hairston *Guilford County. August 25, 1887*

On August 25, 1887, Eugene Hairston, a twenty-year-old black man, was arrested by Kernersville police. He was accused of attempting to rape Mahala Sapp, a seventeen-year-old white woman.[79]† Kernersville police conducted a thorough investigation of the matter and determined that Hairston's guilt was

---

*According to published reports, Lee and Welch stopped by the house of Mourning Harrington for supper. In the course of the evening Harrington's wife discovered that Welch had a pocket full of money and that Lee had a gun. Just how she discovered these facts is unknown; however, after the men left, the woman claimed that she heard a gunshot. This caused suspicion to fall upon Lee. "Found Dead on the Road," Rockingham Rocket, 26 November 1885.

†Mahala C. Sapp, the daughter of a local farmer, claimed that a young black man attacked her as she walked home. In a report given to authorities, Sapp said that as she walked home she saw a black man walking several yards behind her. When they passed through an isolated area the man grabbed her and started to choke the teen. Then he pulled out a small revolver: "If you don't hush I'll shoot you." However, when she persisted the man released her and made his escape (Source: "The Testimony of Miss Mahala C. Sapp-The Dead Man-The Coroner's Jury-Adjourned to September 3rd," Greensboro Morning News, 26 August 1887).

unquestionable. Mahala Sapp swore positively to his being the right person. Not to mention the fact that two farmers also saw Hairston walking near Sapp only minutes before the attack.[81]

However, there were questions about his guilt. On the day after the assault, the magistrate who witnessed Sapp's testimony claimed that she had not positively identified the suspect as her attacker.[82] In addition, authorities made no effort to check Hairston's alibi or search for the gun he allegedly used in the attack. Whatever the case, after Hairston's arrest, authorities soon learned of a plot to lynch the suspect. To prevent such an attack officers transferred Hairston to nearby Greensboro.[83] Yet, such precaution mattered little as less than twelve hours later a mob of masked men entered the city jail and demanded Hairston.[84] When the jailer refused to open Hairston's cell, the men used sledgehammers and some crowbars to batter down the door.[85] As has been often stated, one can only imagine the sheer terror the victim must have felt as the men made their way into his cell. Then they took him to the outskirts of town and swung him from a tree by the neck.[86]

At daybreak, officials summoned a coroner's jury. After conducting a superficial exam, they lowered the body to the ground. They were about to render a verdict and close the case when outraged blacks who attended the hearing expressed the belief that the perpetrators could be discovered if the proper effort were made on the part of the coroner.[87] Perhaps in an effort to placate these blacks, the coroner agreed to adjourn the case to await developments. However, no further developments took place. One week later the coroner officially closed the case, ending efforts to apprehend Hairston's killers.

Jack Blount, Matthew Blount, Patterson Spruill *Washington County. January 26, 1888*

On January 28, 1888, an armed mob of men on horseback rode into Plymouth, North Carolina. At gunpoint, they took from the jailer three black men, Patterson Spruill, John Blount and Blount's brother Matthew, a noted one-armed preacher.[88] Tied together, they dragged the prisoners to some woods a mile from town. There they tied the men to trees. Although they begged for mercy, the mob refused to hear their cries. Instead, the ringleader of the mob told the men that they had a few minutes to pray.[89] Then the mob opened fire with all sorts of weapons—muskets, rifles, shotguns and pistols. They did not cease firing until all the men were dead and their bodies riddled with gunshot.[90]

According to local newspapers, the causes of this brutal act stemmed from the murder of a traveling salesman named John Dawson. As Dawson passed through the small town of Creswell on January 23, 1888, someone hit him on the head, robbed him and threw his lifeless corpse into a shallow grave.[91] Several days later, officials discovered the body when a pedestrian noticed Dawson's knees sticking above the ground.[92] In short order the sheriff arrested four black men, one of whom confessed. While much of the evidence against the men was flimsy, local papers printed the usual commentary by maintaining the evidence against the suspects was conclusive.[93] However, undoubtedly many in the city did not share this sentiment, as in the days following the lynchings acts of arson destroyed a hotel and Plymouth's Episcopal Church.

William Parker   *Beaufort County. March 14, 1888*

On the afternoon of August 14, 1880, someone ambushed and killed General Brian Grimes as he returned from a political rally in the small hamlet of Washington, North Carolina.[94] After the shooting Bryan Satterthwaite, Grimes's twelve-year-old traveling companion, drove the badly wounded man to the nearest house, but Grimes never regained consciousness and died shortly afterward. While the exact cause of the murder is unknown, several days after the shooting local newspapers published a series of articles that maintained the general had been killed to prevent him from testifying in an arson case.[95] As a result authorities interviewed several of the men named in the arson case. This led to the arrest of William Parker, a thirty-one-year-old white man.[96] However, upon examination by a jury the case was dismissed for lack of evidence.

Over the next seven years, the case lay dormant until November 1888 when Parker returned to Washington. "When he got drunk and boasted that he had killed General Grimes he was immediately picked up on a charge of drunkenness and placed in the Washington jail."[97] Several hours later street lamps near the jail suddenly went out, and from the darkness a dozen men emerged. Opening an empty jail cell, they forced the jailer inside and closed the door.[98] Then they broke the lock on Parker's cell and took him to a nearby drawbridge.[99] An hour later, the bridge keeper, who had come to open the span for a steamer, discovered Parker's body. The sheriff was informed and a coroner's jury summoned. The verdict: "William A. Parker had come to his death at the hands of persons unknown to the jury."[100]

Thomas Frazier   *Beaufort County. May 1888*

The evening of Saturday, May 6, 1888, started like most in the rural hamlet of Blount's Creek. After buying supplies in Little Washington, most people stopped by Joshua Cox's store for the latest gossip or a cold soda before heading home. However, on this evening things would be different. About 5:00 P.M., Thomas Frazier, a white mill worker, went to Cox's store and attempted to purchase some wine.[101] When Cox refused to sell him the wine, Frazier grabbed a double barrel shotgun and shot the storeowner.[102]

After the shooting Frazier escaped by running into some nearby woods. However, in a strange coincidence, several hours later Cox's brother captured Frazier when he emerged from the woods.[103] To secure the suspect until authorities arrived the next day, Cox placed Frazier in his brother's store. He also placed an armed guard outside of the building. Yet, Frazier would never keep his date with authorities. Around 3:00 A.M., two dozen masked men overpowered the guard. They took Frazier outside and fired more than a hundred shotgun blasts and bullets into his body. Then the men withdrew.[104]

The next day authorities held an inquest and rendered the verdict that Frazier had come to his death by gunshot wounds at the hands of persons unknown. Many local officials, however, maintained that such violence placed a stain on the people of Beaufort County. In line with this concern, several days after the lynching the editor of the *Washington Progressive* commented, "The people of Beaufort County are aroused and are determined that crime shall be punished."[105] Unfortunately, such a vow did not extend to those who murdered Frazier and authorities, with few protests, closed the case.

John Humphreys   *Buncombe County. July 14, 1888*

On the afternoon of July 14, 1888, a rumor spread across Asheville that a black man had assaulted thirteen-year-old Sally Parker.[106] The news was enough to stir authorities to action and they searched all corners of the city and surrounding countryside. Around 9:00 P.M. they arrested John Humphreys and charged him with the crime.

However, according to the girl, her attacker had on a striped shirt and was barefooted. When arrested, Humphreys had on a white shirt and shoes.[107] Yet, this discrepancy did not deter the police. Several officers maintained that Humphreys had changed clothes after the attack. At gunpoint the officers made Humphreys put on a striped shirt and take off his shoes.[108] Then he was taken before the victim who immediately identified Humphreys as her attacker.

With his identify confirmed, authorities placed Humphreys inside a steel cage in the county jail to prevent lynching. This precaution, however, did not dissuade men who were determined to administer their own brand of justice. Around 3:00 A.M. several dozen men marched into the jail. However, before they reached the cellblock the jailer "supposedly" grabbed his gun and fired on the mob. Most likely this was a ploy to cover his possible involvement in the crime, since he failed to hit anyone despite the fact that the men were less than ten feet away. Whatever the case, after firing a few rounds the deputy surrendered and the mob, using sledgehammer and crowbars, leisurely tore Humphrey's cage apart.[109] Once they ripped the door off of the cage, they battered Humphrey. Then they dragged their bloodied victim to an oak tree, placed a rope around his neck and hoisted him into the air.[110] In the meantime authorities hastily formed a posse. However, by the time they found the prisoner he was dead, and the mob dispersed.

Dave Boone, Frank Stack   *Burke County. September 11, 1888*

Late in the evening of September 11, 1888, an armed mob of more than two hundred men rode into Morganton and demanded the keys to the town's jail. When the jailer refused to comply, the men produced a pair of sledgehammers and broke the locks to cells that contained Frank Stack, a young white man, and Dave Boone, an African American.[111] That the mob seized these two men was no surprise to many in the town. Almost two weeks earlier Boone was charged with murdering Eli Holder, a white man, at a camp meeting.[112] A week later Stack was charged with the murder of Robert Parker, who had killed Stack's brother sometime earlier.[113] At any rate, after breaking into the jail the vigilantes tied the doomed men together and carried them to a nearby railroad bridge. Then they wrapped a plow-line around a crosstie and strung different ends of the rope around Stack and Boone's necks.[114]

With the rope in place the leader of the mob asked the condemned men if they had anything to say. Boone prayed and asserted his innocence. However, Stack asked the leader of the mob to write his family and tell them that he was not guilty of a crime.[115] After Stack finished his plea, the mob threw both men off of the bridge, breaking the men's necks.[116] The next day authorities announced that the men came to their death at the hands of unknown parties.[117] Two days later, a local newspaper reported that Burke County officials had issued warrants and that they expected to arrest the men responsible for the lynchings. However, no arrests were ever made and the murders were quickly forgotten.

John Carson   *Cleveland County. December 2, 1888*

The brutal murder of James Philbeck stunned the small town of Shelby.[118] Needless to say, authorities went right to work on the case. They were unable to generate any leads until one of the officers followed a hunch and questioned some of Philbeck's black field hands. According to one of the workers, several weeks earlier two field hands, John Carson and his brother Lee, had asked other cotton pickers how much money the farmer kept in his house.[119] With this lead the brothers became the primary suspects in the murder.

After a day-long search, the sheriff found the Carson brothers and arrested them. What happened next is somewhat unclear; however, according to local newspapers one of the suspects, John Carson, confessed to the crime.[120] According to this confession, on the night of the murder Carson walked down some railroad tracks to Philbeck's home. Once there, for some unknown reason, he grabbed an axe from a woodpile and slung it through his suspenders. Then he knocked on Philbeck's door. When Philbeck answered, Carson shot the farmer in the face.[121] Then he charged into the home, shot the farmer's wife and took $13.00. After the shooting Carson claimed that he stopped at several of his friends' homes to secure an alibi.[122]

While such a confession makes for interesting reading, it seems strange that Carson would make such an acknowledgement of guilt considering that authorities had no evidence to link him to the crime. Moreover, even Philbeck's wife was unable to identify him.[123] This leads to several questions: Why would Carson go through the effort of establishing an alibi and then confess so easily? Additionally, why would Carson confess to a crime that he knew would lead to his execution? Whatever the case, after the alleged confession, authorities placed Carson in the Cleveland County Jail. However, since tensions were high and many threats made, authorities stationed extra guards around the jail.

When no attempt emerged that evening the sheriff, "foolishly" or possibly in collaboration with local vigilantes, dismissed the extra guards.[124] Several hours later more than two hundred masked men stormed the jail. Then, according to published reports, a "burley negro" pried open the door to Carson's cell.[125] After that, members of the mob took the doomed man about a mile from town and hung him from a small oak tree. No attempt was made by officials to find his killers.

Robert Berrier   *Davidson County. October 15, 1889*

On October 14, 1889, a mob, consisting of men and women, marched into the Lexington jail and demanded twenty-four-year-old Robert Berrier.[126] When the jailer refused their demand, one of the men produced an axe and forced the lock open. Then the mob took Berrier down Main Street to a small grove of trees. There the lynching deviated into a cross between a carnival and a religious camp meeting. While people walked freely and spoke with members of the mob, a Philadelphia man appeared and prayed for Berrier. Then the man sang two songs while members of the mob acknowledged their pleasure with "hearty amens" and such responses as "Lord grant it." [127] After more than an hour and a half, the revival suddenly turned deadly. One of the members of the mob placed the end of a rope around Berrier's neck. Then they threw the other end of the rope across a limb and hoisted the "miserable wretch" from the ground.[128]

The following morning the show continued as hundreds drove out to see the scene of the lynching and view Berrier's body. Moreover, to ensure that all had opportunity to see the mob's handiwork, officials left the corpse hanging until noon when the coroner cut it down. Nonetheless, the question remains why the mob refused to let Berrier have his day in court. The answer to this question lay in the long-running feud between Berrier and his wife. Almost two years earlier Berrier married Elisa Walser. However, the marriage was not a happy one, and after little more than a year Elisa left her husband and returned to her father's home.[129] A short time afterward Elisa filed court papers to recover furniture that her father had given her. When officers arrived to execute the judgment, Berrier fired on the officers.[130] Then he fled to Kansas.[131]

Several months later Berrier learned that his wife had given birth to a baby. He returned to North Carolina and made plans to take the child. After several weeks of secretly watching his wife's family, an opportunity presented itself when his father-in-law headed out of town. In a flash Berrier headed for the Walsers' home and smashed a hole in the door. [132] Then he stuck his pistol through the opening and shot his mother-in-law. After that he rushed inside and seized his baby.[133]

As news of the shooting spread, a posse formed and set out after Berrier. Several days later they found him in a barn in Forsyth County and brought him back to Lexington for a hearing. However, when word reached citizens that a North Carolina law prevented Berrier's wife from testifying against him in court, the people took the law into their hands. The lynching of Berrier, who was white, caused outrage across the state and Gov. Daniel Fowle decided to intervene. In a letter sent to the district solicitor, he commanded that local officials "launch prompt and vigorous action."[134] In part due to this pressure, Davidson County officials arrested twenty-eight suspects. However, the state never prosecuted anyone and the case joined hundreds of other unsolved lynching cases.

John Starling   *Johnston County. May 25, 1890*

Selma, North Carolina, was the scene of a horrible tragedy. At 2:00 A.M. on Sunday, May 25, 1890, a gang of men wearing all kinds of costumes burst into the home of John Starling, a forty-year-old white farmer. They forced him out of his bed and carried him into the yard. There they tied him to a tree and unleashed a deadly barrage. Then the men dispersed.[135]

Another account of the lynching printed in the *Smithfield Herald* newspaper painted a vastly different picture. According to this version, on May 24, 1890, a mob of armed men seized Starling from deputies as they made their way to Smithfield. After placing a rope around his neck the mob dragged the doomed man from a wagon. One hundred yards away they threw a rope across the limb of a tree and hoisted Starling into the air. Then they riddled his body with gunshot. When they were sure he was dead, they cut his body down and dispersed.[136] While the facts surrounding the murder are somewhat unclear, the events after his death are not. In short order, officials closed the case and pretended as if Starling's death never happened.

The events that led to this horrible incident stemmed from the murder of Starling's elderly mother-in-law Mrs. Senie Brown and her nine-year-old grandson. Three months before the lynching, officials had charged Starling with the murder of his mother-in-law and his nephew to ensure that his wife inherited two hundred acres of land owned by Brown. Although officials placed him on trial for the crimes, a jury acquitted him.[137] In spite of this verdict many in the community remained unconvinced of Starling's innocence and they plotted the crime that would lead to his death.

Kinch Freeman   *Hertford County. December 24, 1890*

At 2:00 A.M. on Christmas Eve, 1890, a knock at the door awakened the jailer in the small town of Winton. When he asked what the visitor needed, a voice replied that they had a prisoner for him. However, as he opened the door a gang of masked men burst inside and took his keys. Then several men opened the cell that contained Kinch Freeman, a young black man charged with murder. They placed one end of a rope around the suspect's neck and another end of the rope to the top of Freeman's cell. Then in short order they hoisted him off the ground.[138] So quickly had the mob acted that it failed to unfasten the chains that locked Freeman to the cell floor. As a result, Freeman died a horrible death. With his feet less than three inches from the ground, he jerked and bounced around for more than ten minutes, slowly strangling while members of the mob watched their handiwork with glee.[139] When they were sure that Freeman was dead, the mob filed out of the jail and dispersed.

After the murder, the coroner rushed to the jail, examined the body and conducted an inquest. At daybreak, he took the body down and declared that Freeman came to his death at the hands of unknown parties. It seems improbable that authorities could not identify any of the members of the mob. For one, although the vigilantes wore masks, they nonetheless stayed in the jail more than thirty minutes; this was time in which the jailer had opportunity to observe the men and determine their identities. Second, the mob's long stay and apparent familiarity with the jail suggests that the jailer or other law enforcement officials were possibly involved in the murder. In spite of these questions, the case was quickly closed as most people felt that Freeman was responsible for the crime with which he was charged — namely, the murder of an elderly white couple two months earlier.

Hezekiah Rankin   *Buncombe County. September 24, 1891*

The trouble started in the rail yard. On the evening of September 24, 1891, twenty-three-year-old Fred Tyler, who worked for the Western North Carolina Railroad, pulled an engine into the rail yard. Then he ordered a black railroad worker to uncouple the engine from some freight cars. However, the man, identified as twenty-eight-year-old Hezekiah Rankin, refused: "If you want it done, do it yourself."[140] Annoyed, Tyler threw a piece of coal and struck Rankin on the head.[141]

In a huff, Rankin left the rail yard, walked home and grabbed his pistol. Then he returned to the yard and shot Tyler.[142] Railroad officials summoned the police but when they arrived, they could find no sign of Rankin. However, just a few feet from the officers, hidden inside the roundhouse, the party was just getting started. After the shooting, friends of Tyler chased and captured Rankin. Then they slipped him inside the roundhouse and placed a rope around his neck.[143] Once the police departed, the men dragged Rankin to the banks of the nearby French Broad River. Then as the terrified man begged for his life, they hung Rankin from the limb of a white oak tree.[144]

The next day police found Rankin's body, "his eyes half open with a wild terrified stare with his tongue doubled up by the pressure from the lip almost touching the roof of the mouth, which was wide open."[145] News of the outrage spread rapidly and a large crowd of onlookers descended upon the site.[146] After several hours of this macabre spectacle, the coroner cut the body down. Then he held an inquest to look into the murder. The hearing opened with the testimony of several African American railroad workers, who despite obvious risks bravely identified four railroad workers— W.H. Mayo, Lum Bolich, Erwin Allison and Tom McCoy — as the men responsible for Rankin's death.[147] After these witnesses, authorities called several white railroad workers, but each claimed that they could not remember the names of the men involved in the crime.[148] Nonetheless, two hours later, the jury indicted the four railroad workers as accessories in Rankin's murder.[149] Accordingly, authorities arrested the men and scheduled a trial for the next session of criminal court. However, when the trial opened, officials dismissed the case when it was determined that the Jury of Inquest had been unable to gather sufficient evidence to return a true bill against the men.[150]

Lyman Purdie *Bladen County. May 1, 1892*

On Thursday, April 28, 1892, tension filled the small town of Elizabethtown. Earlier in the day, a farmer found the body of Edward Cain, a young white man, with his throat cut.[151] Authorities were called to the scene and an investigation was launched. Scouring the area, the sheriff discovered a bloody trail that led from the crime scene to the home of Lyman Purdie, a young black man. Inside authorities discovered a wealth of circumstantial evidence: a bloody coat, shoes caked with blood, and most damning, an axe covered with blood.[152] As a result, they arrested Purdie and placed him in the Bladen County jail.

Less than a week later, a mob of more than a hundred men stormed the jail. With sticks and gun butts, they battered Purdie. Then one of the men grabbed a rope, tied it around the doomed man's neck and dragged him out of the jail to the public ferry two hundred yards away.[153] At the ferry, one of the men climbed a pine tree and slung the rope over a low-lying limb. Then several men pulled Purdie toward the sky. To ensure his demise the mob quietly observed his every move until, like a candle, death extinguished the last flicker of life. After that, the men dispersed, leaving Purdie's body as a warning to others.

The next day the coroner declared that Lyman Purdie had come to his death at the hands of a mob to the jury unknown.[154] Later, to justify the action of the mob the *Wilmington Star* printed an article that maintained, "the evidence against Purdie was conclusive."[155]

William Burnett   *Granville County. November 15, 1892*

The night of November 17, 1892, started out like most in the small town of Oxford, North Carolina. Stores closed and the streets quickly emptied at sundown. However, on this night things would be different. About 1:00 A.M., David A. Moore, who served as the town's jailer, was awakened by a knock on the door of his home.[156] When he answered, a gang of masked men surrounded him and took his keys.[157] Then they marched over to the jail and seized William Burnett, a young black man. The next day Burnett's battered body was found hanging from a pine tree just off the town's main street.[158]

News of the hanging quickly spread and hundreds of citizens went to see the awful sight. After several hours of this spectacle, authorities cut the body down and took it to the poor house for burial.[159] Then they announced that "William Burnett had come to his death at the hand of a mob unknown to the jury."[160] No attempt was made to arrest any of the men responsible for his death, as the jailer, the only person who saw the mob, was unable to recognize any of the men.[161]

Why had the mob come after Burnett? Several months earlier, Reuben Overton, a white farmer, caught Burnett as he attempted to get into bed with his daughter.[162] While it is unclear if Burnett had any previous relationship with the Overtons, newspaper articles seem to suggest that the girl and Burnett had a consensual relationship.[163]

Duncan McPhatter   *November 17, 1892*

On the night of November 17, 1892, a mob boarded a Central Carolina Railroad train as it passed through the town of Laurel Hill. With military precision, they searched every car until they found their quarry, Duncan McPhatter. Then, without any resistance from him, they took McPhatter from his guards and tied a rope around his neck. Although he begged for his life, the mob would have none of it. They dragged him from the train and down the railroad tracks to a large tree. There they battered the poor man and for their own benefit forced him to confess to the crime of murder. Then without further ado, several men hoisted him by the neck from a tree.[164]

The cause of this horrific act of violence stemmed from a fight at a political rally. One week earlier, Democrats in Spring Hill, North Carolina, refused to let blacks cast votes. When several black men attempted to challenge this policy, Richmond County officials issued an arrest warrant for the man they identified as the leader of the protest, Duncan McPhatter.[165] However, from this point things did not go as planned. The next day when deputies located McPhatter, he was with his brother Arch, who had similar facial features. Undoubtedly confused, the deputies mistakenly attempted to arrest Arch McPhatter. In the ensuing melee, Arch McPhatter struck one of the deputies. Then he fired a shot that killed the other deputy.[166]

Later that evening, in the belief that Duncan McPhatter fired the blast, authorities issued an arrest warrant charging him with murder. Then the sheriff and a posse set out to arrest the fugitive. After several hours of searching, they found Arch McPhatter in a house near Laurinburg.[167] However, before they could arrest the man he opened fire. Then, despite several bullet wounds, McPhatter escaped.[168] Four days later, the posse captured Duncan McPhatter when he emerged from some woods. They placed him on a train, headed for the Richmond County Jail, and a date with infamy.

The search for Arch McPhatter continued. Two weeks after his brother's death, authorities found and arrested the fugitive in nearby Robeson County. At this point authorities got their biggest surprise: during an interrogation McPhatter told authorities that he fired the shots that killed the deputy.[169] Such an admission, if true, meant that Duncan McPhatter was innocent of any crime. This also meant that the mob had violated one of the central tenets of vigilante justice, namely, justification for their action. Yet, considering the virulent racism of the period, Richmond County officials had little desire to investigate the death of a black man, especially one involved in political activity. Instead, the sheriff transferred Arch McPhatter to Wilmington for safekeeping and made plans to try him for Deputy Livingston's death. However, before he could complete the preparations, McPhatter died from the wounds he received earlier, ending this tragic episode.[170]

Daniel Slaughter   *Alleghany County. February 22, 1894*

On February 6, 1894, a large crowd gathered in rural Alleghany County to attend a wedding reception. All went well until Daniel Slaughter started an argument with an old man.[171] As the argument heated, the hosts forced Slaughter to leave. After a few minutes he stormed back into the house and renewed the argument with the man. This time several partygoers attempted to defuse the situation by separating the men. However, this angered Slaughter and he stabbed one of the men, John Bare, in the heart.[172] Then as he made his way to the door, he stabbed another man Edward Long in the chest and fled.[173]

Less than two miles away authorities captured Slaughter, and there was a great deal of fear that he would be lynched. As a result, authorities hastily rushed their prisoner to the Alleghany County Jail in nearby Sparta.[174] Nonetheless, two weeks later the worst fears of authorities would be realized when a dozen men charged into the jail. Few of the vigilantes expected the reception that they received, for as soon as the jailer saw the members of the mob, he grabbed his gun and opened fire. In the ensuing gunfight he wounded several of the men.[175] But this did not stop the remaining men, who despite a hail of bullets charged into the cell and seized Slaughter. Then they departed into the night. One mile away they hung Slaughter from the branch of a chestnut tree.

In this instance this was not the end of the story. One of the vigilantes was so badly wounded that the other members of the mob left him beside the road to die.[176] Less than an hour later authorities discovered the man, identified as Alexander Reese, and brought him back to the jail in Sparta where he slowly recovered. More importantly, Reese announced his willingness to identify and testify against the other men that participated in Slaughter's murder.[177] However, Reese's incarceration did not go unnoticed. Several days after his arrest, rumors spread that friends of Slaughter as well as Reese's former confederates planned to lynch him to keep him from testifying. For that reason, they transported Reese to Winston for safekeeping.[178] His arrest was anticlimactic as a jury failed to convict Reese or any of the men he identified.

James Bergeron *Craven County. December 26, 1894*

On Christmas Eve, 1894, James Bergeron, angered that a neighbor, Ben Thompson, had cheated him, sought to settle score. With a gun in his hand, Bergeron charged into Thompson's house and attempted to kill his neighbor. But his gun misfired. Fortunately for Thompson, the sound of the gunfire alerted neighbors who rushed to the scene and restrained Bergeron until police arrived.[179]

This did not end the flare-up. Following his arrest, Bergeron convinced authorities to accompany him home so he could get his wife to sign his bond.[180] However, before they headed for his home, the justice of the peace foolishly returned Bergeron's shotgun and pistol.[181] Several miles away Bergeron fired a load of buckshot into the officer.[182] Then he calmly walked home.

The next day a posse captured Bergeron and locked him up in a store nearby until he could be transported to New Bern the next day.[183] However,

Bergeron's stay would be much shorter than expected. Several hours after he was placed in the store, a dozen masked men disarmed the men guarding Bergeron.[184] Then with the prisoners and guards in tow, the mob marched to a tall tree. While several men readied a rope, others held the desperado up so they could place a noose around his neck.[185] Just before they were ready to execute Bergeron, he screamed, "I killed Watson but you ought not to kill me. I did not know what I was doing," referring to the fact that he had been drinking heavily the day before he killed Watson.[186] However, none of the vigilantes were inclined to hear Bergeron's plea. They answered by placing a noose around his neck and hoisting his body into the air.[187] Then as he thrashed about, several men unloaded their guns.

Arriving at the scene the next day, the coroner rendered a verdict: Bergeron had come to his death at the hands of parties unknown.[188] Authorities undertook no further efforts to identify or arrest any of the men responsible for the crime. Undoubtedly, many people felt that Bergeron had gotten what he deserved. An article printed in the *New Bern Daily Journal* best sums up this feeling: "While it is to be regretted that the murderer met his fate in the manner he did instead at the hands of the law, there is no expression of opinion that he got any more than rightly belonged to him."[189]

Lewis Patrick   *Carteret County. June 14, 1899*

On June 9, 1899, residents of the small fishing village of Bogue found one of their most prominent citizens, merchant E.B. Weeks, strangled to death inside of his store. After searching the crime scene, authorities found the footprints of a single intruder and concluded that a young black man named Lewis Patrick was responsible for the crime.[190] Just how authorities came to this conclusion is unknown; however, the next day police arrested Patrick and charged him with the crime when one of the members of the posse identified a piece of pork Patrick had in his possession as coming from Weeks's store.[191]

Later that day officials took Patrick to Beaufort and placed him in the Carteret County Jail. However, many citizens in the town deeply resented his presence. Four nights later, this resentment boiled into action. Around 11:00 P.M. a crowd of heavily armed masked men arrived at the town's dock by boat. After securing their boats, the men moved silently through the street until they reached the jail. Once there they placed a pistol to the jailer's head and seized Patrick.[192] Then they pushed their boats off and sailed off into the night.

The next morning when word of the brazen attack reached the Carteret County sheriff, he summoned a launch and set off across the inlet for Bogue. When he arrived he found no sign of Patrick. However, he alertly noted that he found few of the men who lived in the village, "their absences being accounted for as away fishing."[193] With no sign of Patrick, the sheriff concluded that the mob took the prisoner to the middle of Bogue Sound, attached weights to his body and pushed the doomed man over the side of the boat.[194] However, several days later the sheriff discovered the awful truth when a foul odor and a flock of buzzards and sea birds notified them of Patrick's badly decomposed body tied to a tree riddled with bullets.[195] After conducting an inquest, officials buried the body. Authorities made no attempt to arrest or prosecute the guilty parties, as most viewed Patrick as an undesirable newcomer who deserved the fate he received, even if it came at the hands of a mob.

Silas Martindale   *Moore County. March 10, 1901*

One of the most shocking acts in the history of Moore County occurred on March 8, 1901. Shortly after midnight a mob of fifty men broken into the Moore County Jail and seized Silas Martindale, a twenty-five-year-old white man.[196] At gunpoint, they forced Martindale down Main Street to the outskirts of Carthage. When they reached a black jack tree, they tied a rope around his neck and hanged him.[197] However, just watching Martindale strangle to death did not satisfy the mob. Several times members of the mob lowered the doomed man to the ground in order to extort a confession. However, when he refused to confess the mob angrily hoisted the doomed man off the ground and let him strangle to death.[198]

The next day the coroner arrived and cut Martindale's body down. Then he issued arrest warrants for several prominent citizens suspected of participating in the crime.[199] However, when the suspects produced alibis, authorities released the men and closed the case.[200] Yet, this does not explain why the mob inflicted such a terrible punishment on Martindale. According to published reports, several months earlier, officials charged Martindale with the sexual assault of a white schoolteacher.

John Osborne   *Union County. July 3, 1903*

One night Mrs. Lizzie Wentz, an elderly white woman, reported that a young black man raped and robbed her.[201] The next day, Plummer Stewart, a nephew of Wentz, set out to find the assailant. For two days he searched, but found no clue of the guilty man. However, three days after the assault Stewart learned, from a neighbor, that John Osborne, "known to be a negro of desperate character had been in the neighborhood on the night of the attack."[202]

With this discovery, Stewart and several men arrested Osborne and headed back to Wentz's home. However, when they brought the suspect before Wentz she was unable to identify Osborne. Nonetheless, Stewart remained convinced that Osborne was guilty. For that reason, he called the local justice of the peace and organized a hearing for the suspect. While it is highly questionable if such a hearing had any legal bearing, it nonetheless produced some interesting findings. For one, Diana McCombs, a black woman who lived near Wentz, testified that Osborne stopped by her home the night before the attack. In addition, she claimed that Osborne had no money when he stopped by her house, but when he visited her home the next day he had a fifty-cent piece, a quarter, a dime and three pennies.[203] Just how McCombs made this discovery is unknown; however, amazingly the amounts she described were exactly the same amount and denomination of coins taken from Wentz's home.[204] At any rate, after this one-sided hearing officials decided to transport Osborne to the Union County Jail in Monroe, until they could schedule a trial for him later in the month.

About two miles from Wentz's home several men ran out of some woods and grabbed the reins of the horse. The guards supposedly opened fire.[205] However, either they were extremely poor shots or they were involved in conspiracy to murder Osborne, for they failed to wound or nick any of the attackers, despite the fact the members of the mob were less than six feet away. At any rate, after this exchange the mob swarmed the wagon and seized Osborne. They dragged him to a nearby white oak tree, tied a scarf and a plough line around his neck and asked the doomed man about the crime. But he refused to make a confession. Then they threw the end of the plough line over a small limb and drew Osborne off the ground.[206] There he died with his feet less than two inches from the ground.[207] The next day, the coroner celebrated Independence Day by holding a jury of inquest. However, as usual the jury found that "Osborne came to his death at the hand of unknown persons."[208] After this announcement authorities made no effort to arrest the men responsible for Osborne's murder, as most felt he got what he deserved. Perhaps nothing sums up this feeling better than an article published by the *Charlotte Observer* several days after the murder: "Never has the work of any crowd of men been looked upon with more satisfaction than is the lynching of John Osborne."[209]

John Daniels *Onslow County. February 7, 1919*

On January 25, 1919, Onslow County officials arrested two young black men, John Daniels and Daniel Petteway. Officials charged the men with the murder of a white man, Grover Dickey, the manager of the Roper Lumber Company farm.[210] Earlier in the day as Dickey reprimanded Petteway for leaving the pig pen gate open, John Daniels slipped behind the manager and struck him with a fence post.[211] Then, as he lay on the ground Daniels struck Dickey several more times.[212]*

The sheriff was notified and in short ordered arrested Daniels and Pette-

*Several hours later Dickey died.

way and placed them in the Onslow County Jail. However, less than a week later a mob of more than twenty masked men stormed the jail. At gunpoint, they seized Petteway. However, when they reached Daniels's cell he told the men "that he would kill the first man who came into his cell."[213] In reply, the men fired several shots and Daniels fell to the floor. Then they seized the wounded man and disappeared into the darkness. Several hours later officials found Daniels's body hanging by the neck from a drawbridge.[214] Officers found no sign of Petteway.

Yet, persistent rumors remained that the mob had released Petteway.* For that reason, Onslow County officials, anxious to charge someone with Dickey's murder, continued to search for him. After several years of persistent searching, in January 1922 news reached Onslow officials that Petteway was working with a road construction crew in Kinston.[215] As a result, Kinston police were dispatched. However, when Petteway saw the officers, he turned and fled. Just before he reached the safety of some nearby woods, one of the officers fired a shot and Petteway fell wounded. After this, the officers easily captured the fugitive and transported him to a nearby hospital.[216] However, for Petteway his pending return to Onslow County caused a great deal of fear. According to Petteway, the mob only spared his life because they believed that he was innocent. But ominously they told him to never return to Onslow County or suffer Daniels's fate.[217] With this in mind, several days later Petteway, perhaps with the assistance of sympathetic doctors and nurses, escaped from the hospital.[218] Although officials launched an extensive search, they never found Petteway again.

Willie McDaniel   *Mecklenburg County. June 30, 1929*

On Sunday morning, June 30, 1929, the body of twenty-three-year-old Willie McDaniel was found in a clump of bushes on the edge of a cotton field.[219] Authorities conducted a cursory investigation and turned the body over to black undertaker.[220] Later that day authorities held a coroner's inquest, during which they announced that McDaniel "came to his death of a broken neck caused by a person or persons unknown."[221] This revelation set off a firestorm in nearby Charlotte. Several reporters rushed to the scene and launched their own investigation, one of whom maintained that he found a tree near the crime scene that showed evidence of having been the location of the hanging. Police on the other hand rejected this theory since the tree was more than three hundred yards from where they found McDaniel's body. Instead the officers expressed the belief that McDaniel was hanged in the loft of a nearby barn. After his death, they concluded, several men placed his dead body at the edge of the cotton field.[222]

---

*The rumors that Petteway was alive were quite possibly substantiated by the possible involvement of law officers in Daniels's lynching.

This however did not end the controversy surrounding McDaniel's death. The day after the inquest Sallie McDaniel, the victim's wife, and several other black sharecroppers charged that McDaniel had come to his death by gunshot. This charge was significant since during the inquest several of the sharecroppers testified that they had seen Mell Grier, a white landowner, chasing McDaniel with a shotgun.[223]

Whatever the case, following the hearing Jake Newell, an attorney hired by McDaniel's friends, announced that the family would exhume the body to determine the cause of death. Several days later they dug the body up and conducted a second autopsy. However, like the first, this examination failed to find any gunshot wounds but it did positively confirm that McDaniel's death came as a result of a broken neck.[224]

The exhumation of the body was a dramatic proceeding. After three feet of dirt was excavated the coffin was removed bottom side up and the body of the slain man laid out on the lid. Few of the people were prepared for what happened next, as the only clothes on McDaniel's body was a piece of heavy brown wrapping paper.[225] As a result, an old woman who was a cousin of McDaniel bitterly complained that she "had carried a suit of clothes to the undertaker and had been given assurances that the body would be dressed in the garments."[226]

The exhumation nonetheless captured the attention of the district solicitor John G. Carpenter. On the day after the second autopsy he announced that the Grand Jury would investigate McDaniel's murder. "I am determined to get to the bottom of this thing and I am starting an investigation at once.... It was a terrible thing and the people of Mecklenburg County have a right to have it cleared up."[227] Despite this announcement, after several visits to the crime scene, on July 19, 1929, the Grand Jury announced that "it was unable to arrive at a solution or even find a clue that might lead to a subsequent denouement."[228]

Yet, there was evidence that pointed to several suspects, namely, Mell Grier. During the coroner's inquest George Hurd, a black sharecropper who worked on the Grier farm alongside Willie McDaniel, testified that he and McDaniel went with Grier to get some flour from Charlotte. When they returned to the farm, McDaniel asked Grier if he was going to pay him for moving the flour. Grier refused to pay. McDaniel then asked Grier if he would pay for some blackberries that his wife had picked earlier for the Grier household. This made Grier angry and an argument ensued. Grier threw a rock at McDaniel. However, before Grier could pick up another stone McDaniel jumped from the wagon and grabbed Grier. In the midst of the scuffle, Grier broke away and ran to his house where he grabbed his shotgun.[229]

Emma Mosley, a black house girl at the Grier home, testified that she saw the fight. When Grier ran out on the porch with the shotgun, he aimed at the fleeing McDaniel but his brother-in-law swung at the gun and prevented him from firing.[230] However, the most dramatic testimony came from Jim Edmonds, an elderly black tenant, with whom McDaniel and his wife lived. On the witness stand Edmonds maintained that after McDaniel fled, Grier hunted him all afternoon in the field and woods nearby.[231] That night Hurd claimed that he went to Grier's home and asked his boss to patch things up and "let Willie come back."[232] In response Grier replied, "He'll come back all right."[233] The next day after the discovery of McDaniel's body, Hurd said he told Grier that he was the last person seen with McDaniel and that he had a gun. Then he asked Grier if he had committed the murder. Grier responded by saying, "Uncle Jim I didn't do it. He brought it on hisself [sic]."[234] After Edmonds's testimony officials called another black tenant, Fred Mosley. Like many of the other farm workers, Mosley testified that he saw Grier with a shotgun. Moreover, he maintained that before the murder Grier asked him if McDaniel had entered his home. When he told Grier that he had not entered, the landowner insisted on checking for himself.[235]

Yet, despite this testimony, officials refused to investigate Grier or to identify him as a person of interest. Instead they chose to hastily bury the case with the victim. Only the efforts of a lawyer hired by the McDaniel family forced them to take action. Even then they refused to charge the most obvious suspect. Perhaps since Grier was a prominent landowner, officials felt they stood little chance of conviction, or maybe they felt the evidence did not support an arrest. Whatever the case, shortly after the Grand Jury released its findings, Mecklenburg County officials quickly relegated the McDaniel's murder case to the files of the unsolved. However, like a flickering candle, over the next two years the case continued to spark to life periodically. In October 1929, black workers marched in Charlotte to protest the murder.[236] The next year the American Communist Party, as part of the efforts to enlist black workers, published an editorial in newspapers across the South condemning McDaniel's murder.[237] Despite these occasional flickers, by 1931 the last spark was extinguished and the case was forgotten.

Appendix II

North Carolina Lynchings, 1865–1941

St #	Victim	Race*	Sex†	Offense	Date	County
1	Negro, Unnamed	B	M	Unknown	? ?, 1865	Chatham
2	Negro, Unnamed	B	M	Unknown	Feb. ?, 1865	Robeson
3	Negro, Unnamed	B	M	Unknown	Feb. ?, 1865	Robeson
4	Negro, Unnamed	B	M	Unknown	Feb. ?, 1865	Robeson
5	Negro, Unnamed	B	U	Trespassing	Aug. 1(?), 1865	Duplin
6	Negro, Unnamed	B	U	Trespassing	Aug. 1(?), 1865	Duplin
7	Negro, Unnamed	B	U	Trespassing	Aug. 1(?), 1865	Duplin
8	Negro, Unnamed	B	U	Trespassing	Aug. 1(?), 1865	Duplin
9	Negro, Unnamed	B	U	Trespassing	Aug. 1(?), 1865	Duplin
10	Negro, Unnamed	B	U	Trespassing	Aug. 1(?), 1865	Duplin
11	Negro, Unnamed	B	U	Unknown	Feb. ?, 1866	Lenoir
12	Negro, Unnamed	B	U	Unknown	Feb. ?, 1866	Lenoir
13	Negro, Unnamed	B	U	Unknown	Feb. ?, 1866	Lenoir
14	Negro, Unnamed	B	U	Unknown	Feb. ?, 1866	Lenoir
15	Negro, Unnamed	B	M	Race Prejudice	Feb. 14, 1866	Lenoir
16	Negro, Unnamed	B	M	Race Prejudice	? ?, 1866	Pitt
17	Walker, Mac	B	M	Unknown	Oct. ?, 1866	Harnett
18	Negro, Unnamed	B	M	Race Prejudice	Jan. ?, 1866	Beaufort
19	Negro, Unnamed	B	M	Race Prejudice	Feb. ?, 1866	Duplin
20	Negro, Unnamed	B	M	Rape	Dec. ?, 1866	Greene
21	White, Unnamed	W	M	Rape	Dec. ?, 1866	Greene
22	Negro, Unnamed	B	M	Rape	Dec. ?, 1866	Greene
23	Negro, Unnamed	B	M	Rape	Dec. ?, 1866	Greene
24	Negro, Unnamed	B	M	Rape	Dec. ?, 1866	Greene
25	Negro, Unnamed	B	M	Rape	Dec. ?, 1866	Greene
26	Negro, Unnamed	B	M	Rape	Dec. ?, 1866	Greene
27	Norcom, James	B	M	Dispute with Landower	Nov. ?, 1867	Washington
28	Cooper, Henderson	B	M	Rape	Nov. ?, 1866	Granville
29	Beebe, Archie	B	M	Attempted rape	Feb. 11, 1867	Cumberland

*B=Black, W=White
†M=Male, F=Female, U=Unknown

167

St #	Victim	Race*	Sex†	Offense	Date	County
30	Negro, Unnamed	B	M	Unknown	Nov. ?, 1868	Alamance
31	Negro, Unnamed	B	M	Unknown	Aug. ?, 1869	Orange
32	Morrow, Dan	B	M	Arson	Aug. 7, 1869	Orange
33	Morrow, Jeff	B	M	Arson	Aug. 7, 1869	Orange
34	Shepperd, M.L.	W	M	Political Activity	Aug. 18, 1869	Lenoir
35	Wright, Woods	B	M	Arson	Dec. ?, 1869	Orange
36	Guy, Cryus	B	M	Arson	Dec. ?, 1869	Orange
37	Child, Unnamed	B	U	Unknown	Dec. ?, 1869	Alamance
38	Negro, Unnamed	B	M	Robbery	Jan. 24, 1869	Lenoir
39	Negro, Unnamed	B	M	Robbery	Jan. 24, 1869	Lenoir
40	Negro, Unnamed	B	M	Robbery	Jan. 24, 1869	Lenoir
41	Negro, Unnamed	B	M	Robbery	Jan. 24, 1869	Lenoir
42	Negro, Unnamed	B	M	Arson	July ?, 1869	Orange
43	Child, Unnamed	B	U	Unknown	Mar. ?, 1869	Alamance
44	Stephens, John	W	M	Political Activity	May 21, 1869	Caswell
45	Cogden, Lewis	B	M	Stealing	? ?, 1869	Greene
46	Jones, Amos	B	M	Political Activity	May 28, 869	Jones
47	Colgrove, O.R.	W	M	Political Activity	May 28, 869	Jones
48	Blue, Child	B	F	Father's Testimony	Feb. ?, 1869	Moore
49	Blue, Child	B	U	Father's Testimony	Feb. ?, 1869	Moore
50	Blue, Child	B	U	Father's Testimony	Feb. ?, 1869	Moore
51	Blue, Child	B	U	Father's Testimony	Feb. ?, 1869	Moore
52	Blue, Child	B	U	Father's Testimony	Feb. ?, 1869	Moore
53	Blue, Mother	B	F	Hus. Testimony	Feb. ?, 1869	Moore
54	Outlaw, Wyatt	B	M	Political Activity	Feb. 26, 1870	Alamance
55	Puryear, William	B	M	Political Activity	Mar. ?, 1870	Alamance
56	Negro, Unnamed	B	M	Race Prejudice	Apr. 29, 1871	Chatham
57	Negro, Unnamed	B	U	Race Prejudice	Apr. 29, 1871	Chatham
58	Weston, Child	B	U	Race Prejudice	May ?, 1871	Rutherford
59	Weston, Child	B	U	Race Prejudice	May ?, 1871	Rutherford
60	Weston, Silas	B	M	Race Prejudice	May ?, 1871	Rutherford
61	Weston, Child	B	U	Race Prejudice	May ?, 1871	Rutherford
62	Taylor, John	B	M	Rape	June 10, 1881	Rockingham
63	Church, Elijah	B	M	Murder	Oct. 6, 1881	Alexander
64	Davis, Edmund	B	M	Attempted rape	Oct. 17, 1881	Union
65	Negro, Unnamed	B	M	Attempted rape	Apr. 11, 1883	Bertie
66	White, Lawrence	B	M	Murder	Nov. 8, 1883	Rowan
67	Campbell, Charles	B	M	Murder	Oct. 16, 1883	Iredell
68	Johnson, Dockery	B	M	Attempted rape	Sep. 20, 1883	Richmond
69	McCullough, Erwin	B	M	Murder	Apr. 1, 1884	Gaston
70	Smith, Charles	B	M	Robbery	Dec. 24, 1884	Johnston
71	Davis, Thomas	B	M	Robbery	Dec. 24, 1884	Johnston
72	Johnson, George	B	M	Rape	Sep. 6, 1884	Iredell
73	Lee, John	W	M	Murder	Dec. 18, 1885	Richmond
74	Boggan, John	B	M	Criminal assault (rape)	Jul. 2, 1885	Anson
75	Stratten, Lee	B	M	Rape	Mar. 4, 1885	Union
76	Mebane, Bud	B	M	Rape & murder	Oct. 3, 1885	Caswell
77	Finch, Harriet	B	F	Murder	Sep. 29, 1885	Chatham
78	Finch, Jerry	B	M	Murder	Sep. 29, 1885	Chatham
79	Pattisall, John	B	M	Murder	Sep. 29, 1885	Chatham

St #	Victim	Race*	Sex†	Offense	Date	County
80	Tyson, Lee	B	M	Murder	Sep. 29, 1885	Chatham
81	Powell, T. C.	W	M	Murder	Nov. 13, 1886	Edgecombe
82	Hairston, Eugene	B	M	Assault/rape	Aug. 25, 1887	Guilford
83	White, Benjamin	B	M	Criminal assault (rape)	May 8, 1887	Edgecombe
84	Carson, John	B	M	Murder	Dec. 2, 1888	Cleveland
85	Blount, Jack	B	M	Murder	Jan. 26, 1888	Washington
86	Blount, Matthew	B	M	Murder	Jan. 26, 1888	Washington
87	Spruill, Patterson	B	M	Murder	Jan. 26, 1888	Washington
88	Humphreys, John	B	M	Rape	Jul. 15, 1888	Buncombe
89	Parker, Wm. A.	W	M	Murder	Mar. 13, 1888	Beaufort
90	Frazier, Thomas	W	M	Murder	May 6, 1888	Beaufort
91	Smith, Alonzo	B	M	Arson & burglary	Sep. 2, 1888	Granville
92	Tanner, John	B	M	Murder	Sep. 2, 1888	Granville
93	Tanner, Henry	B	M	Murder	Sep. 2, 1888	Granville
94	Berrier, Robert	W	M	Murder	Oct. 14, 1889	Davidson
95	Sigmund, John	B	M	Attempted rape	Sep. 6, 1889	Gaston
96	Stack, Franklin	W	M	Murder	Sep. 11, 1889	Burke
97	Boone, David	B	M	Murder	Sep. 11, 1889	Burke
98	Freeman, Kinch	B	M	Murder	Dec. 23, 1890	Hertford
99	Starling, John	W	M	Making threats	May 24, 1890	Johnston
100	Best, Mack	B	M	Attempted rape	Sep. 6, 1891	Sampson
101	Rankin, Hezekiah	B	M	Murder	Sep. 25, 1891	Buncombe
102	Whitley, Alexander	W	M	Murder	Jun. 9, 1892	Stanly
103	Purdie, Lyman	B	M	Murder	May 1, 1892	Bladen
104	Burnett, Carter	B	M	Assaulted girl (rape)	Nov. 15, 1892	Granville
105	McPhatter, Duncan	B	M	Murder	Nov. 17, 1892	Richmond
106	Allison, Thomas	W	M	Murder	Sep. 12, 1892	Surry
107	Ray, Bob	B	M	Murder	Jan. 6, 1893	Moore
108	English, Holland	W	M	Murder	Apr. 1, 1894	Mitchell
109	Bergeron, James	W	M	Murder	Dec. 26, 1894	Beaufort
110	Slaughter, Daniel	W	M	Murder	Feb. 22, 1894	Alleghany
111	Wofford, Dick	B	M	Assaulted girl (rape)	Nov. 22, 1894	Polk
112	Chambers, Robert	B	M	Attempted rape & arson & arson	Apr. 21, 1896	Mitchell
113	Willis, Nathan	B	M	Murder	Nov. 29, 1897	Brunswick
114	Johnson, Thomas	B	M	Rape & murder	May 29, 1898	Cabarrus
115	Kiser, Joseph	B	M	Rape & murder	May 29, 1898	Cabarrus
116	Maney, George	W	M	Murder	Jan. 13, 1899	Cherokee
117	Jones, Henry	B	M	Rape & murder	Jan. 11, 1899	Chatham
118	Patrick, Lewis	B	M	Murder	Jun. 14, 1899	Carteret
119	Mills, Avery	B	M	Murder	Aug. 28, 1900	Rutherford
120	Ratliffe, George	B	M	Assaulted girl (rape)	Mar. 5, 1900	Haywood
121	Rittle, George	B	M	Informer	Mar. 20, 1900	Moore
122	Huff, Luke	B	M	Murderous assault	Aug. 21, 1901	Anson
123	Jones, D. B.	B	M	Assault (rape)	Jun. 18, 1901	Lenoir
124	Martindale, James	W	M	Assaulted woman	Mar. 8, 1901	Moore
125	Jones, Thomas	B	M	Rape	Aug. 25, 1902	Wayne
126	Gillespie, Harrison	B	M	Murder	Jun. 11, 1902	Rowan
127	Gillespie, James	B	M	Murder	Jun. 11, 1902	Rowan
128	Walker, James	B	M	Murder	Mar. 25, 1902	Beaufort

St #	Victim	Race*	Sex†	Offense	Date	County
129	Ponton, Manna	B	M	Rape/Murder	Aug. 22, 1903	Halifax
130	Osborne, John	B	M	Criminal assault (rape)	Jul. 2, 1903	Union
131	Whitehead, Dick	B	M	Assaulted child (rape)	May 18, 1904	Northampton
132	Moore, John	B	M	Murderous assault	Aug. 27, 1905	Craven
133	Gillespie, John	B	M	Murder	Aug. 6, 1906	Rowan
134	Gillespie, Nease	B	M	Murder	Aug. 6, 1906	Rowan
135	Dillingham, Jack	B	M	Murder	Aug. 6, 1906	Rowan
136	Johnson, J. V.	W	M	Murder	May 28, 1906	Anson
137	Negro, Unnamed	B	M	Fraud	Jan. 7, 1908	Johnston
138	Negro, Unnamed	B	M	Robbery	Oct. 8, 1910	Rockingham
139	McNeely, Joseph	B	M	Murder	Aug. 26, 1913	Mecklenburg
140	Wilson, James	B	M	Rape & murder	Jan. 28, 1914	Johnston
141	Perry, Mrs. Joe	B	F	Unknown	Mar. 12, 1915	Vance
142	Perry, Child	B	U	Unknown	Mar. 12, 1915	Vance
143	Black, Joseph	B	M	Making threats	Apr. 5, 1916	Greene
144	Rouse, Lazarus	B	M	Unknown	Aug. 4, 1916	Lenoir
145	Richards, John	B	M	Murder	Jan. 12, 1916	Wayne
146	Bazemore, Peter	B	M	Criminal assault (rape)	Mar. 23, 1918	Bertie
147	Taylor, George	B	M	Criminal assault (rape)	Nov. 5, 1918	Wake
148	Elliott, Walter	B	M	Attacked woman (rape)	Aug. 20, 1919	Franklin
149	Green, Powell	B	M	Murder	Dec. 27, 1919	Franklin
150	Daniels, John	B	M	Murder	Feb. 6, 1919	Onslow
151	Jeffress, John	B	M	Attempted assault (rape)	Aug. 25, 1920	Alamance
152	Roach, Edward	B	M	Attempted rape	Jul. 7, 1920	Person
153	Artis, Norman	B	M	Peeping Tom	Sep. 30, 1920	Wayne
154	Whitfield, Jerome	B	M	Attacked woman (rape)	Aug. 14, 1921	Jones
155	Williams, Alfred	B	M	Race prejudice	Jan. 24, 1921	Warren
156	Bullock, Plummer	B	M	Race prejudice	Jan. 24, 1921	Warren
157	Daniels, Ernest	B	M	In white woman's room	Sep. 18, 1921	Chatham
158	Blackwell, Bayner	B	M	Murder	Aug. 6, 1922	Onslow
159	Bryant, Wife	B	F	Unknown	May 25, 1926	Duplin
160	Bryant, Dock	B	M	Unknown	May 25, 1926	Duplin
161	Miller, Broadus	B	M	Murder	Jul. 3, 1927	Burke
162	Bradshaw, Thomas	B	M	Criminal assault (rape)	Aug. 2, 1927	Nash
163	McDaniel, Willie	B	M	Unknown	Jun. 29, 1929	Mecklenburg
164	Wiggins, Ella May	W	F	Strike activity	Sep. 14, 1929	Gaston
165	Moore, Oliver	B	M	Rape	Aug. 20, 1930	Edgecombe
166	Rogers, Dock	B	M	Assault	Aug. 27, 1933	Pender
167	Ward, Sweat	B	M	Murder	Aug. 23, 1935	Franklin
168	Melker, Robert	B	M	Arguing with white man	Apr. 13, 1941	Wilkes

Notes

Preface

1. "Lynching Near LaGrange," *Wilmington Morning Star*, 20 June 1901.

Introduction

1. "Lynching in Sampson," *Wilmington Star*, 7 September 1891.

2. *Ibid.*

3. Between 1890 and 1930, lynch mobs claimed 458 victims in Georgia, 214 in Tennessee and 152 in South Carolina. In contrast during the same period mob violence claimed 99 lives in North Carolina. Famous lynchings from the era include Sam Hose, 1899; William "Froggie" James, Cairo, Illinois, 1909; Leo Franks, Marietta, Georgia, 1915; Ed Johnson, Chattanooga, Tennessee, 1906; and Edward Coy in Texarkana, Arkansas, 1892.

4. Ida B. Wells-Barnett, "Lynching Law in America," *Arena*, vol. 23.1, January 9, 1909, 15–24.

5. W. Fitzhugh Brundage, *Under the Sentence of Death: Lynching in the South* (Chapel Hill: University of North Carolina Press, 1997), 3.

6. Walter Lockhart, "Lynching in North Carolina" (M.A. Thesis, University of North Carolina, 1972), 53; and Walter White, *Rope and Faggot* (New York: Alfred A. Knopf, 1929), 205-206.

7. Walter Lockhart, "Lynching in North Carolina" (M.A. Thesis, University of North Carolina, 1972), 53.

8. *Ibid.*

9. Philip Dray, *At the Hands of Persons Unknown* (New York: Modern Library, 2003), 461.

10. W. Fitzhugh Brundage, *Under the Sentence of Death: Lynching in the South* (Chapel Hill: University of North Carolina Press, 1997), 6.

11. *Ibid.*, 10–11.

12. Major works of this genre include Arthur Raper, *The Tragedy of Lynching* (Chapel Hill: University of North Carolina Press, 1933); and Carl Hovland and Robert R. Sears, "Minor Studies of Aggression: Correlations of Economic Indices With Lynching," *Journal of Psychology*, vol. ix (1940).

13. Stewart Tolnay and E.M. Beck, *A Festival of Violence: An Analysis of Southern Lynchings, 1882–1930* (Urbana: University of Illinois Press, 1995), 111–139.

14. Major studies that support his theory are Edward L. Ayers, *Vengeance and Justice: Crime and Punishment in the Nineteenth Century South* (New York: Oxford University Press, 1984); Bertram Wyatt-Brown, *Southern Honor: Ethics and Behavior in the Old South* (New York: Oxford University Press, 1982); Elliot J. Gorn, "Gouge and Bite, Pull Hair and Scratch: The Social Significance of Fighting in the Southern Backcountry," *American Historical Review* vol. 90 (1985); and W. Fitzhugh Brundage, *Lynching in the New South: Georgia and Virginia* (Champaign: University of Illinois Press, 1993).

15. Brundage, 3.

16. Important case studies include Louis Burnham, *Behind the Lynching of Emmett Louis Till* (New York: Freedom Associates, 1955); Leonard Dinnerstein, *The Leo Frank Case* (New York: Columbia University Press, 1968); Howard Smead, *Blood Justice: The Lynching of Mark Charles Parker* (New York: Oxford University Press, 1981); James T. McGovern, *Anatomy of a Lynching: The Killing of Claude Neal* (Baton Rouge: Louisiana State University Press, 1982); Stephen Whitfield, *A Death in the Delta: The Story of Emmett Till* (Baltimore: John Hopkins University Press, 1992); Dennis B. Downey and Raymond Hyser, *No Crooked Death: Coatsville, Pennsylvania, and the Lynching of Zacharia Walker* (Urbana: University Illinois Press, 1991); Marco Rimanelli, *1891 New Orleans Lynching and U.S.-Italian Relations: A Look Back* (New York: Peter Lang, 1992); Harry Farrell, *Swift Justice: Murder and Vengeance in a California Town* (New York: St. Martin's Press, 1992); Domenic Capeci, *The Lynching of Cleo Wright* (Lexington: University of Kentucky Press, 1998); Joan E. Cashin, "A Lynching in Wartime Carolina: The Death of Saxe Joiner," in *Under Sentence of Death: Lynching in the South* (1997); Patrick J. Huber, "Caught Up in the Violent Whirlwind of Lynching: The 1885 Quadruple

Lynching in Chatham County, North Carolina," *North Carolina Historical Review*, vol. LXXV (1998); Mark Curriden and Leroy Phillips, *Contempt of Court: The Turn of the Century Lynching That Launched a Hundred Years of Federalism* (New York: Faber and Faber, 1999); Monte Akers, *Flames After Midnight: Murder, Vengeance, and the Desolation of a Texas Community* (Austin: University of Texas Press, 1999); James Madison, *A Lynching in the Heartland* (New York: Palgrave, 2002); Michael Fedo, *Lynching in Duluth* (St. Paul: Minnesota Historical Society, 2000); Richard Gambino, *Vendetta: The True Story of the Largest Lynching in U.S. History* (New York: Doubleday, 2000); Robert Seitz Frey and Nancy Thompson Frey, *The Silent and the Damned: The Murder of Mary Phagen and the Lynching of Leo Frank* (Lanham, M.D.: Cooper Square Press, 2002); Laura Wexler, *Fire in a Canebrake* (New York: Scribner's, 2003); and J. Timothy Cole, *The Forest City Lynching of 1900* (Jefferson, N.C.: McFarland, 2003).

17. "What Is a Lynching," *Asheville Citizen*, 15 July 1941.

18. Frank Shay, *Judge Lynch: His First Hundred Years* (New York: Ives Washburn, 1938), 7; and Walter Lockhart, "Lynching in North Carolina," 52.

19. Stephen J. Leonard, *Lynching in Colorado 1859–1919* (Boulder: Univ. of Colorado Press, 2002), 9.

20. R.C. Lawrence, "Lynchers of the Law," *The State*, April 21, 1945.

21. Hugh Lefler, *North Carolina: History, Geography, Government* (New York: Harcourt, Brace & World, 1959), 404.

Chapter 1

1. Handbook of Texas Online, s.v. <http://www.tsha.utexas.edu/handbook/online/articles/LL/jgl1.html>(December 10, 2006).

2. There was considerable fear that blacks, who formed a majority in sixteen North Carolina counties, would form a political base for the Republican Party.

3. J. Kelly Turner and J.N.O. Bridgers, *History of Edgecombe County North Carolina* (Raleigh: Edward & Broughton Printing, 1920), 247.

4. Jeffrey J. Crow, Paul D. Escott and Flora J. Hatley, *A History of African-Americans in North Carolina* (Raleigh: North Carolina Department of Cultural Resources, 2002), 91.

5. Jesse Parker Bogue, "Violence and Oppression in North Carolina During Reconstruction 1865–1873," (Ph. D. diss., University of Maryland, 1973), 212.

6. *Ibid.*

7. *Senate Executive Documents*, No. 16, Part 2, 41st Congress, 3rd Session (Washington, D.C.: Government Printing Office, 1871), 54.

8. *Ibid.*, 44.

9. *Ibid.*, 48.

10. *Ibid.*, 8.

11. Richard Zuber, *North Carolina During Reconstruction* (Raleigh: North Carolina Department of Cultural Resources, 1969), 29.

12. *Ibid.*, 29–33.

13. Joseph Roulhac Hamilton, *Reconstruction in North Carolina* (New York: Columbia University Press, 1914), 480.

14. Eric Anderson, *Race and Politics in North Carolina, 1872–1901: The Black Second* (Baton Rouge: Louisiana State University Press, 1981), 56–57.

15. *Ibid.*, 57.

16. *Ibid.*

17. *Ibid.*, 56.

18. Frenise A. Logan, *The Negro in North Carolina, 1876–1894* (Chapel Hill: University of North Carolina Press, 1964), 185; and Clarence Carson, "Ninety Degrees in the Shade," quoted in Maurice R. Davie, *Negroes in American Society* (New York: McGraw-Hill, 1949), 348.

19. Joe Mobley, "In the Shadow of White Society: Princeville, a Black Town in North Carolina, 1865–1915," *North Carolina Historical Review* (July 1986), 11; and Piel, 168.

20. Anderson, 321.

21. *Ibid.*

22. *Ibid.*

23. "A Negro Lynched," Raleigh *State Chronicle*, 12 May 1887.

24. Mobley, 11.

25. *Ibid.*

26. "Lynched," Raleigh *News & Observer*, 4 September 1888. The first two men were charged with murder while Smith was charged with arson.

27. *Ibid.*

28. Oliver H. Orr, *Charles Brantley Aycock* (Chapel Hill: University of North Carolina Press, 1961), 1.

29. *Ibid.* , 1.

30. R.D.W. Connor and Clarence Hamilton Poe, *The Life and Speeches of Charles Brantley Aycock* (New York: Doubleday, 1912), 68–69.

31. *Ibid.*

32. *Ibid.*

33. Glenda Elizabeth Gilmore, *Gender & Jim Crow: Women and the Politics of White Supremacy in North Carolina, 1896–1920* (Chapel Hill: University of North Carolina Press, 1996), 85.

34. Oliver H. Orr, *Charles Brantley Aycock* (Chapel Hill: University of North Carolina Press, 1961), 123–24.

35. Jeffrey J. Crow, Paul D. Escott and Flora J. Hatley, *A History of African-Americans in North Carolina* (Raleigh: North Carolina Department of Cultural Resources, 2002), 86. The number of actual deaths is difficult to determine since many terrified blacks presumably buried slain relatives rather than report their deaths to authorities.

36. Orr, 137. Fearing black retaliation, whites in Wilmington sent telegraphs to towns throughout eastern North Carolina requesting armed help. When a telegraph reached Goldsboro, Aycock led more than five hundred armed men to the train depot. However, before the men could depart news reached the mob that the riot was over.

37. Gilmore, 121.

38. "Mr. Aycock in Rutherford," *Charlotte Observer*, 3 July 1900.

39. Jeffrey J. Crow, Paul D. Escott and Flora J. Hatley, *A History of African-Americans in North Carolina* (Raleigh: North Carolina Department of Cultural Resources, 2002), 117.

40. "Dr. D.T. Tayloe, Wife and Children Poisoned," *Washington Progress*, 20 March 1920.

41. "Found Walker's Ghastly Corpse Swinging in Air," Raleigh *News & Observer*, 26 March 1902.

42. *Ibid.*

43. *Ibid.*

44. "Dr. D. Tayloe, Wife and Children Poisoned," *Washington Progress*, 20 March 1920.

45. "A Determined Mob," Williamston *Enterprise*, 28 March 1902.

46. *Ibid.*

47. *Ibid.*

48. "Jim Boston Lynched," *Washington Progress*, 27 March 1902.

49. Orr, 239.

50. *Ibid.*

51. *Ibid.*, 272.

52. "Dragged from the Jail and Lynched," Raleigh *News & Observer*, 12 June 1902; and "Lynching Must be Stopped," Raleigh *Progressive Farmer*, 24 June 1902.

53. "Dragged from Her House and Ravished by a Fiend," Kinston *Daily Free Press*, 23 August 1902.

54. *Ibid.*

55. "Jones Tied to a Log and Shot to Death," Raleigh *News & Observer*, 26 August 1902.

56. "Confessed His Crime," *Goldsboro Weekly Argus*, 28 August 1902.

57. "Jones Tied to a Log and Shot to Death," Raleigh *News & Observer*, 26 August 1902.

58. "Confessed His Crime," *Goldsboro Weekly Argus*, 28 August 1902.

59. "Tied to a Log and Riddled with Shot and Bullets," Kinston *Daily Free Press*, 23 August 1902; and "Confessed His Crime," *Goldsboro Weekly Argus*, 28 August 1902.

60. The sheriff's absence may have been intentional as he was informed of the capture more than five hours earlier.

61. "Confessed His Crime," *Goldsboro Weekly Argus*, 28 August 1902.

62. "Getting the News of a Lynching," Kinston *Daily Free Press*, 26 August 1902.

63. Walter Samuel Lockhart III, "Lynching in North Carolina" (M.A. Thesis University of North Carolina, 1972), 35; and "Confessed His Crime," *Goldsboro Weekly Argus*, 28 August 1902.

64. *Ibid.*

65. "Jones Tied to a Log and Shot to Death," Raleigh *News & Observer*, 26 August 1902.

66. "Getting the News of a Lynching," Kinston *Daily Free Press*, 26 August 1902.

67. Anderson, 291.

68. Benjamin Justeseen, *George Henry White: An Even Chance in the Race of Life* (Baton Rouge: Louisiana State University Press, 2001), 26.

69. John Hope Franklin, *The Free Negro in North Carolina 1790–1860* (Chapel Hill: University of North Carolina Press, 1943), 140. Stanley was hardly alone in 1850 more than one-fifth of Craven's black population was free.

70. Franklin, 169.

71. Justeseen, Benjamin. *George Henry White: An Even Chance in the Race of Life* (Baton Rouge: Louisiana State University Press, 2001), 38.

72. *Ibid.*, 141.

73. *Ibid.* and Robert Winston, *It's a Far Cry* (New York: Henry Holt, 1937), 210.

74. Anderson, 209.

75. Congressional Record, 56th Congress, 1st session, 1365; *New York Times*, 1 Feb 1900; and Eric Anderson, *Race and Politics in North Carolina 1872–1901*, 287.

76. Anderson, 288.

77. "What the Negro White Really Said," Raleigh *News & Observer*, 10 February 1900.

78. *Ibid.*

79. R.D.W. Connor, *North Carolina Rebuilding and Ancient Commonwealth* (Chicago: American Historical Society, 1929), 559.

80. "Paid Extreme Penalty for His Crime," *New Bern Weekly Journal*, 29 August 1905. It appears that the man's sole purpose for entering the store was robbery. Reports printed in local papers, however, suggest that the robber also raped the shopkeeper.

81. "The Neuse Sees a Deed of Horror," Raleigh *News & Observer*, 29 August 1905.

82. "Paid Extreme Penalty for His Crime," *New Bern Weekly Journal*, 29 August 1905.

83. Connor, 559.

84. Lockhart, 76.

85. *Ibid.*, 78.

86. "White Man Is Lynched," *Charlotte Observer*, 29 May 1906.

87. "Torn from Cell, Hanged and Shot," Raleigh *News & Observer*, 29 May 1906.

88. Lockhart, 82.

89. Connor, 560.

90. "Fourteen in Anson Jail, Alleged Lynchers Behind Bars," *Charlotte Observer*, 1 June 1906; and Lockhart, 82.

91. Lockhart, 84

92. Glenda Gilmore, *Gender & Jim Crow* (Chapel Hill: University of North Carolina Press, 1996), 144.

93. "To Avenge the Outrage," Raleigh *News & Observer*, 8 August 1906.

94. Gilmore, 144.

95. *Ibid.*

96. Lockhart, 88.

97. "To Avenge the Outrage," Raleigh *News & Observer*, 8 August 1906.

98. "A Child Avenged; Negroes Lynch One of Their Own Race for Assault," Raleigh *News & Observer*, 20 May 1904.

99. "Negroes Lynch Stranger," *Littleton News Reporter*, 27 May 1904.

100. "A Child Avenged; Negroes Lynch One of Their Own Race for Assault," Raleigh *News & Observer*, 20 May 1904.

101. "Torn to Pieces, Negroes' Body Strewn Along Railroad Track," Raleigh *News & Observer*, 10, January 1908.

102. *Ibid.*

103. *Ibid.*

104. *Ibid.*

105. *Ibid.*

106. Kenneth O'Reilly, "The Jim Crow Policies of Woodrow Wilson," *Journal of Blacks in Higher Education* (Autumn 1997): 117–19.

107. Richard Wormster, *The Rise and Fall of Jim Crow* (New York: St. Martin's Press, 2003), 119.

108. Michael J. Klarman, *From Jim Crow to Civil Rights: The Supreme Court and the Struggle for Racial Equality* (New York: Oxford University Press, 2004), 68. No cabinet member was more determined in this endeavor than the longtime editor of the Raleigh *News & Observer*, Josephus Daniels. As Wilson's secretary of the Navy, Daniels segregated all work, restroom and cafeteria facilities in the department.

109. *Ibid.*

110. *Ibid.*

111. Frank W. Sweet, *Legal History of the Color Line: The Rise of the One Drop Rule* (Palm Coast, F.L.: Backintyme Publishing, 2005), 418–19.

112. "Joe McNeely Is Shot by a Mob," *Charlotte Observer*, 26 August 1913.

113. *Ibid.*

114. "Wilson Displays Nerve of Iron," *Charlotte Observer*, 24 August 1913.

115. "Joe McNeely Is Shot by a Mob," *Charlotte Observer*, 26 August 1913.

116. *Ibid.*

117. "Wilson Recovery Very Doubtful," *Charlotte Observer*, 25 August 1913.

118. "Sheriff Talks," *Charlotte Observer*, 27 August 1913.

119. "Joe McNeely Is Shot by a Mob," *Charlotte Observer*, 26 August 1913.

120. "Majesty of the Law Trampled Upon by Mecklenburg Mob," *Charlotte Observer*, 27 August 1913.

121. *Ibid.*

122. *Ibid.*

123. "This Outraged Community's Demand," *Charlotte Observer*, 27 August 1913.

124. "Majesty of the Law Trampled Upon by Mecklenburg Mob," *Charlotte Observer*, 27 August 1913.

125. "This Outraged Community's Demand," *Charlotte Observer*, 27 August 1913.

126. *Ibid.*

127. "Mayor Offers Reward of $1,000 for Lynchers," *Charlotte Observer*, 27 August 1913.

128. "Majesty of the Law Trampled Upon by Mecklenburg Mob," *Charlotte Observer*, 27 August 1913.

129. "Mob Lynches Jim Wilson and Lets Worth Sanders Go," Raleigh *News & Observer*, 29 January 1914; and "Lynching at Wendell," *Nashville Graphic*, 29 January 1914.

130. *Ibid.*

131. "Mob Lynches Jim Wilson and Lets Worth Sanders Go," Raleigh *News & Observer*, 29 January 1914.

132. "Lynching at Wendell," *Nashville Graphic*, 29 January 1914.

133. "Mob Lynches Jim Wilson and Lets Worth Sanders Go," Raleigh *News & Observer*, 29 January 1914.

134. *Ibid.*

135. *Ibid.*

136. *Ibid.*

137. *Ibid.*

138. "Lynching at Wendell," *Nashville Graphic*, 29 January 1914.

139. "Wayne County Folk Invoke Lynch Law for Negro Slayer," *Kinston Free Press*, 12 January 1916.

140. "Negro Slayer Lynched by Mob," Raleigh *News & Observer*, 13 January 1916.

141. "Could Have Been Averted," Wilmington *Morning Star*, 14 January 1916; and Mark Curriden and Leroy Phillips, *Contempt of Court* (New York: Anchor Books, 1999), 151.

142. "Could Have Been Averted," Wilmington *Morning Star*, 14 January 1916.

143. "Wayne County Folk Invoke Lynch Law for Negro Slayer," *Kinston Free Press*, 12 January 1916.

144. *Ibid.*

145. "Mob Lynches JNO Richards at Goldsboro," Wilmington *Morning Star*, 13 January 1916.

146. *Ibid.*

147. *Ibid.*

148. "Negro Slayer Lynched by Mob," Raleigh *News & Observer*, 13 January 1916.

149. "Goldsboro Quiet After Lynching," Raleigh *News & Observer*, 14 January 1916.

150. James Allen, et al., *Without Sanctuary: Lynching Photography in America* (Santa Fe: Twin Palms Publishers, 2000), 173. The photograph taken of Richards's lynching shows him suspended by a rope under his arms. Additionally, his pants are lowered, suggesting possible castration.

151. "Precaution Taken Against Lynching Negroes in Wayne," *Kinston Free Press*, 13 January 1916.

152. "Negro Slayer Lynched by Mob," Raleigh *News & Observer*, 13 January 1916; "Could Have Been Averted," Wilmington *Morning Star*, 14 January 1916; "Precaution Taken Against Lynching Negroes in Wayne," *Kinston Free Press*, 13 January 1916.

153. "Goldsboro Lynching Is Being Investigated," Wilmington *Morning Star*, 16 January 1916.

154. *Ibid.*

155. "Col. Langston in Reply to Criticism," Raleigh *News & Observer*, 24 January 1916.

156. "Judge Clark's Reply to Governor Craig," Wilmington *Morning Star*, 18 January 1916.

157. *Ibid.*

158. K.B. Johnson to Judge Walter Clark, 28 January 1916, Papers of Governor Locke Craig, General Correspondence, North Carolina Department of Cultural Resources, Raleigh, North Carolina; Reverend W.A. Piland to Judge Walter Clark, 28 January 1916, Papers of Governor Locke Craig, General Correspondence, North Carolina Depart-

ment of Cultural Resources, Raleigh, North Carolina; John Langston to Judge Walter Clark, 19 January 1916, Papers of Governor Locke Craig, General Correspondence, North Carolina Department of Cultural Resources, Raleigh, North Carolina.

159. Crow, 123.

160. John Inscoe, "The Clansmen on Stage and Screen: North Carolina Reacts," *North Carolina History Review*, LXIV (April 1987).

161. Gilmore, 135.

162. *Ibid.*

163. Inscoe, 141.

164. *Ibid.*, 142.

165. *Ibid.*

166. *Ibid.*

167. *Ibid.*, 144.

168. *Ibid.*

169. *Ibid.*, 145.

170. "The Clansman Wins Here," *Charlotte Observer*, 12 October 1905.

171. Phillip Dray, *At the Hands of Persons Unknown: The Lynching of Black America* (New York: Modern Library, 2003), 197.

172. Gilmore, 137.

173. *Ibid.*

174. Charles Flint Kellogg, *NAACP: A History of the National Advancement of Colored People* (Baltimore: John Hopkins Press, 1967), 143.

175. William M. Tuttle, *Race Riot: Chicago in the Red Summer of 1919* (New York: Antheneum, 1974), 189, 230, 244.

176. Thurston Brown Interview, interview by author. Tape recording, Warrenton, North Carolina, 9 June 2002.

177. Dray, 64.

178. "Negro Commits Awful Crime Upon Six-Year-Old Girl, Clubs Mother of Victim and Shoots a Former Official," *Kinston Free Press*, 5 April 1916.

179. *Ibid.*

180. "Negro Taken from Jail Here This A.M. by Mob from Neighbor County; Shot to Death and Left on Greene Co. Road," *Kinston Free Press*, 5 April 1916.

181. *Ibid.*

182. *Ibid.*

183. *Ibid.*

184. "Greene County Farmers Take Joe Black, Negro, from Lenoir Jail and Shoot Him to Death," Raleigh *News & Observer*, 6 April 1916. Joseph Black was charged with providing weapons to his son.

185. "Shaw Will Abandon Attempt (to) Bring Lynchers to Trial for Murder," *Kinston Free Press*, 5 April 1916; and "Father of Little Girl's Assailant Lynched by Mob," Wilmington *Morning Star*, 6 April 1916.

186. *Ibid.*

187. *Ibid.*

188. "Father of Little Girl's Assailant Lynched by a Mob," Wilmington *Morning Star*, 6 April 1916.

189. "Craig Will Try to Send Some of the Lynchers to Prison," *Kinston Free Press*, 7 April 1916; and "Father of Little Girl's Assailant Lynched by a Mob," Wilmington *Morning Star*, 6 April 1916.

190. "Craig Should Take Precaution to Get Troops [*sic*] Snow Hill," *Kinston Free Press*, 12 April 1916.

191. *Ibid.*

192. "Corner's Jury of Inquest Accused No One of Killing Rouse," *Kinston Free Press*, 5 August 1916.

193. *Ibid.*

194. James Harmon Chadburn, *Lynching and the Law* (Chapel Hill: University of North Carolina Press, 1933), 31.

195. A. Philip Randolph, "Keynote Address to the Policy Conference of the March on Washington Movement," in *Negro Protest Thought in the Twentieth Century*, edited by Francis L. Broderick and August Meier (New York: Bobbs-Merrill, 1965).

196. *Ibid.* Between 1895 and 1919, race riots occurred in more than fifty locations across the country. Perhaps the most notable riots flared up in Atlanta; Brownsville, T.X.; Chicago; Springfield, I.L.; Houston T.X.; and Wilmington, N.C.

197. Hugh Davis Graham and Ted Robert Gurr, *Violence in America* (New York: Bantam Books, 1969), 402.

198. Hugh Davis Graham and Ted Robert Gurr, *Violence in America* (New York: Bantam Books, 1969), 402.

Chapter 2

1. *Ibid.*

2. Norlina City Council, "Official History of Norlina," (City of Norlina, 2005), 1.

3. "Norlina Seaboard Junction Makes Rapid Strides in Twelve Years," *Norlina Headlight*, 14 March 1924.

4. *Ibid.*

5. Timothy B. Tyson, *Radio Free Dixie: Robert Williams and the Roots of Black Power* (Chapel Hill: University of North Carolina Press, 1999), 19.

6. Ben Green, *Before His Time: The Untold Story of Harry T. Moore, America's First Civil Rights Martyr* (New York: Free Press, 1999), 18.

7. "Norlina Seaboard Junction Makes Rapid Strides in Twelve Years," *Norlina Headlight*, 14 March 1924.

8. *Ibid.*; and Warren County Heritage Book Committee, ed., *Warren County Heritage* (Waynesville, N.C.: Warren County Heritage Committee, 2002), 165.

9. "Negro Suffrage a Failure," *Warren Record*, 12 January 1900; "Suffrage Club, Negro Suffrage the Result of Military Despotism," *Warren Record*, 26 January 1900; "White Supremacy Parade," *Warren Record*, 7 October 1904. "The President's Hostile Attitude to the South, Record of the Two Parties Contrasted," *Warren Record*, 27 March 1903.

10. Tiring of Warrenton in 1909, he sold the paper and returned to Scotland Neck, where he purchased the local newspaper, the *Commonwealth*. Five years later he sold the *Commonwealth* and moved to Norlina.

11. Warren County Heritage Book Committee, ed., 165. Henderson also served as minister of Oak Level Church of Christ in Drewy and as president of Franklinton Christian College.

12. "Caught a Man in His House," *Norlina Headlight*, 20 August 1915.

13. Manley Wade Wellman, *County of Warren, North Carolina 1586–1917* (Chapel Hill: University of North Carolina Press, 1959), 213.

14. *Ibid.*, 209.

15. "Bullock's Father Has Heavy Loss: Has Lost Greater Part of His Money Over Son's Case," *Hamilton Herald*, 4 March 1922.

16. Charles Jones, interview by author, Norlina, North Carolina, 7 June 2002.

17. Norlina is located less than twenty miles from Vance County.

18. "Shot Dead in Effort to Quell Riotous Negroes," Raleigh *News & Observer*, 20 August 1902.

19. *Ibid.*

20. "The Murder on the Train," Raleigh *News & Observer*, 22 August 1902.

21. *Ibid.*

22. Charles Jones, interview by author, Norlina, North Carolina, 7 June 2002.

23. *Ibid.*

24. *Ibid.*

25. *Ibid.*

26. "Dr. H.L. Hawkins to Howard Jones editor of the *Warren Record*," 22 September 1911.

27. Charles Jones, interview by author, Norlina, North Carolina, 7 June 2002.

28. Arthur E. Barleau and Florette Henri, *The Unknown Soldier, African-Americans in World War I* (New York: Da Capo Press, 1996), 175.

29. *Ibid.*, 171.

30. Editors of Ebony, *Ebony Pictorial History*, Vol. II (Nashville: Southwestern, 1971), 148.

31. "Negro Lynched in Franklin County," Raleigh *News & Observer*, 22 August 1919.

32. *Ibid.*

33. *Ibid.*

34. "Solicitor Starts Lynching Probe," Raleigh *News & Observer*, 24 August 1919.

35. "Negro Lynched in Franklin County," Raleigh *News & Observer*, 22 August 1919.

36. "Walter Tyler Is Lynched on a Public Highway Near Louisburg," *Franklin Times*, 22 August 1919.

37. *Ibid.*

38. *Ibid.*

39. *Ibid.*

40. *Ibid.*

41. Irving Cheek, "Negro Lynched in Franklin County," Raleigh *News and Observer*, 22 August 1919. To achieve the greatest shock value, the body was stripped and castrated. For most of the day the body hung from the tree near a main highway, where hundreds including women and children drove from the surrounding area to view the body.

42. "Solicitor Starts Lynching Probe," *Franklin Times*, 24 August 1919.

43. *Ibid.*

44. *Ibid.* and "Walter Tyler Is Lynched on a Public Highway Near Louisburg," *Franklin Times*, 22 August 1919.

45. "Powell Green Lynched," *Franklin Times*, 2 January 1919.

46. *Ibid.*

47. "Six Witnesses Fail to Implicate Any of Lynch Party," Raleigh *News & Observer*, 29 December 1919.

48. "Powell Green Lynched," *Franklin Times*, 2 January 1919.

49. "Within Hours After Negro Kills Franklinton White Man, Mob Lynches Slayer," Raleigh *News & Observer*, 28 December 1919.

50. *Ibid.*

51. "Six Witnesses Fail to Implicate Any of Lynching Party," Raleigh *News & Observer*, 29 December 1919.

52. "Within Hours After Negro Kills Franklinton White Man, Mob Lynches Slayer," Raleigh *News & Observer*, 28 December 1919.

53. "Powell Green Lynched in Franklinton," *New York World*, 29 December 1919; and Charles Jones, interview by author, Norlina, North Carolina, 7 June 2002.

54. *Ibid.*

55. *Ibid.*

56. "Bickett Denounces Lynchers of Green; Effort to Punish Them Crucified the Elementary Principle of Justice," Savannah *Morning News*, 29 December 1920.

57. "Outsider Linked Up with Lynching," Raleigh *News & Observer*, 31 December 1919.

58. *Ibid.*

59. "Lynch Negro for Assault on Young Girl at Roxboro," Raleigh *News & Observer*, 8 July 1920.

60. *Ibid.*

61. "Declare Roach Innocent of Crime for Which He Was Lynched," *Baltimore Commonwealth*, 13 August 1920.

62. "Race Riot at Roxboro," *Boston Daily Globe*, 24 October 1896.

63. *Ibid.*

64. *Ibid.*

65. *Ibid.*

66. "Declares Roach, Innocent of the Crime for Which He Was Lynched," *Baltimore Commonwealth*, 13 August 1920.

67. "Lynching Epidemic Causes Alarm and Indignation Among Southern Whites," *Norfolk Journal and Guide*, 24 July 1920.

68. *Ibid.*

69. James Weldon Johnson to Governor Thomas W. Bickett, 8 July 1920, Governor Walter Bickett Collection, General Correspondence, North Carolina State Archives, Raleigh North Carolina.

70. J.M. Avery, president of the Durham NAACP, to Walter White, Assistant Secretary of NAACP, 13 July 1920, Papers of the National Association for the Advancement of Colored People (NAACP) Anti-Lynching Files, North Carolina, C-363, Manuscript Division, Library of Congress.

71. "Lynch Negro for Assault on Young Girl at Roxboro," Raleigh *News & Observer*, 8 July 1920.

72. Walter Bickett to Jas. W. Johnson, 13 July 1920, Governor Walter Bickett Collection, General Correspondence, North Carolina State Archives, Raleigh, North Carolina.

73. "Lynch Negro for Assault on Young Girl at Roxboro," Raleigh *News & Observer*, 8 July 1920.

74. "Lynch Probe in Person County Stops Abruptly," Raleigh *News & Observer*, 15 July 1920.

75. *Ibid.*

76. *Ibid.*

77. *Ibid.*

78. Crow, 197.

79. Gavin, 107.

80. Crow, 126.

81. "Two Negroes Shot to Death by Mob as They Ran Toward Woods," Raleigh *News & Observer*, Tuesday, 21 January 1921. It is quite possible NAACP operatives visited Norlina, since after the lynching of Plummer Bullock and Alfred Williams the Raleigh *News & Observer* blamed the ill feeling that led to the lynchings on a negro organizer from Washington, D.C., who had been in the town several times before the riot.

82. "Editorial," *Warren Record*, 4 March 1921.

Chapter 3

1. It is quite possible that Matthew Bullock served in France during World War I.

2. Frank Bullock, interview by Reverend Leon White, June 1991, Oak Level United Church of Christ, Drewy, N.C.; and "Eight Wounded at Norlina Deport Early Sunday Morning," Raleigh *News & Observer*, 24 January 1921.

3. Frank Bullock, interview by Reverend Leon White, June 1991, Oak Level United Church of Christ, Drewy, N.C.

4. Reverend William Bullock and his eleven siblings lived in Batavia, New York, from 1905 to 1916. While in the city, his children had little experience in dealing with Southern Jim Crow customs.

5. "Deported and Perhaps Doomed Unless Ottawa Grants Trial," *Toronto Evening Telegram*, 14 January 1922.

6. With few places to meet, the train depot became a favorite meeting place for African American men.

7. "Eight Wounded in Race Outbreak at Norlina Depot Early Sunday Morning," Raleigh *News & Observer*, 24 January 1921. Whites wounded in the attack included Raby Traylor and his brother Lloyd Traylor, W.J. Upchurch, H.A. Rainey; and H.A. Inscoe. African Americans wounded in the attack included Claude Jones, Jerome Hunter and Robert Moss.

8. *Ibid.*

9. Editors of *Makers of America: Biographies of Leading Men of Thought and Actions, the Men Who Constitute the Bone and Sinew of American Prosperity and Life* (Washington, D.C.: B.F. Johnson, 1915–1917), 567–72.

10. "Colored People Put Little Faith in Gov. Morrison," *Hamilton Spectator*, 21 February 1921.

11. Warrenton had an all black fire department and a black jailer.

12. Warren County Heritage Book Committee, ed., *Warren County Heritage*, 81.

13. *Ibid.*

14. "Two Negroes Shot to Death by Mob as They Ran Toward Woods," Raleigh *News & Observer*, 25 January 1921.

15. *Ibid.* Green's brother was O.C. Green, the owner of the black mortuary.

16. *Ibid.*

17. *Ibid.* Braving the hail of bullets from the mob, the man escaped down a side street. However, it is not known if he was injured.

18. *Ibid.*

19. Death Certificate for Plummer Bullock, 24 January 1921, Registration District 93–8060 No. 302, North Carolina State Board of Health, Bureau of Vital Statistics, vol. 597, 1909–1930; and Death Certificate for Alfred Williams, 24 January 1921, Registration District 93–8060 No. 305, North Carolina State Board of Health, Bureau of Vital Statistics, vol. 597, 1909–1930.

20. "Fourteen Placed in State Prison for Safekeeping," Raleigh *News & Observer*, 25 January 1921. On the day after the lynching, local officials arrested five blacks for carrying firearms.

21. Tasker Polk to Joseph Blount Cheshire, 11 March 1921, Joseph Blount Cheshire Papers, Wilson Library, University of North Carolina, Chapel Hill; and E.W. Baxter to Joseph Blount Cheshire, 23 March 1921, Joseph Blount Cheshire Papers, Wilson Library, University of North Carolina, Chapel Hill.

22. "Mr. Polk Views the Situation," *Warren Record*, 24 February 1921.

23. *Ibid.*

24. *Ibid.*

25. "Good Advice in Right Way," *Warren Record*, 25 February 1921.

26. "Resolutions of Greenwood Baptist Church," *Warren Record*, 4 March 1921. In addition to action by Warrenton's black churches, a host of black leaders issued appeals urging restraint.

27. "Editorial" *Warren Record*, 4 March 1921.

28. Leon White, interview by author, Whitakers, North Carolina, 9 June 2002.

29. Thurston Brown, interview by author, Warrenton, North Carolina, 9 June 2002.

30. Although the exact method Bullock used to make his escape is unknown, the presence of a record snowfall undoubtedly aided his escape.

31. "Police Seeking Young Bullock, Whereabouts Not Known," Batavia *Evening News*, 5 February 1921; and "Bullock Fleeing from Angry Mob," Batavia *Evening News* 30 January 1921.

32. "Resolute Fight to Hold Negro Under Our Flag," *Toronto Globe*, 19 January 1922. After two unsuccessful attempts, he gained entry by pretending to be a member of a group of black churchgoers.

Chapter 4

1. "Editorial," *Warren Record*, January 28, 1921.

2. Robert D. W. Connor, *NC Rebuilding an Ancient Commonwealth*, vol. 4 (Chicago and New York: American Historical Society, 1929), 25.

3. Eric Anderson, *Race and Politics in North*

Carolina, 1872–1901: The Black Second (Baton Rouge: Louisiana State University Press, 1981), 162–63.

4. This law was extremely important since it meant that children with as little as 12 percent African American blood could be classified as black and forced to attend all-black segregated schools.

5. Woodard was only five years older than Polk. Both men had served as solicitors and in the legislature during the same periods. Moreover, since their homes were only forty miles apart it is highly likely they had additional contact.

6. T.S. Inborden to *The Crisis*, 26 January 1921, Papers of the NAACP Legal Files, Group I, Box 41, Manuscript Division, Library of Congress, Washington, D.C.

7. Rev. J.W.M to James Weldon Johnson, 17 February 1921, Papers of the NAACP Legal Files, Group I, Box 41, Manuscript Division, Library of Congress, Washington, D.C.

8. "Mr. Polk Views the Situation," *Warren Record*, 25 February 1921.

9. "Editorial," *Warren Record*, 28 January 1921.

10. Jerome Hunter Description, Register of Prisoners 1884–1955, Records of the North Carolina State Highway and Public Works Commission, Prison Department, North Carolina State Archives, Raleigh North Carolina.

11. "Negro Gets Eight Years in Prison," Raleigh *News & Observer*, 26 May 1921. Charlie Smith was not tried since he was ill with tuberculosis and was not expected to live.

12. *Ibid.*

13. "Hunter Gets Eight Years," *Warren Record*, 27 May 1921.

14. *Ibid.*

15. "Negro Gets Eight Years in Prison; Six Other Blacks Implicated in Norlina Riot Case Get a Year Each," Raleigh *News & Observer*, 26 May 1921. After serving eight years in prison, Jerome Hunter moved to New York where he died in the early 1970s. James Hunter served one year on the chain gang and also moved to New York; according to family members he died in the mid-1980s. As for the other men, they disappeared after they served their prison sentences.

Chapter 5

1. The Fugitive Slave Law of 1850 required that only a sworn affidavit was needed to claim blacks who were thought to be runways. The apprehended individual had no right to trial by jury, nor could the fugitive present any testimony that challenged their capture.

2. Robin W. Winks, *The Blacks in Canada: A History* (Montreal: McGill-Queens University Press, 1997), 134.

3. Anna Henderson letter to W.E.B. Du Bois, Ottawa, Canada, 16 January 1922, NAACP Legal Files Group I, Box 41, Manuscripts Division, Library of Congress, Washington, D.C.

4. "Bullock Must Return to the United States," *Hamilton Spectator*, 18 January 1922.

5. "Counsel Engaged to Defend Matt Bullock, Arrested at Hamilton Who Fears Lynching," Toronto *Evening Telegram*, 13 January 1922. Only thirty-eight at the time, Treleaven had a distinguished record as an attorney. After graduation from Osgood Hall in 1908, his quick wit and penchant for detail caught the eye of prominent attorney, S.D. Bigger, who made him a junior partner in his law firm. Over the next decade, Treleaven gained a reputation as a defender of the working-man by aiding poor European immigrants and assisting blacks. *City of Hamilton Scrapbook*, compiled by Special Collections Department, Hamilton Public Library: Hamilton, Ontario, 2001, vol. 3, 16.

6. J.D. Howell to NAACP, 7 March 1922, NAACP Legal Files, Group 1, Box D-41, Manuscript Division, Library of Congress, Washington, D.C.

7. J.D. Howell telegram to J. Weldon Johnson, 12 January 1921, NAACP Legal Files, Group 1, Box D-41, Manuscript Division, Library of Congress, Washington, D.C.

8. AM Henderson to W.E.B. Du Bois, 13 January 1922, NAACP Legal Files, Group 1, Box D-41, Manuscript Division, Library of Congress, Washington, D.C.

9. Mildred Dawson to James Weldon Johnson, 6 February 1921 NAACP Legal Files, Group 1, Box D-41, Manuscript Division, Library of Congress, Washington D.C; and Frank Mickey to Edward Mickey, 2 March 1921 NAACP Legal Files, Group 1, Box D-41, Manuscript Division, Library of Congress, Washington, D.C.

10. The NAACP was also heavily involved in defending suspects in the Elaine Arkansas case.

11. Phillip Dray, *At the Hands of Persons Unknown: The Lynching of Black America* (New York: Modern Library, 2003), 263–66.

12. James W. Johnson letter to Mr. Wickersham, 4 February 1922, NAACP Legal Files, Group 1, Box D-41, Manuscript Division, Library of Congress, Washington, D.C.

13. Since Bullock had spent much of his life in the Buffalo suburb of Batavia, New York, many people knew his family, and few were prepared to see him meet the fate of Plummer.

14. Marshall Brown letter to Robert W. Bagnall, 29 December 1922, NAACP Legal Files, Group 1, Box D-41, Manuscript Division, Library of Congress, Washington, D.C.

15. *Ibid.*

16. "Bullock Must Return to the United States," *Hamilton Spectator*, 18 January 1922; "Sees No Hope for Bullock if Sent Back," *Toronto Globe*, 20 January 1922; "2nd Monster Mass Meeting Called to Aid Matthew Bullock, Local Branch NAACP Appeals to Governor to Prevent Extradition," *Buffalo Booster*, 26 January 1922; "Lynching," *Hamilton Herald*, 20 January 1922; "Bullock to Have Fair Trial," *Washington Bee*, 21 January 1922; and "Congressman Dyer and Walter White Address Large Crowd Last Week," *Washington Tribune*, 25 March 1922.

17. Sandra Wilson, *In Search of Democracy: The NAACP Writing of James Weldon Johnson, Walter*

White and Roy Wilkins (1920–1977) (New York: Oxford University Press, 1999), 46.

18. "F.F. Treleaven to Confer with King's Cabinet," *Hamilton Spectator*, 23 January 1922; and "Sees No Hope for Bullock If Sent Back," *Toronto Globe*, 20 January 1922.

19. "Sees No Hope for Bullock If Sent Back," *Toronto Globe*, 20 January 1922.

20. Amelia Anderson letter to Mary White Ovington, 26 January 1922, NAACP Legal Files, Group 1, Box D-41, Manuscript Division, Library of Congress, Washington, D.C.

21. *Ibid.*

22. Joyce Ross, *J.E. Spingarn and the Rise of the NAACP 1911–1923* (New York; Viking Press, 1982), 60.

23. "Third Annual Session of the National Race Congress Hold Enthusiastic Opening," *Washington Bee*, 11 October 1919.

24. *Ibid.*

25. *Ibid.*

26. *Ibid.*

27. John H. Finley, *Dictionary of African-American Biography* (New York: Scribner's, 1928), 2758.

28. Elliott P. Skinner, *African-Americans and U.S. Policy Toward Africa 1850–1924* (Washington, D.C.: Howard University Press, 1992), 412.

29. "The National Race Congress," *Washington Bee*, 13 October 1917.

30. R.L. Vann was editor of the Pittsburgh *Courier*, Nan H. Burrough was local leader of black women's groups and I.N. Ross was an AME bishop.

31. "The Race Congress," *Washington Bee*, 24 August 1918.

32. "The National Race Congress Collected Over Two Thousand Dollars; No Report Made," *Washington Bee*, 3 January 1920.

33. "The Financial Secretary for the Riot Funds Speaks; The Report Doesn't Report," *Washington Bee*, 10 January 1920.

34. *Ibid.*

35. Since AME ministers made up a large contingent of the NRC's membership, it is quite possible that J.D. Howell was a member or was familiar with NRC leaders and programs.

36. "National Race Congress of America," *Washington Bee*, 14 May 1921.

37. "Deportation of Bullock Ordered by D.H. Reynolds," *Hamilton Herald*, 18 January 1922.

38. John Weaver, "Black Man, White Justice: The Extradition of Matthew Bullock, an African American Residing in Ontario, 1922," *Osgood Hall Law Journal* 34 (Winter 1996): 639.

39. "Matthew Bullock Stays in Canada, Wins His Freedom by Good Record," *Toronto Globe*, 27 January 1922; and "Bullock Is Free Once More," *Hamilton Herald*, 28 January 1922.

40. "Assistance Was Appreciated by Bullock Family," *Hamilton Spectator*, 30 January 1922.

Chapter 6

1. Matthew Bullock, Extradition Application, 19 January 1922, NAACP Legal Files, Group 1, Box D-41, Manuscript Division, Library of Congress, Washington, D.C.

2. Jeffrey J. Crow, Paul D. Escott and Flora J. Hatley, *A History of African-Americans in North Carolina* (Raleigh: North Carolina Department of Cultural Resources, 2002), 112.

3. Crow, 112.

4. *Ibid.*, 113.

5. *Ibid.*

6. Nathaniel F. Magruder, "The Administration of Governor Cameron Morrison of North Carolina 1921–1925" (Ph.D. diss., University of North Carolina, 1968), xx.

7. *Ibid.*

8. *Ibid.*

9. *Ibid.*, 344.

10. On several occasions fugitives were kidnapped by bounty hunters and retuned to the United States without the benefit of a trial.

11. "Sleuth Trailed Bullock," *Toronto Evening Telegram*, 18 February 1922.

12. U.S. Department of State, "Webster-Ashburton Treaty," 9 August 1842, *United States Treaties etc. 1841–1845.*

13. Harry Fletcher to Cameron Morrison, 24 January 1922, Papers of the NAACP. Part 7, The Anti-Lynching Campaign 1912–1955, Series A, Anti-Lynching Investigative Files, 1912–1953, reel 15, Perkins Library, Duke University, and Weaver, 646. During the John Anderson case, Canadian courts rejected the concept of double criminality; however, in later cases Canadian courts upheld double criminality.

14. H.P Fletcher to Jose de Olivares, 21 February 1922, Papers of the NAACP. Part 7, The Anti-Lynching Campaign 1912–1955, Series A, Anti-Lynching Investigative Files, 1912–1953, reel 15. Perkins Library, Duke University.

15. Telegram: Fletcher to Morrison, 18 February 1922, Papers of the NAACP. Part 7, The Anti-Lynching Campaign, 1912–1955. Series A, Anti-Lynching Investigative Files, 1912–1953, reel 15. Perkins Library, Duke University.

16. Patrick Brode, *The Odyssey of John Anderson* (Toronto: University of Toronto Press, 1989), 1–119.

17. *Ibid.*, 32.

18. *Ibid.*

19. "Negro Fire Bug Caught," *Durham Daily Sun*, 23 July 1902; "Rogers' Case Now Goes to Courts," *Boston Guardian*, 30 August 1902; and "In Darkest Boston," Raleigh *News & Observer*, 19 August 1902.

20. "Rogers' Case Now Goes to Courts," Boston, *Guardian*, 30 August 1902.

21. *Ibid.*

22. "In Darkest Boston," Raleigh *News & Observer*, 19 August 1902.

23. *Ibid.*

24. "Negro Fire Bug Caught," *Durham Daily Sun*, 23 July 1902; and "Rogers' Case Now Goes to Court," Boston *Guardian*, 30 August 1902; and "In Darkest Boston," Raleigh *News & Observer*, 19 August 1902.

25. "Rogers Case Goes to Court," Boston *Guardian*, 30 August 1902.

26. "The Monroe Roger Case," *Charlotte Observer*, 1 September 1902.

27. "U.S. Asks Canada to Hand Him Over," *Hamilton Herald*, 18 February 1922.

28. "American Sleuths Trail Bullock to Hiding Place," *Toronto Evening Telegram*, 18 February 1922.

29. "Asserts Lynching Is Misunderstood," *Hamilton Spectator*, 22 February 1922.

30. *Ibid.*; "Fair Trial for Bullock is Promised by Governor," *Toronto Evening Telegram*, 20 February 1922; and "Lynching Only Killing of a Criminal," *Chicago Whip*, 25 February 1922.

31. "Negro Rapist Get Usual Treatment at Hands Maddened Men," *Kinston Free Press*, 15 August 1921.

32. "Negro Lynched by Mob at Pittsboro Early on Sunday," Raleigh *News & Observer*, 19 September 1921.

33. "Negro Rapist Get Usual Treatment at Hands Maddened Men," *Kinston Free Press*, 15 August 1921.

34. *Ibid.*

35. *Ibid.*

36. *Ibid.*

37. *Ibid.*

38. *Ibid.*

39. "Negro Lynched by Mob at Pittsboro Early on Sunday," Raleigh *News & Observer*, 19, September 1921.

40. *Ibid.*

41. *Ibid.*

42. *Ibid.*

43. *Ibid.*

44. *Ibid.*

45. Walter White to Amelia Anderson, February 20, 1922, Papers of the NAACP. Part 7, The Anti-Lynching Campaign, 1912–1955. Series A, Anti-Lynching Investigative Files, 1912–1953, reel 15. Perkins Library, Duke University.

46. White's threat led to a series of letters between the NAACP to J.D. Howell and W.H. Jernigan of the NRC. Since the NAACP's investment was minimal and the potential benefits great, White had little choice but to remain an active participant in the case.

47. Walter White to R. McCants Andrews, 20 February 1922, and R. McCants Andrews to Walter White, 18 February 1922, Papers of the NAACP. Part 7, The Anti-Lynching Campaign, 1912–1955. Series A, Anti-Lynching Investigative Files, 1912–1953, reel 15. Perkins Library, Duke University.

48. "Another Adjournment in the Bullock Case," *Hamilton Herald*, 24 February 1924.

49. *Ibid.*

50. Transcript of Hearing, 24 February 1924, Matthew Bullock Case, Canadian Department of Justice, series A-5, vol. 993. Public Archives of Canada.

51. J.D. Olivares telegram to Secretary of State, 28 February 1922, and opinion of C.W. Bell, 28 February 1922, Papers of the NAACP. Part 7, The Anti-Lynching Campaign, 1912–1955. Series A, Anti-Lynching Investigative Files, 1912–1953, reel 15. Perkins Library, Duke University.

52. *Ibid.*

53. W. Carr to A. Halstead, 2 February 1922. Matthew Bullock Case, Canadian Department of Justice, series A-5, vol. 993. Public Archives of Canada.

54. S.J. Dickson to Albert Caudron, 24 February 1922. Matthew Bullock Case, Canadian Department of Justice, series A-5, vol. 993. Public Archives of Canada.

55. Nathaniel Fuqua Magruder, "The Administration of Governor Cameron Morrison of North Carolina, 1921–1925" (Ph.D. diss. University of North Carolina, 1968), 3.

56. Hugh Lefler, *North Carolina: History, Geography, Government* (New York: Harcourt, Brace & World, 1959), 373.

57. Magruder, 3.

58. D.L. Corbitt, ed., *Public Papers and Letters of Cameron Morrison* (Raleigh: Edwards & Broughton Company State Printers, 1927), xxxiv.

59. "North Carolina State Bonds, Mississippi State Bonds," *New York Times*, 23 May 1911. Although the North Carolina legislature repudiated the bonds as Reconstruction-era fraud, investment houses nonetheless recognized the bonds as legitimate. When North Carolina refused to honor the bonds, investment houses refused to extend credit to the state.

60. "Andrews, Edward L. Telegram for the Council of Foreign Bondholders," *New York Times*, May 1923.

61. "Defaulting American States," *London Daily Telegram*, 2 May 1911.

62. Cecil K. Brown, *The State Highway System of North Carolina* (Chapel Hill: University of North Carolina Press, 1931), 124.

63. *Ibid.*, 125.

64. Cameron Morrison to Fletcher, February 24, 1922, Papers of the NAACP. Part 7, The Anti-Lynching Campaign, 1912–1955. Series A, Anti-Lynching Investigative Files, 1912–1953, reel 15. Perkins Library, Duke University.

65. "Bullock Free Man Again; No Witnesses Appeared," Toronto *Evening Telegram*, 3 March 1922.

66. E.J. Newcombe to C. Snider, 20 April 1922. Matthew Bullock Case, Canadian Department of Justice, series A-5, vol. 993. Public Archives of Canada; and E.J. Newcombe letter to Mr. Narroway, 29 August 1922. Matthew Bullock Case, Canadian Department of Justice, series A-5, vol. 993. Public Archives of Canada.

67. Collin Snider to Newcombe, 25 April 1922. Matthew Bullock Case, Canadian Department of Justice, series A-5, vol. 993. Public Archives of Canada.

Chapter 7

1. "Southern Negro Granted Freedom by Judge Snider," *Hamilton Spectator*, 3 March 1922.

2. Furnifold Simmons led the push by the Democratic Party to establish white supremacy in North Carolina. Simmons later became the leader of North Carolina's Democratic Party.

3. Max Abernethy, "Morrison Has Last Say Bullock Affair," *Kinston Free Press* 4 March 1922; and "Morrison Declares Bullock's Release a Blow to Justice," Raleigh *News & Observer*, 4 March 1922.

4. *Ibid.*

5. "Ku Klux After Negro Bullock," *Charlotte Observer*,18 March 1922. Arthur Talmage Abernethy was pastor of the First Christian Church of Asheville.

6. *Ibid.*

7. Arthur Abernethy, *The Jew a Negro, Being a Study of the Jewish Ancestry from an Impartial Standpoint* (Moravian Falls, N.C.: Dixie Publishing, 1910), 11.

8. "The Roaring 20s and the Roots of American Fascism, Part 5: Preachers & Klansmen," <http://www.spiritone.com/~gdy52150/1920sp5.html>(2001–2004), Glen Yeadon.

9. "Secrets of the Ku Klux Klan Exposed," *New York World*, 6 September 1921.

10. *Toronto Star*, 13 March 1922.

11. The Ku Klux Klan underwent a dramatic revival in North Carolina under the leadership of Judge Henry Grady. By 1922 the organization enrolled more than 10,000 members.

12. Howell refused to reveal the country Bullock entered.

Chapter 8

1. R.D.W. Conner, *North Carolina: Rebuilding an Ancient Commonwealth, 1584–1924* (Chapel Hill: University of North Carolina Press, 1929), 562.

2. *Ibid.*

3. "Brutal Criminal Assault Upon Graham Women," *Greensboro Patriot*, 16 July 1920.

4. "Machine Guns Guard Negroes in Alamance Jail," *Gaston Gazette*, 19 July 1920.

5. "Shoot and shoot straight for prisoners protection orders Governor Bickett," Norfolk *Journal and Guide*, 24 July 1920.

6. "Recent Shooting of Graham Citizens by Durham Militiamen," Raleigh *News & Observer*, 20 July 1920.

7. "Governor Orders Inquiry Made of Troops Conduct," Raleigh *News & Observer*, 23 July 1920.

8. *Ibid.*

9. *Ibid.*

10. *Ibid.*

11. *Ibid.*

12. "Machine Gunmen Defend Actions," *Kingsport Times*, 6 August 1920.

13. "Concerted Plan to Attack Graham Jail, He Declares," Raleigh *News & Observer*, 3 August 1920.

14. *Ibid.*

15. *Ibid.*

16. "Three Men Saved from Mob by Governor Bickett Freed by Court," *New York Age*, 2 October 1920.

17. Grand Jury Indictment, North Carolina versus John Jeffress. Alamance County Minute Docket, Superior Court Vol. 12–14, 1920–1926, Microfilm, North Carolina State Archives, Raleigh, North Carolina; and "Court Ready for Trial But Crowd Refused to Wait," Raleigh *News & Observer*, 26 August 1920.

18. *Ibid.*

19. *Ibid.*

20. *Ibid.*

21. "Angry Mob Storms Building to Get Negro Prisoners," Raleigh *News & Observer*, 3 December 1920.

22. *"Ibid.*

23. "Wayne County Folk Invoke Lynch Law for Negro Slayer," *Kinston Free Press*, 12 January 1916; "Negro Slayer Lynched by Mob," Raleigh *News & Observer*, 13 January 1916; "Could Have Been Averted," Wilmington *Morning Star*, 14 January 1916; "Mob Lynches JNO Richards At Goldsboro," Wilmington *Morning Star*, 13 January 1916; and "Goldsboro Quiet After Lynching," Raleigh *News & Observer*, 14 January 1916.

24. *Ibid.*

25. "Judge Calvert Fixes Sentence at Four Years," Wilmington *Morning Star*, 19 February 1921.

Chapter 9

1. "Judge Sinclair Expected to Join Gilliam in Investigation," Raleigh *News & Observer*, 3 April 1925.

2. "Philadelphia Traveling Salesman Arrested in Edenton on Charge of Criminal Assault on Local Girl," Williamston *Enterprise*, 27 March 1925.

3. "Judge Sinclair," Raleigh *News & Observer*, 3 April 1925.

4. "Needleman Still in Serious Condition at Washington Is Friendly to Williamston," Williamston *Enterprise*, 3 April 1925.

5. "Judge Sinclair," Raleigh *News & Observer*, 3 April 1925.

6. *Ibid.*

7. *Ibid.*

8. *Ibid.*

9. "Needleman Still in Serious Condition at Washington is Friendly to Williamston," Williamston *Enterprise*, 3 April 1925.

10. "Sinclair Expected to Join Gilliam in Investigation," Raleigh *News & Observer*, 3 April 1925.

11. "Needleman Accuses D. Griffin; Dramatic Scene When Victim Says—That's the Man," Williamston *Enterprise*, 7 May 1925.

12. *Ibid.*

13. *Ibid.*

14. *Ibid.*

15. "Needleman Gives Pathetic Account of Brutal Attack," Raleigh *News & Observer*, 8 May 1925.

16. *Ibid.*

17. "Gurkin Tells His Side of the Crime; Put Entire Responsibility for Crime on Dennis Griffin," Williamston *Enterprise*, 10 May 1925.

18. "Dramatic Scene," Williamston *Enterprise*, 7 May 1925.

19. *Ibid.*

20. "Governor Ignores Martin Sheriff in Offering Reward," Raleigh *News & Observer*, 4 April 1925.

21. *Ibid.*

22. Undoubtedly, Mclean was aware of the case of Leo Frank. Only ten years earlier the lynching of Frank and the failure of Georgia to prosecute his murderers led many Northern industrialists to shun Georgia. It is highly probably that Mclean feared a similar outcome if he failed to vigorously prosecute those responsible for mutilating Needleman.

23. "Three Men Arrested Suspected of Being Members of Mob," *Tarboro Southerner*, 31 March 1925; and Ferrnie Sparrow & Effie Griffin Marriage License, Martin County Licenses 1921–1927, vol. 7, 26 March 1925, Microfilm, North Carolina State Archives, Raleigh, North Carolina.

24. Ferrnie Sparrow & Effie Griffin Marriage License. The couple married at her parents' home several hours after the assault on Needleman.

25. *North Carolina v. Joe Needleman*, Grand Jury Minutes, 4 May 1924, Martin County Minute Docket, vol. 10. 1924–1930, Microfilm, North Carolina State Archives, Raleigh, North Carolina. Stone was born in England. He immigrated to United States in 1908.

26. "Grand Jury Shows Quick Action, Charge by Judge Sinclair is Model for Conciseness," Williamston *Enterprise*, 5 May 1925.

27. "Hear Needleman Case at Special Term in May," Raleigh *News & Observer*, 10 April 1925.

28. "Grand Jury Shows Quick Action, Charge by Judge Sinclair is Model for Conciseness," Williamston *Enterprise*, 5 May 1925.

29. "Tommy Lilley Shoots Self with Small Caliber Rifle, Not Expected to Recover," Williamston *Enterprise*, 5 May 1925.

30. "Grand Jury Shows Quick Action, Charge by Judge Sinclair is Model for Conciseness," Williamston *Enterprise*, 5 May 1925.

31. "Gurkin Tells His Story of Crime, Puts Entire Responsibility for Crime on Dennis Griffin," Williamston *Enterprise*, 7 May 1925.

32. *Ibid.*

33. *Ibid.*

34. "Needleman Accuses D. Griffin; Dramatic Scene When Victim Says— That's the Man," Williamston *Enterprise*, 7 May 1925.

35. "Needleman Points Out Griffin as the Man That Mutilated Him," *Tarboro Southerner*, 8 May 1925.

36. "Needleman Accuses D. Griffin," Williamston *Enterprise*, 7 May 1925.

37. "Griffin Denies Everything. Claims He Was Not in Mob That Mutilated Needleman," Williamston *Enterprise*, 8 May 1925. Kinston is located fifty miles south of Williamston. Considering the poor state of North Carolina roads in 1925 a trip between the towns took approximately one-and-a-half to two hours.

38. *Ibid.*

39. *Ibid.*

40. *Ibid.* Robertsonville is located ten miles from Williamston.

41. "Dennis Griffin Attempts Prove Alibi at Trial," *Tarboro Southerner*, 9 May 1925.

42. *Ibid.*

43. *Ibid.*

44. "Griffin Denies Everything," Williamston *Enterprise*, 8 May 1925.

45. "Trial of Alleged Mob Members Nearing Its Close," Greenville *Reflector*, 11 May 1925.

46. *Ibid.*

47. *Ibid.*

48. "Mob Leaders Guilty, Needleman to Go Free, Griffin and Bullock May Get Sentence of Sixty Years," Wilmington *Morning Star*. 13 May 1925.

49. *Ibid.*

50. *Ibid.*

51. *Ibid.*

52. "Dennis Griffin Gets 30 Years," Williamston *Enterprise*, 11 May 1925.

53. "Leader of Williamston Mob Is Given Sentence of Thirty Years in State Penitentiary," Raleigh *News & Observer*, 14 May 1925.

54. "Leader of Williamston Mob Is Given Sentence of Thirty Years in State Penitentiary," Raleigh *News & Observer*, 14 May 1925.

55. "Attorney General Rules That Dennis Griffin Can Be Released Under Bond," Williamston *Enterprise*, 26 May 1925.

56. "Kinston People Trying to Aid Young Sparrow," *Gastonia Gazette*, 18 December 1926.

57. "Federal Officers on the Way to Williamston to Serve Summonses," *Washington Daily News*, 28 July 1927. After his escape, Bullock was never recaptured.

58. "Needleman Enters Suit for $100,000 Against Mutilators," Williamston *Enterprise*, 29 July 1927.

59. "Defendants in Needleman Suit File Their Answer in Washington Federal Court," Williamston *Enterprise*. 26 August 1927.

60. *Ibid.*

61. "Needleman's Suit for $100,000 Ended," Statesville *Landmark*, 2 July 1928; and "Needleman $100,000 Suit is Compromised," *Gastonia Gazette*, 28 June 1928.

62. "Sheriff Takes Negro from City as Big Crowd Begins to Form," *Asheville Citizen*, 20 September 1925.

63. Charlotte is approximately 150 miles from Asheville.

64. "Sheriff Takes Negro from City as Big Crowd Begins to Form," *Asheville Citizen*, 20 September 1925.

65. *Ibid.*

66. *Ibid.*

67. *Ibid.*

68. *Ibid.*

69. *Ibid.*

70. "Convict Eleven of Rushing Jail and Nine Plead Guilty," Raleigh *News & Observer*, 15 November 1925.

Chapter 10

1. William H. Richardson, "No More Lynchings," in Albert Shaw, *The American Review of Reviews* (January-June 1924), 401–404.

2. William Richardson, "North Carolina Crushes Mob Rule," *Dearborn Independent* Magazine (April 1926): 7, 23–24.

3. *Ibid.*

4. "Earp Child Assailant Falls Before Pursuers," *Nashville Graphic*, 4 August 1927.

5. *Ibid.*

6. *Ibid.*

7. *Ibid.*

8. "Mob Trails Man Who Escaped and Then Lynch Him," *Chicago Whip*, 20 August 1927.

9. "Earp Child Assailant Falls Before Pursuers," *Nashville Graphic*, 4 August 1927.

10. "Enraged Sandhill Citizens Pursue Prisoner 75 miles," Raleigh *News & Observer*, 5 August 1922; and "Tourist Shot, Wife Assaulted," Carthage *Moore County News*, 10 August 1922.

11. "Tourist Shot, Wife Assaulted," Carthage *Moore County News*, 10 August 1922.

12. *Ibid.*

13. *Ibid.*

14. "Enraged Sandhill Citizens Pursue Prisoners 75 miles," Raleigh *News & Observer*, 5 August 1922.

15. "Tourist Shot, Wife Assaulted," Carthage *Moore County News*, 10 August 1922.

16. *Ibid.*

17. "Enraged Sandhill Citizens Pursue Prisoners 75 miles," Raleigh *News & Observer*, 5 August 1922.

18. *Ibid.*; and "Tourist Shot, Wife Assaulted," Carthage *Moore County News*, 10 August 1922.

19. *Ibid.*

20. Included in this number was Attorney General James Manning.

21. "Withdraw Troops on Guard at Pen," Raleigh *News & Observer*, 6 August 1922; and Nathaniel Fuqua Magruder, 357.

22. *Ibid.*

23. "Two Negroes Tried on Capital Charge Sentenced to Death," Carthage *Moore County News*, 17 August 1922.

24. *Ibid.*

25. *Ibid.*

26. "Enraged Sand hill Citizens Pursue Prisoners 75 miles," Raleigh *News & Observer*, 5 August 1922; and "Tourist Shot, Wife Assaulted," Carthage *Moore County News*, 10 August 1922.

27. Ben Dixon MacNeil, "Moore County Negroes to Die in Prison September 15," Raleigh *News & Observer*, 16 August 1923.

28. *Ibid.*

29. *Ibid.*

30. *Ibid.*

31. *Ibid.*

32. *Ibid.*

33. *Ibid.*

34. Brundage, 259.

35. Brock Barkley, "Negroes to Get Protection, Says Chief Executive; Trusty System in State Prison May Go–Governor Thinks It Unwise," *Asheville Citizen*, 29 September 1923; and "To Ask Morrison for State Troops," *Hickory Daily Record*, 28 September 1923.

36. "National Guard Units Arrive in Spruce Pine," *Asheville Citizen*, 29 September 1929; and "Deported Negroes to Return to Highway Work Today in Mitchell County Under Guard of Soldiers," Raleigh *News & Observer*, 29 September 1923.

37. "Negro Labor to Work Today in Mitchell County Under Guard of Soldiers," Raleigh *News & Observer*, 29 September 1923; and "Governor to Make No Reports Other Than in the Press," *Asheville Citizen*, 29 September 1923.

38. *Ibid.*

39. *Ibid.*

40. "Negro Eating Crackers When Officers Came," *Asheville Citizen*, 30 September 1923; "Morganton Boys Are at Spruce Pine," Morganton *News Herald*, 4 October, 1923; "Hopes Negro's Capture Will Allay Feelings in Mitchell," Raleigh *News & Observer*, 30 September 1923; and "Goff is Captured, Taken to Raleigh," *Hickory Daily Record*, 1 October 1923.

41. "Goff is Captured, Taken to Raleigh" *Hickory Daily Record*, 1 October 1923. Goss claimed that he had lured the woman out of the house to steal some shoes.

42. *Ibid.*

43. "Threat Against Prison Camp Brings Call for Guardsmen," Raleigh *News & Observer*, 29 September 1923.

44. *Ibid.*

45. "Attempt Made to Have the Mayor of Town Ousted," *Asheville Citizen*, 1 October 1923. Many citizens in Spruce Pine maintained that the mayor was improperly elected since the citizens of Spruce Pine had not voted for him. Several months before the rape the Spruce Pine town council elected the mayor when Chas Patterson, who had been duly elected, won a seat in the House of Representatives.

46. *Ibid.*

47. "Eleven Negroes Return and Are Guarded at Camp," *Asheville Citizen*, 2 October 1923.

48. *Ibid.*

49. Ben Dixon MacNeil, "Sabbath Quiet Pervades the Valleys of Mitchell," Raleigh *News & Observer*, 1 October 1923.

50. *Ibid.*

51. Tom Rusher, *Until He Is Dead* (Boone, N.C.: Parkway Publishers, 2003), 24–25.

52. *Ibid.*

53. *Ibid.*, 25.

54. "Death Penalty Is Imposed on Goss," Raleigh *News & Observer*, 23 October 1923.

55. Oddly enough the neighbor was Alice Thomas's son, Wilburn Thomas.

56. *North Carolina vs. John Goss*, 22 Oct 1923, Mitchell County Clerk of Superior Court, Court Docket 15, Microfilm, North Carolina State Archives, Raleigh, North Carolina, 42.

57. "John Goss Dies Admitting Crime," Raleigh *News & Observer*, 8 December 1923.

58. *Ibid.*

59. "Morganton Girl Died: Negro Slayer Hunted by Mob of 2000 Men," *Burlington Daily Times*, 27 June 1927.

60. "$500 Reward for Capture of Young Girl's Assailant," Gastonia *Daily Gazette*, 22 June 1927.

61. *Ibid.*

62. *Ibid.*

63. *Ibid.*

64. *Ibid.*

65. "Long Hunt for Negro Outlaw Ended Sunday When He Was Shot Down Near Linville Falls," Morganton *News Herald*, 7 July 1927.

66. *Ibid.*

67. *Ibid.*

68. *Ibid.*

69. *Ibid.*

70. *Ibid.*

71. *Ibid.*

72. "Vain Effort Being Made to Discredit Burleson," Morganton *News Herald*, 21 July 1927.

73. *Ibid.*

74. *Ibid.*

75. *Ibid.*

76. *Ibid.*

77. *Ibid.*

78. "Burleson Brings Slander Suit Against Gragg and Dula, Asking Damage to Total $60,000," Morganton *News Herald*, 28 July 1927.

79. "Gregg Offers Apology to Commodore Burleson," Morganton *News Herald*, 4 August 1927.

80. "Burleson Suits Against Gragg and Dula Settled," Morganton *News Herald*, 1 September 1927.

81. "Negro Desperado Kills Three," Statesville *Landmark*, 16 November 1906.

82. Ken Traylor and Delas M. House, *Asheville Ghosts and Legends* (Asheville: Haunted America, 2006), 62.

83. *Ibid.*

84. "Mob Riddled Him," *Chillicothe Constitution*, 16 November 1906.

85. "The Men Shot Will Harris," Statesville *Landmark*, 20 November 1906.

86. "Jury Thanks the Lynchers," *Los Angeles Times*, 17 November 1906.

Chapter 11

1. John Bell, *Hard Times: The Beginning of the Great Depression in North Carolina 1929–1933* (Raleigh: North Carolina Office of Archives and History, 1982), 8.

2. Anita Price Davis, *North Carolina During the Great Depression: A Documentary Portrait of a Decade* (Jefferson, N.C.: McFarland, 2003), 34.

3. "Seven Men Accused in Gastonia Killing of Woman Striker," *New York Times*, 16 September 1929.

4. *Ibid.*

5. "Negro Arrested Here Upon Alleged Confession to Killing White Man," *Wilmington Star*, 20 January 1930.

6. *Ibid.*

7. "Both Sides Scout Points as Testimony in Begun in English Murder Case," *Wilmington Star*, 10 July 1930.

8. "Mob Effort Frustrated by Prisoner's Removal from Kenansville Jail," *Wilmington Star*, 21 January 1930.

9. "Stephen English Held for Murder of His Young Wife," *Wilmington Star*, 7 March 1930.

10. *Ibid.*

11. "26 Years Ago Today They Strung Oliver Moore from a Pine Tree," Tarboro *Weekly Southerner*, 20 August 1952.

12. Clifford Young, "A Case Study of the Tarboro Lynching" (M.A. Thesis, University of North Carolina, 1931), 45.

13. "Oliver Moore Assailant of Two White Girls at Tobacco Barn Has Been Arrested," Tarboro *Weekly Southerner*, 21 August 1930.

14. "Negro Lynched in Wilson County Early Tuesday by Crowd of 200 Masked Men," Raleigh *News & Observer*, 19 August 1930.

15. *Ibid.*

16. Young, 48.

17. "Negro Lynched in Wilson County Early Tuesday by Crowd of 200 Masked Men," Raleigh *News & Observer*, 19 August 1930.

18. "Women, Children, Turn Lynching into a Picnic," *The Afro-American*, 30 August 1930.

19. "Resources of Entire State Behind Investigation of Lynching of Negro Man," Tarboro *Daily Southerner*, 20 August 1930.

20. "Morbid Crowd Swarms Around Body of Negro Lynched by Mob," Raleigh *News & Observer*, 20 August 1930.

21. *Ibid.*

22. Young, 49.

23. "Morbid Ground Swarms Around Bloody Body of Negro Lynched by Mob," Raleigh *News & Observer*, 20 August 1930.

24. *Ibid.*

25. Young, 60.

26. *Ibid.*, 56

27. *Ibid.*

28. E. Turney Cobb, "Race Relations in Edgecombe County, North Carolina 1700–1975" (Honors Thesis, University of North Carolina, 1975), 55.

29. Young, 56–57.

30. "A Problem for the Negro to Solve," *Rocky Mount Telegram*, 12 August 1931.

31. Letter to the Editor, *Rocky Mount Telegram*, 22 August 1931.

32. *Ibid.*

33. C.F. Rich to NAACP, 5 February 1931, Papers of the NAACP. Part 7, The Anti-Lynching Campaign 1912–1955, Series A, Anti-Lynching Investigative Files, 1912–1953, reel 15. Perkins Library, Duke University. Rocky Mount is fifteen miles from Tarboro.

34. *Ibid.*

35. *Ibid.*

36. *Ibid.*

37. Letter from H.K. William to Tyre Taylor, Secretary to Governor Gardner, 25 August 1930. Papers of Governor O. Max Gardner, General Cor-

respondence, North Carolina State Archives, Raleigh, North Carolina.

38. There was considerable evidence that the governor, like many whites, considered Moore was guilty of the crime.

39. Delegation headed by the Rev. T.A. Powers to Lawrence A. Oxley, State Director Division of Negro Welfare, 5 September 1933. Papers of Governor John Christopher Blucher Ehringhaus, Gen. Correspondence, North Carolina State Archives, Raleigh, North Carolina.

40. *Ibid.*

41. *Ibid.* During this exchange he wounded Piner's wife.

42. *Ibid.*

43. *Ibid.*

44. *Ibid.*

45. *Ibid.*

46. *Ibid.*

47. C.G. Powell to the Sheriff of Pender County, 1 September 1933. Papers of Governor John Christopher Blucher Ehringhaus, Gen. Correspondence, North Carolina State Archives, Raleigh, North Carolina.

48. At the time of the assault Kellum was fifty-five years old and was best known as a real estate attorney. He later became solicitor for New Hanover and Pender counties.

49. Transcript of Dock Rogers' Hearing, 8 September 1933, Papers of Governor John Christopher Blucher Ehringhaus, Gen. Correspondence, North Carolina State Archives, Raleigh, North Carolina, 1.

50. *Ibid.*, 58–78.

51. *Ibid.*, 59; and "Inquiry Fails to Disclose Names of Negro's Slayers in Pender County Lynching," Wilmington *Morning Star*, 3 September 1933.

52. *Ibid.*

53. "Negro's Death Being Probed by Solicitor," Wilmington *Morning Star*, 3 September 1933.

54. Transcript of Dock Rogers' Hearing, 8 September 1933, Papers of Governor John Christopher Blucher Ehringhaus, Gen. Correspondence, North Carolina State Archives, Raleigh, North Carolina, 51.

55. *Ibid.*

56. *Ibid.*, 73.

57. *Ibid.*

58. *Ibid.*, 74.

59. *Ibid.*

60. Woodus Kellum to Governor Ehringhaus, 22 November 1933, Papers of Governor John Christopher Blucher Ehringhaus, Gen. Correspondence, North Carolina State Archives, Raleigh, North Carolina.

61. *Ibid.*

62. "Charles G. Stokes 67 Decapitated," *Franklin Times*, 9 August 1935.

63. *Ibid.*

64. *Ibid.*

65. Curtis Todd, Secretary Raleigh Branch of NAACP, to Governor J.C. Ehringhaus, 30 July 1935, Papers of Governor John Christopher Blucher Ehringhaus, Gen. Correspondence, North Carolina State Archives, Raleigh, North Carolina.

66. NAACP Report on Sweat Ward's Death, 30 July 1935, Papers of the NAACP. Part 7, The Anti-Lynching Campaign 1912–1955, Series A, Anti-Lynching Investigative Files, 1912–1953, reel 15. Perkins Library, Duke University.

67. *Ibid.*

68. *Ibid.*

69. *Ibid.*

70. *Ibid*

71. Dray, 342.

72. Tony W. Catledge, "Sitting in Josiah's Chair," *Biblical Recorder*, 7 November 2005, 2.

73. *Ibid.*

74. *Ibid.*

75. "Bonus Action Sped to Bar Long Fight on Lynching Bill," *New York Times*, 26 April 1935.

76. Walter White, *A Man Called White: The Autobiography of Walter White* (Athens: University of Georgia Press, 1995), 169–70.

77. "Bonus Action Sped to Bar Long Fight on Lynching Bill," *New York Times*, 26 April 1935; and "Votes Bars Shelving of Anti-Lynching Bill," *New York Times*, 27 April 1935.

78. Robert Zangrando, *The NAACP Crusade Against Lynching, 1909–1950* (Philadelphia: Temple University Press, 1980), 141–42.

79. "Lynch & Anti-Lynch," *Time*, 26 April 1937.

Chapter 12

1. "African American History," Microsoft® Encarta® Online Encyclopedia 2007, http://encarta.msn.com© 1997–2007 Microsoft Corporation.

2. *Ibid.*

3. *Historical Chronology of the North Carolina State Bureau of Investigation, 1937–2005* (Raleigh, N.C: North Carolina State Bureau of Investigation, 2007).

4. Investigations of Lynchings, etc, Public Law 114–15, North Carolina General Statutes (1937).

5. "Negroes Flogged by Band in Wayne: Five Unmasked White Men Take Prisoners from Jail: Inquiry Opens Tuesday," Raleigh *News & Observer*, 10 February 1939.

6. "Crowd Threatens Gil; Attacker," Raleigh *News & Observer*, 16 August 1941.

7. "Violence Flares in Alleged Rape," Raleigh *News & Observer*, 17 August 1941.

8. *Ibid.*

9. *Ibid.*

10. *Ibid.*

11. *Ibid.*

12. *Ibid.*

13. "Jury May Receive Mob Case Today," Raleigh *News & Observer*, 23 April 1942; and "Five Persons Convicted in Person Mob Cases," Raleigh *News & Observer*, 24 April 1942.

14. *Ibid.*

15. "Four Are Held in Gun Death," *Charlotte Observer*, 14 April 1941.

16. *Ibid.*

17. "4 Plead Guilty in the Melker Case," *Gastonia Daily Gazette*, 23 April 1941.

18. "Four Are Held in Gun Death," *Charlotte Observer*, 14 April 1941.

19. "Four Held for Melker Death," *Gastonia Daily Gazette*, 15 April 1941.

20. *Ibid.*

21. *Ibid.*

22. "4 Get Pen for Melker Death," *Gastonia Daily Gazette*, 24 April 1941.

23. "Protest Story Negro Lynching," *Gastonia Daily Gazette*, 3 July 1941.

24. "Not Surprising," *Gastonia Daily Gazette*, 17 July 1941; "Time for a Retraction," *Gastonia Daily Gazette*, 10 July 1941; "What Is a Lynching," *Asheville Citizens*, 15 July 1941; and "Negro Editor Condemns Lynching Report," *Gastonia Gazette*, 21 July 1941.

25. "Bush Escapes in Lynch Puzzle: Surrenders to FBI Rushed to Raleigh," *Raleigh Times*, 26 May 1947.

26. "Seven Rich Square Men Charged with Kidnapping," Weldon *Roanoke News*, 29 May 1947.

27. "Negro Jailed for Burglary Assault," *Jackson News*, 1 May 1947; and "Second Man Held in Rich Square Case," *Jackson News*, 2 May 1947.

28. "Police Chief Gives Story of Attack on White Woman," *Raleigh Times*, 25 June 1947.

29. *Ibid.*

30. *Ibid.*

31. According to Outland, Cherry told him that Boone initiated the crime.

32. "Negro Jailed for Burglary Assault," *Jackson News*, 1 May 1947.

33. "Armed Mob Flee with Prisoner," *Raleigh Times*, 23 May 1947.

34. "Lynching Feared in Eastern North Carolina County: Accused Negro Seized by Mob," Burlington *Daily Times-News*, 23 May 1947.

35. "Mob Takes Negro from Northampton Jail: Unarmed Jailer Turns Keys Over to Masked Crowd," Statesville *Daily Record*, 23 May 1947.

36. "Lynching Feared in Eastern North Carolina County: Accused Negro Seized by Mob," Burlington *Daily Times-News*, 23 May 1947.

37. *Ibid.*

38. State Bureau of Investigation, Report of Godwin Bush Abduction, 5 August 1947, Papers of Governor Gregg Cherry, Northampton County Lynching, North Carolina State Archives, Raleigh, North Carolina.

39. *Ibid.*

40. *Ibid.*

41. "Think New Fled from Masked Men," *New York Times*, 25 May 1947.

42. "Negro Escapes Mob, Belief: Searches Fail to Locate Body," *Raleigh Times*, 24 May 1947.

43. "Attempted Attack on Lasker Woman: 3 Arrests Made," *Jackson News*, 5 June 1947.

44. State Bureau of Investigation, Report of Godwin Bush Abduction, 5 August 1947, Papers of Governor Gregg Cherry, Northampton County Lynching, North Carolina State Archives, Raleigh, North Carolina; and "Surrenders to FBI," *Raleigh Times*, 26 May 1947.

45. "Mobs in Lynch Puzzle," *Raleigh Times*, 28 May 1947.

46. "Governor Pledges Jackson Mob Will Be Caught and Prosecuted," *Kingsport News*, 27 May 1947.

47. *Ibid.*

48. *Ibid.*

49. State Bureau of Investigation, Report of Godwin Bush Abduction, 5 August 1947, Papers of Governor Gregg Cherry, Northampton County Lynching, North Carolina State Archives, Raleigh, North Carolina.

50. *Ibid.*

51. *Ibid.*

52. *Ibid.*

53. *Ibid.*

54. "May Never Be Caught," *Raleigh Times*, 27, May 1947.

55. *Ibid.*

56. *Ibid.*

57. *Ibid.*

58. *Ibid.*

59. *Ibid.*

60. "Officer's Wife Praises Mob," Raleigh *Carolinian*, 7 June 1947.

61. "Attempted Attack on Lasker Woman 3 Arrests Made," *Jackson News*, 5 June 1947; and "Another Attack in Northampton: Three Men Jailed in New Case," *Raleigh Times*, 2 June 1947.

62. *Ibid.*

63. *Ibid.*

64. "Attempted Attack on Lasker Woman: Three Arrests Made," *Jackson News*, 5 June 1947; and "Another Attack in Northampton: Three Men Jailed in New Case," *Raleigh Times*, 2 June 1947. To prevent the outbreak of further violence the men were taken to Halifax for safekeeping.

65. "Selection of Jury Begins in Jackson Assault Trial," *Raleigh Times*, 24 June 1947.

66. "Jury Sentences Cherry to Die August 29: Negro Found Guilty on Both Charges of 1st Degree Burglary," *Jackson News*, 26 June 1947.

67. *Ibid.*

68. *Ibid.*

69. *Ibid.*

70. *Ibid.*

71. *Ibid.*

72. "Cherry is Convicted, Sentenced to Death," *Raleigh Times*, 24 June 1947. Amazingly Cherry was the only witness called by the defense.

73. *Ibid.*

74. "Admit Guilt," *Raleigh Times*, 28 June 1947.

75. "Northampton Jury Fails to Indict Accused: Governor Cherry Orders Hearing," Weldon *Roanoke News*, 7 August 1947.

76. *Ibid.*

77. *Ibid.* After the trial Bush moved to New York and died in 1973.

78. *Ibid.*

79. Laura Wexler, *Fire in a Canebrake: The Last Mass Lynching in America* (New York: Scribner's, 2003), 13–14.

80. *Ibid.*, 57–60.

81. *Ibid.*, 22, 57–60.

82. *Ibid.*, 60.

83. *Ibid.*, 61–64.

84. *Ibid.*
85. *Ibid.*, 66.
86. *All Things Considered*, "FBI Re-Examines 1946 Lynching Case," National Public Radio, 25 July 2006.
87. "Cherry Demands Justice in Bush Case: To Reopen Jail Raid," *Raleigh Times*, 6 August 1947.
88. "Attempted Lynching of Negro Leads to Re-Arrest of Seven," Council Bluff *World News*, 17 August 1947.
89. Unsigned Letter to Governor Cherry, 9 August 1947, Papers of Governor R. Gregg Cherry, Northampton County Lynching, North Carolina State Archives, Raleigh, North Carolina.
90. Donald Nunnery to Governor Cherry, 2 August 1947, Papers of Governor R. Gregg Cherry, Northampton County Lynching, North Carolina State Archives, Raleigh, North Carolina.
91. *Ibid.*
92. L. Barnwell Washington to R. Gregg Cherry. 7 August 1947, Papers of Governor R. Gregg Cherry, Northampton County Lynching, North Carolina State Archives, Raleigh, North Carolina.
93. Leonard Cally Moore to R. Gregg Cherry, 4 September 1947, Papers of Governor R. Gregg Cherry, Northampton County Lynching, North Carolina State Archives, Raleigh, North Carolina.
94. "Jailer Arrested in Lynch Attempt," *Long Beach Press*, 3 September 1947.
95. "Grand Jury Again Declines to Hold Northampton Pair," Burlington *Daily News*, 14 September 1947.
96. *Ibid.*

Chapter 13

1. David Bryon Davis, *Inhumane Bondage: The Rise and Fall of Slavery in the New World* (New York: Oxford University Press, 2006), 196.
2. W. Fitzhugh Brundage, *Lynching in the New South: Georgia and Virginia 1880–1930* (Champaign: University of Illinois Press, 1993), 4.
3. *Ibid.*, 6.
4. "The Barbarous South," London *Pall Mall Gazette*, 17 Jan. 1922.
5. "Editorial," Toronto *Globe*, 16 January 1922.
6. "Prove That You Will Not Lynch Bullock: Canada," *Chicago Defender*, 28 January 1922.

Appendix I: Notes

1. "Lynch Law," Greensboro *North State*, 16 June 1881.
2. *Ibid.*
3. *Ibid.*
4. *Ibid.*; and "Horrible Crime in Rockingham," Statesville *Landmark*, 10 June 1881.
5. "Lynch Law," Greensboro *North State*, 16 June 1881.
6. *Ibid.*
7. "A Ravisher Lynched," *Atlanta Constitution*, 20 October 1881.
8. *Ibid.*
9. *Ibid.*
10. "A Ravisher Lynched," Statesville *Landmark*, 21 October 1881.
11. "A Ravisher Lynched," *Atlanta Constitution*, 20 October 1881.
12. *Ibid.*
13. *Ibid.*
14. "Bloodshed and Vengeance," Statesville *Landmark*, 19 October 1883.
15. *Ibid.*
16. *Ibid.*
17. *Ibid.*
18. *Ibid.*
19. "Homicide and Lynching in Rowan," *Salisbury Watchman*, 15, November 1883.
20. *Ibid.*
21. *Ibid.*
22. *Ibid.*
23. *Ibid.*
24. *Ibid.*
25. "Lynching at Monroe," Raleigh *News & Observer*, 6 March 1885.
26. *Ibid.*
27. *Ibid.*
28. *Ibid.*
29. *Ibid.*
30. *Ibid.*
31. "Lynch Law," *Chatham Record*, 1 October 1885.
32. *Ibid.* and Patrick Huber, "Caught Up in the Violent Whirlwind of Lynching: The 1885 Quadruple Lynching in Chatham County, North Carolina," *North Carolina Historical Review*, vol. LXXV, no. 7 (April 1998): 155.
33. "Lynch Law," *Chatham Record*, 1 October 1885; and "Four Lynched," Raleigh *News & Observer*, 30 September 1885.
34. Patrick Huber, "Caught Up in the Violent Whirlwind of Lynching: The 1885 Quadruple Lynching in Chatham County, North Carolina," *North Carolina Historical Review*, vol. LXXV, no. 7 (April 1998): 155.
35. *Ibid.*
36. Huber, 155.
37. "Lynch Law," *Chatham Record*, 1 October 1885; and "Four Lynched," Raleigh *News & Observer*, 30 September 1885.
38. *Ibid.*
39. *Ibid.*; and Huber, 150.
40. *Ibid.*
41. *Ibid.*
42. *Ibid.*
43. *Ibid.*
44. Huber, 144.
45. "Four Lynched," Raleigh *News & Observer*, 30 September 1885.
46. *Ibid.*
47. *Ibid.*; and Huber, 144–45.
48. *Ibid.*
49. "Four Lynched," Raleigh *News & Observer*, 30 September 1885.
50. *Ibid.*
51. *Ibid.*

52. Raleigh *News & Observer*, 7 July 1885; Raleigh *News & Observer* 8 July 1885; and Huber, 149.
53. "Four Lynched," Raleigh *News & Observer*, 30 September 1885.
54. Raleigh *News & Observer*, 16 July 1885; and Raleigh *News & Observer*, 11 July 1885.
55. Huber, 153.
56. *Ibid.*
57. Raleigh *News & Observer*, 16 July 1885. When the note was found to be a fraud, all of the men were released.
58. Huber, 154.
59. *Ibid.*
60. "Four Lynched," Raleigh *News & Observer*, 30 September 1885.
61. "The Lynching of Bud Mebane," Raleigh *News & Observer*, 6 October 1894.
62. *Ibid.*
63. *Ibid.*
64. *Ibid.*
65. *Ibid.*
66. "John Lee Lynched," *Rockingham Rocket*, 24 December 1885.
67. *Ibid.*
68. *Ibid.*
69. *Ibid.*
70. *Ibid.*
71. *Ibid.*
72. *Ibid.*
73. *Ibid.*
74. *Ibid.*
75. "Judge McRae and the Late Lynching," *Rockingham Rocket*, 24 December 1895.
76. "Found Dead on the Road," *Rockingham Rocket*, 26 November 1885.
77. "The Testimony of Miss Mahala C. Sapp—The Dead Man—The Coroner's Jury—Adjourned to September 3rd," *Greensboro Morning News*, 26 August 1887.
78. "Attempted Outrage," *Greensboro North State*, 1 September 1887; and *Ibid.*
79. "The Lynching," *Greensboro North State*, 1 September 1887.
80. "Attempted Outrage," *Greensboro North State*, 1 September 1887.
81. "Lynched," *Greensboro Morning News Extra*, 26 August 1887.
82. *Ibid.*
83. *Ibid.*
84. *Ibid.*
85. "North Carolina Lynching," *San Antonio Daily Ledger*, 28 January 1888; and "Three Men Lynched: The Great Tragedy in Plymouth North Carolina," *Atlanta Constitution*, 29 January 1888.
86. *Ibid.*
87. *Ibid.*
88. "Three Men Lynched: The Great Tragedy in Plymouth North Carolina," *Atlanta Constitution*, 29 January 1888.
89. *Ibid.*
90. *Ibid.*
91. "Judge Lynch at Washington," *New Bern Daily Journal*, 14 March 1888.
92. "Assassination in North Carolina," Raleigh *News & Observer*, 16 August 1880.
93. *Ibid.*
94. William S. Powell, *Dictionary of North Carolina Biography*, vol. II. (Chapel Hill: University of North Carolina Press, 1979), 376.
95. *Ibid.*
96. *Ibid.*
97. *Ibid.*
98. "Horrible Murder," *Washington Progressive*, 8 May 1888.
99. *Ibid.*
100. *Ibid.*
101. *Ibid.*
102. *Ibid.*
103. "No Mercy from the Mob: A Negro Quickly Hanged for His Crime," *New York Times*, 16 July 1888.
104. *Ibid.*
105. *Ibid.*
106. *Ibid.*
107. *Ibid.*
108. "Hung from a Railroad Bridge," *Morganton Star*, 12 September 1889.
109. *Ibid.*
110. "Two Men Strung Up by Mob at Morganton," Raleigh *News & Observer*, 12 September 1889.
111. "Hung from a Railroad Bridge," *Morganton Star*, 12 September 1889.
112. *Ibid.*
113. *Ibid.*
114. *Ibid.*
115. "The Murder of Farmer Philbeck of Cleveland County Under Arrest," Statesville *Landmark*, 6 December 1888; and "The Murderers," *Charlotte Chronicle*, 2 December 1888.
116. *Ibid.*
117. *Ibid.*
118. "The Murder of Farmer Philbeck of Cleveland County Under Arrest," Statesville *Landmark*, 6 December 1888.
119. *Ibid.*
120. "The Murderers," *Charlotte Chronicle*, 2 December 1888.
121. "Lynching a Desperado," *New York Times*, 4 December 1888.
122. *Ibid.*
123. "Bob Berrier Lynched," *Davidson Dispatch*, 16 October 1889.
124. "Devotional Exercises at a Lynching," *Chicago Daily Tribune*, 23 October 1889.
125. "Bob Berrier Lynched," *Davidson Dispatch*, 16 October 1889.
126. *Ibid.*
127. *Ibid.*
128. *Ibid.*
129. *Ibid.*
130. *Ibid.*
131. Raleigh *News & Observer*, 24 October 1889.
132. "Lynched at Selma," Raleigh *News & Observer*, 27 May 1890.
133. "J.E. Starling Lynched," *Smithfield Herald*, 31 May 1890.
134. "Lynched at Selma," Raleigh *News & Observer*, 27 May 1890.

135. "Lynched in His Cell," *Washington Post*, 25 December 1890.

136. *Ibid.*

137. "Was Lynched," *Asheville Citizen*, 25, September 1891.

138. *Ibid.*

139. *Ibid.*

140. *Ibid.*

141. *Ibid.*

142. *Ibid.*

143. *Ibid.*

144. "The Coroner's Inquest," *Asheville Citizen*, 26 September 1891.

145. *Ibid.*

146. *Ibid.*

147. "Asheville Lynchers Go Free," Statesville *Landmark*, 5 November 1891.

148. "Lynching in Bladen," Wilmington *Morning Star*, 3 May 1892.

149. *Ibid.*; and "Taken from Jail; and Lynched," *New York Times*, 3 May 1892.

150. *Ibid.*

151. *Ibid.*

152. *Ibid.*

153. "Colored Man Lynched," *Oxford Public Ledger*, 18 November 1892.

154. *Ibid.*

155. *Ibid.*

156. *Ibid.*

157. *Ibid.*

158. *Ibid.*

159. *Ibid.*

160. "Colored Man Lynched," *Oxford Public Ledger*, 18 November 1892.

161. "Lynching at Laurel Hill," Raleigh *News & Observer*, 19 November 1892.

162. "Death of a Brave Officer," *Rockingham Rocket*, 19 November 1892; and "Lynching at Laurel Hill," Raleigh *News & Observer*, 19 November 1892.

163. *Ibid.*

164. *Ibid.*

165. *Ibid.*

166. Charles David Phillips, "Exploring Relations Among Forms of Social Control: The Lynching and Execution of Blacks in North Carolina, 1889–1918," *Law & Society Review*, vol. 21, no. 3 (1987): 361.

167. "State News," Statesville *Landmark*, 8 December 1892.

168. "Double Murder at a Wedding," *Atlanta Constitution*, 19 February 1894.

169. *Ibid.*

170. *Ibid.*

171. *Ibid.*

172. "That Allegheny Lynching," Statesville *Landmark*, 1 March 1899.

173. *Ibid.*

174. "Lyncher to Give State's Evidence," *New York Times*, 15 March 1894.

175. "An Allegheny Lyncher in Danger of Being Lynched," Statesville *Landmark*, 8 March 1894.

176. "A Double Tragedy," *Washington Gazette*, 3 January 1895.

177. "Lynched by a Mob at Idalia," *New Berne Daily Journal*, 28 December 1894.

178. "A Double Tragedy," *Washington Gazette*, 3 January 1895.

179. "Lynched by a Mob at Idalia," *New Berne Daily Journal*, 28 December 1894.

180. "A Double Tragedy," *Washington Gazette*, 3 January 1895.

181. *Ibid.*

182. *Ibid.*

183. *Ibid.*

184. *Ibid.*

185. *Ibid.*

186. "Lynched by a Mob at Idalia," *New Berne Daily Journal*, 28 December 1894.

187. "E.B. Weeks Prominent and Respected Citizen Found Dead," *New Bern Daily Journal*, 10 June 1899.

188. "Dead or Alive," *New Bern Daily Journal*, 15 June 1899.

189. *Ibid.*

190. *Ibid.*

191. *Ibid.*

192. "Patrick Was Lynched," *Portsmouth Herald*, 21 June 1899.

193. "Lynching at Carthage," Statesville *Landmark*, 12 March 1901.

194. *Ibid.*

195. *Ibid.*

196. *Ibid.*

197. "News Tidbits," *Robinsonian*, 15 March 1901.

198. "Lynching in Union County," Statesville *Landmark*, 7 July 1903.

199. "Fiend Pays the Penalty for His Heinous Crime at the End of a Rope," *Charlotte Observer*, 3 July 1903.

200. *Ibid.*

201. *Ibid.*

202. *Ibid.*

203. *Ibid.*

204. *Ibid.*

205. "Same Old Verdict in Osborne Matter," *Charlotte Observer*, 4 July 1903.

206. *Ibid.*

207. "Negro Lynched at Jacksonville," Raleigh *News & Observer*, 7 February 1919.

208. *Ibid.*

209. *Ibid.*

210. *Ibid.*

211. *Ibid.*

212. "Many Chances to Die, Negro Still Lives," Statesville *Landmark*, 12 January 1922; and "Negro Once Freed by Mob Fears Rope Will Be Fate," *Kinston Free Press*, 11 January 1922.

213. *Ibid.*

214. *Ibid.*

215. "Daniel Petteway is Again at Liberty: Escapes Hospital," *Kinston Free Press*, 16 January 1922.

216. "Hanged in Barn Police Theory," *Charlotte Observer*, 5 July 1929.

217. "Mecklenburg Has Mystery Murder," Statesville *Landmark*, 8 July 1929.

218. "Hanged in Barn Police Theory," *Charlotte Observer*, 5 July 1929.

219. *Ibid.*

220. "Mecklenburg Has Mystery Murder," Statesville *Landmark*, 8 July 1929.

221. "Grand Jury to Hear of Case," *Charlotte Observer*, 8 July 1929; and "Death Caused by a Broken Neck," Statesville *Landmark*, 7 July 1929.

222. *Ibid.*

223. "Grand Jury to Hear of Case," *Charlotte Observer*, 8 July 1929.

224. *Ibid.*

225. "Busy Ten-Day Session by Grand Jury," *Charlotte Observer*, 19 July 1929.

226. "Mecklenburg Has Mystery Murder," Statesville *Landmark*, 8 July 1929.

227. *Ibid.*

228. *Ibid.*; and "Negro's Body to be Dug Up in Clue Hunt," *Charlotte Observer*, 6 July 1929.

229. *Ibid.*

230. *Ibid.*

231. *Ibid.*

232. "Negro's Body to be Dug Up in Clue Hunt," *Charlotte Observer*, 6 July 1929.

233. Doral Apel, *Imagery of Lynching: Black Men, White Woman and the Mob* (Camden, N.J.: Rutgers University Press, 2004), 60.

234. "A Fiend and Propaganda," *Kingsport Times*, 6 February 1930.

Bibliography

Interviews

Brown, Thurston, retired mortician. Interview by author, 9 June 2002, Warrenton, NC. In possession of author, Rocky Mount, NC.

Bullock, Frank. Interview by the Reverend Leon White, June 1991. In possession of the Reverend Leon White and Oak Level Christian Church, Drewy, NC.

Bullock, India. Interview by the Reverend Leon White, June 1991. In possession of the Reverend Leon White and Oak Level Christian Church, Drewy, NC.

Jones, Charles, farmer. Interview by author, 7 June 2002, Norlina, NC. In possession of author, Rocky Mount, NC.

White, Leon. Pastor Oak Level Christian Church. Interview by Author, 9 June 2002, Franklinton Center, Whitakers, NC.

Archival Materials

Alfred Williams Death Certificate: Warren County Vital Statistics Records, North Carolina Department of Archives and History, Raleigh.

Cameron Morrison Papers: North Carolina Department of Archives and History, Raleigh.

Ferrnie Sparrow & Effie Griffin Marriage License: Martin County Licenses 1921–1927, vol. 7, March 26, 1925, North Carolina Department of Archives and History, Raleigh.

John Christopher Blucher Ehringhaus Papers: North Carolina Department of Archives and History, Raleigh.

Joseph Blount Cheshire Papers: Wilson Library Special Collections, University of North Carolina.

Locke Craig Papers: North Carolina Department of Archives and History, Raleigh.

Matthew Bullock Extradition File: Canadian Department of Justice, Canadian National Archives, Ottawa, Canada.

NAACP (National Association for the Advancement of Colored People) Papers. Manuscript Division, Library of Congress.

North Carolina v. John Goss: Mitchell County Minute Docket, Superior Court, vol. 14, 1921–1923, North Carolina Department of Archives and History, Raleigh.

North Carolina v. John Jeffress: Alamance County Minute Docket, Superior Court, vol. 12–14, 1920–1926, North Carolina Department of Archives and History, Raleigh.

O. Max Gardner Papers: North Carolina Department of Archives and History, Raleigh.

Plummer Bullock Death Certificate: Warren County Vital Statistics Records, North Carolina Department of Archives, Raleigh.

R. Gregg Cherry Papers: North Carolina Department of Archives and History, Raleigh.

Register of Prisoners 1884–1955: Records of the North Carolina State Highway and Public Works Commission, Prison Department, North Carolina Department of Archives and History, Raleigh.

Walter Bickett Papers: North Carolina Department of Archives and History, Raleigh.

Warren County Jury Roster, Norlina Riot, Warren County Clerk of Court, Warrenton NC.

Government Documents

Congressional Record, 56th Congress, 1st session, 1365, U.S. Government Printing Office.

U.S. Department of State, "Webster-Ashburton Treaty." 9 August 1842, *Unites States Treaties etc. 1841–1845.*

U.S. Senate, *Senate Executive Documents*, no. 16,

191

Part 2, 41st Congress, 3rd Session. 1871. U.S. Government Printing Office.

State Laws/General Statutes

Investigations of Lynchings, etc, Public Law 114–15, North Carolina General Statutes, 1937.

Newspapers

Asheville Citizen, 1891, 1922–1947
Atlanta Constitution, 1881
Baltimore Afro-American, 1922
Baltimore Commonwealth, 1920
Batavia Evening News, 1922
Boston Daily Globe, 1896
Boston Guardian, 1902
Buffalo Booster, 1922
Burlington Daily Times-News, 1947
Carolina Times, 1930
Carthage Moore County News, 1922
Charlotte Chronicle, 1888
Charlotte Observer, 1890–1947
Chatham Record, 1885
Chicago Defender, 1921–1922
Chicago Daily Tribune, 1889
Chicago Whip, 1922
Chillicothe Constitution, 1906
Council Bluff World News, 1947
Davidson Dispatch, 1889
Durham Daily Sun, 1902
Durham Sun, 1921–1922
Franklin Times, 1919–1935
Gaston Gazette, 1920–1925
Gastonia Daily Gazette, 1941
Goldsboro Daily Messenger, 1868
Goldsboro Weekly Argus, 1902–1912
Greensboro Patriot, 1920
Greensboro News, 1921–1947
Greensboro Morning News, 1887
Greensboro North State, 1881, 1887
Greenville Reflector, 1925
Greenwood Commonwealth, 1930
Hamilton Herald, 1922
Hamilton Spectator, 1922
Hickory Daily Record, 1923
Jackson News, 1947
Kingsport Times, 1920–1947
Kinston Free Press, 1902–1923
Littleton News Reporter, 1904
London Evening Free Press, 1922
London Daily Telegram, 1911
London Pall Mall Gazette, 1922
Long Beach Press, 1947
Lumberton Robinsonian, 1901
Morganton Star, 1889
Morganton News Herald, 1923–1928

Morning New Bernian, 1921
Murfreesboro Roanoke News, 1947
Nashville Graphic, 1914–1923
New Orleans Times-Picayune, 1930
New Bern Daily Journal, 1888, 1894, 1899
New Bern Weekly Journal, 1905
New York Age, 1920
New York Times, 1865–1935
New York Tribune, 1921–1922
New York World, 1919–1922
Norfolk, Journal and Guide. 1920–1947
Norlina Headlight, 1914, 1915, 1924
Oxford Public Ledger, 1892
Portsmouth Herald, 1899
Raleigh State Chronicle, 1887–1888
Raleigh Carolinian, 1931–1947
Raleigh Daily Standard, 1868–1869
Raleigh Progressive Farmer, 1902
Raleigh News & Observer, 1914–1925
Raleigh Times, 1900–1948
Rock Hill Evening Herald, 1931–1965
Rockingham Rocket, 1885
Rocky Mount Telegram, 1915–1925
Salisbury Watchman, 1883
San Antonio Daily Ledger, 1888
Savannah Morning News, 1920–1921
Smithfield Herald, 1890
Statesville Daily Record, 1947
Statesville Landmark, 1928
Tarboro Southerner, 1898
Tarboro Weekly Southerner, 1952
Star of Zion, 1915–1925
Toronto Christian Guardian, 1922
Toronto Evening Telegram, 1922
Toronto Globe, 1922
Warren Record, 1900–1922
Washington Bee, 1916–1920
Washington Gazette, 1895
Washington Tribune, 1921–1922
Washington Daily News, 1925–1929
Washington Post, 1890
Washington Progress, 1888, 1920
Weldon Roanoke News, 1947
Williamston Enterprise, 1925
Wilmington Morning Star, 1916–1925
Wilmington Star, 1891
Windsor Border Cities Star, 1922
Winston Salem Journal, 1918–1922

Books

Abernethy, Arthur. The Jew a Negro, Being a Study of the Jewish Ancestry from an Impartial Standpoint. Moravian Falls, NC: Dixie Publishing, 1910.

Akers, Monte. Flames After Midnight: Murder, Vengeance and the Desolation of a Texas Com-

munity. Austin: University of Texas Press, 1999.

Alexander, Roberta Sue. *North Carolina Faces the Freedmen: Race Relations During Presidential Reconstruction 1865–1867*. Durham: Duke University Press, 1985.

Allen, James, et al. *Without Sanctuary: Lynching Photography in America*. Santa Fe: Twin Palms Publishers, 2000.

Anderson, Eric. *Race and Politics in North Carolina, 1872–1901: The Black Second*. Baton Rouge: Louisiana State University Press, 1981.

Apel, Dora. *Imagery of Lynching: Black Men, White Women and the Mob*. Camden, N.J.: Rutgers University Press, 2004.

Ayers, Edward. *The Promise of the New South: Life After Reconstruction*. New York: Oxford University Press, 1992.

_____. *Vengeance and Justice: Crime and Punishment in the Nineteenth Century South*. New York: Oxford University Press, 1984.

Barleau, Arthur, and Florette Henri. *The Unknown Soldier: African-Americans in World War I*. New York: Da Capo Press, 1996.

Bates, Beth. *Pullman Porters and the Rise of Protest Politics in Black America, 1925–1945*. Chapel Hill: University of North Carolina Press, 2000.

Bell, John. *Hard Times: The Beginning of the Great Depression in North Carolina*. Raleigh: North Carolina Office of Archives and History, 1928.

Bennett, Lerone. *Before the Mayflower: A History of Black America*. Chicago: Johnson Publishing, 1987.

Blassingame, John. *The Slave Community*. New York: Oxford University Press, 1979.

Blaustein, Albert, and Robert L. Zangrando. *Civil Rights and the New Negro*. Chicago: Northwestern University Press, 1991.

Brode, Patrick. *The Odyssey of John Anderson*. Toronto: University of Toronto Press, 1989.

Broderick, Francis, and August Meier. *Negro Protest Thought in the Twentieth Century*. New York: Bobbs-Merrill, 1965.

Brown, Cecil. *The State Highway System of North Carolina*. Chapel Hill: University of North Carolina Press, 1931.

Brundage, W. Fitzhugh. *Under the Sentence of Death: Lynching in the South*. Chapel Hill: University of North Carolina Press, 1997.

_____. *Lynching in the New South: Georgia and Virginia, 1880–1930*. Urbana: University of Illinois Press, 1993.

Bumbalough, Barbara F. *Come with Me to Germantown: Ridgeway, North Carolina Revisited*. Warrenton, NC: Record Printing, 1998.

Burnham, Louis. *Behind the Lynching of Emit Louis Till*. New York: Freedom Associates, 1955.

Capeci, Dominic. *The Lynching of Cleo Wright*. Lexington: University of Kentucky Press, 1998.

Carborne, John. *The Civil War in Coastal North Carolina*. Raleigh: North Carolina Department of Cultural Resources, 2000.

Carter, Dan. *Scottsboro: A Tragedy of the American South*. Baton Rouge: Louisiana State University Press, 1969.

Cecelski, David. *Along Freedom Road: Hyde County North Carolina, and the Fate of Black Schools in the South*. Chapel Hill: University of North Carolina Press, 1994.

_____, and Timothy B. Tyson, ed. *Democracy Betrayed: The Wilmington Race Riot of 1898 and Its Legacy*. Chapel Hill: University of North Carolina Press, 1998.

Chadbourn, James H. *Lynching and the Law*. Chapel Hill: University of North Carolina Press, 1933.

Chalmers, David. *Hooded Americanism: The History of the Ku Klux Klan*. Durham: Duke University Press, 1987.

Colburn, David. *Racial Change and Community Studies: St. Augustine, Florida, 1877–1980*. New York: Columbia University Press, 1985.

Cole, Timothy. *The Forest City Lynching of 1900: Populism, Racism, and White Supremacy in Rutherford County, North Carolina*. Jefferson NC: McFarland, 2003.

Collins, Winfred. *The Truth about Lynching and the Negro in the South*. New York: Neale Publishing, 1918.

Conner, R.D.W. *North Carolina: Rebuilding an Ancient Commonwealth 1584–1924*. Chapel Hill: University of North Carolina Press, 1929.

_____, and Clarence Hamilton Poe. *The Life and Speeches of Charles Brantley Aycock*. New York: Doubleday, 1912.

Corbitt, D.L., ed. *Public Papers and Letters of Cameron Morrison: Governor of North Carolina 1921–1925*. Raleigh: Edwards & Broughton Company State Printers, 1927.

Cortner, Richard, *A Mob Intent on Death: The NAACP and the Arkansas Riot Cases*. Middletown, C.T.: Wesleyan University Press, 1988.

Cozart, Leland. *Venture of Faith: The History of Barber-Scotia College 1867–1969*. Concord, NC: Barber-Scotia College, 1972.

Crow, Jeffrey, Paul Escott, and Flora J. Hatley. *A History of African-Americans in North Carolina*. Raleigh: North Carolina Division of Archives and History, 1992 & 2002.

Crow, Jeffrey, and Robert Winters, eds. *The*

Black Presence in North Carolina. Raleigh: North Carolina Museum of History, 1978.

Curriden, Mark, and Leroy Phillips. *Contempt of Court: The Turn-of-the-Century Lynching That Launched a Hundred Years of Federalism.* New York: Faber & Faber, 1999.

Cutler, James. *Lynch Law: An Investigation into the History of Lynching in the United States.* New York: Longman's Greens, 1905.

Davie, Maurice. *Negroes in American Society.* New York: McGraw-Hill, 1949.

Davis, Anita P. *North Carolina During the Great Depression: A Documentary Portrait of a Decade.* Jefferson, NC: McFarland, 2003.

Davis, David B. *Inhumane Bondage: The Rise and Fall of Slavery in the New World.* New York: Oxford University Press, 2006.

Dinnerstein, Leonard. *The Leo Frank Case.* New York: Columbia University Press, 1968.

Downey, Dennis, and Raymond M. Hyser. *No Crooked Death: Coatesville, Pennsylvania and the Lynching of Zachariah Walker.* Urbana: University of Illinois Press, 1991.

Dray, Phillip. *At the Hands of Person Unknown: The Lynching of Black America.* New York: Modern Library, 2003.

Du Bois, W.E.B. *Black Reconstruction in America 1860–1880.* New York: Atheneum, 1992.

Durrill, Wayne. *War of Another Kind: A Southern Community in the Great Rebellion.* New York: Oxford University Press, 1990.

Ebony Pictorial History of Black America, vol. II. Nashville: Southwestern, 1971.

Edmonds, Helen. *The Negro and Fusion Politics in North Carolina: 1894–1901.* Chapel Hill: University of North Carolina Press, 1951.

Ellsworth, Scott. *Death in a Promised Land: The Tulsa Race Riot of 1921.* Baton Rouge: Louisiana State University Press, 1992.

Evans, William McKee. *Ballots & Fence Rails: Reconstruction on the Lower Cape Fear.* Athens: University of Georgia Press, 1995.

Fairclough, Adam. *Race and Democracy: The Civil Rights Struggle in Louisiana, 1915–1972.* Athens: University of Georgia Press, 1995.

Farrell, Harry. *Swift Justice: Murder and Vengeance in a California Town.* New York: St. Martin's Press, 1992.

Fedo, Michael. *The Lynchings in Duluth.* St. Paul: Minnesota Historical Society Press, 2000.

Finley, John. *Dictionary of American Biography.* New York: Scribner's, 1928.

Forner, Eric. *Reconstruction: America's Unfinished Revolution, 1863–1877.* New York: Harper & Row, 1988.

Franklin, John Hope. *The Free Negro in North Carolina, 1790–1860.* Chapel Hill: University of North Carolina Press, 1943.

_____. *Reconstruction After the Civil War.* Chicago: University of Chicago Press, 1961.

_____, and Alfred A. Moss, Jr. *From Slavery to Freedom: A History of African-Americans.* New York: Knopf, 2000.

Frazier, Franklin E. *The Negro Church in America.* New York: Schocken Books, 1974.

Frey, Robert, and Nancy Thompson Frey. *The Silent Damned: The Murder of Mary Phagen and the Lynching of Leo Frank.* New York: Cooper Square Press, 2002.

Gaillard, Frye. *Becoming Truly Free: 300 Years of Black History in the Carolinas, a Charlotte Observer Summary.* Charlotte: Charlotte Observer Publishing, 1985.

Gambino, Richard. *Vendetta: The True Story of the Largest Lynching in U.S. History.* New York: Doubleday, 2000.

Gilmore, Glenda Elizabeth. *Gender and Jim Crow.* Chapel Hill: University of North Carolina Press, 1996.

Ginzburg, Ralph. *One Hundred Years of Lynching.* New York: Lancer Books Classic Press, 1962.

Godwin, John. *Black Wilmington and the North Carolina Way: Portrait of a Community in the Era of Civil Rights Protests.* Lanham, M.D.: University Press of America, 2000.

Goings, Harry. *The NAACP Comes of Age.* Bloomington: Indiana University Press, 1990.

Graham, Hugh, and Ted Robert Gurr. *Violence in America.* New York: Bantam Books, 1969.

Green, Ben. *Before His Time: The Untold Story of Harry T. Moore, America's First Civil Rights Martyr.* New York: Free Press, 1999.

Greenwood, Janet. *Bittersweet Legacy: The Black and White Better Classes in Charlotte, 1850–1910.* Chapel Hill: University of North Carolina Press, 1994.

Hall, Jacquelyn, and James Leloudis. *Like A Family: The Making of a Southern Cotton Mill World.* Chapel Hill: University of North Carolina Press, 1987.

Hamilton, Roulhac J. G. *Reconstruction in North Carolina.* Gloucester, MA: Peter Smith, 1914.

Hanchett, Thomas. *Sorting Out the New South City: Race, Class, and Urban Development in Charlotte, 1875–1975.* Chapel Hill: University of North Carolina Press, 1998.

Harding, Vincent. *There is a River: The Black Struggle for Freedom in America.* New York: Harcourt Brace, 1981.

Harlan, Louis, ed. *The Booker T. Washington Papers,* vol. 3. Urbana: University of Illinois Press, 1974.

Harney, Robert, ed. *Gathering Place: Peoples and Neighbourhoods of Toronto, 1834–1945.* Toronto: Multicultural History Society of Canada, 1985.

Harris, Trudier. *Exorcising Blackness: Historical and Literary Lynching and Burning Rituals.* Bloomington: Indiana University Press, 1984.

Harrison, Alferdteen. *Black Exodus: The Great Migration from the American South.* Jackson: University of Mississippi Press, 1991.

Henri, Florette. *Black Migration: Movement North 1900–1920.* Garden City, N.Y.: Anchor Press, 1975.

Henry-Simmons, Linda, and Phillip Henry. *The Heritage of Blacks in North Carolina.* Charlotte, NC: North Carolina Heritage Foundation, 1990.

Heritage of Warren County. Waynesville, NC: Walsworth Publishing, 2002.

Higginbotham, Evelyn Brooks. *Righteous Discontent: The Women's Movement in the Black Baptist Church.* Cambridge, MA: Harvard University Press, 1993.

Hobbs, S.H. *North Carolina: Economic and Social.* Chapel Hill: University of North Carolina Press, 1930.

Honey, Michael. *Southern Labor and Black Civil Rights: Organizing Memphis Workers.* Urbana: University of Illinois Press, 1993.

Hubbard, Stephen. *Against All Odds: The Story of William Peyton Hubbard, Black Leader and Municipal Reformer.* Toronto: Dundurn Press, 1987.

Hughes, Langston. *Fight for Freedom: The Story of the NAACP.* New York: Norton, 1962.

Ikard, Robert. *No More Social Lynchings.* Franklin, TN: Hillsboro Press, 1997.

Inscoe, John. *Appalachians and Race.* Lexington: University Press of Kentucky, 2001.

Jack, Robert. *History of the NAACP.* Boston: Meador, 1943.

Jakoubek, Robert. *Walter White and the Power of Organized Protest.* Brookfield, CT: Milbrook Press, 1994.

Jordan, William. *Black Newspapers and America's War for Democracy 1914–1920.* Chapel Hill: University of North Carolina Press, 2001.

Justesen, Benjamin. *George Henry White: An Even Chance in the Race of Life.* Baton Rouge: Louisiana State University Press, 2001.

Kantrowitz, Stephen. *Ben Tillman and the Reconstruction of White Supremacy.* Chapel Hill: University of North Carolina Press, 2000.

Kellog, Charles F. *NAACP: A History of the National Association for the Advancement of Colored People.* Baltimore: Johns Hopkins Press, 1967.

Kelly, Robin. *Race Rebels; Culture, Politics and the Black Working Class.* New York: Free Press, 1996.

Kennedy, Louise Venable. *The Negro Peasant Turns Cityward.* New York: AMS Press, 1968.

Klarman, Michael. *From Jim Crow to Civil Rights: The Supreme Court and the Struggle for Racial Equality.* New York: Oxford University Press, 2004.

Kluger, Richard. *Simple Justice.* New York: Random House, 1975.

Kolchin, Peter. *American Slavery 1619–1877.* New York: Hill & Wang, 1979.

La Forest, G.V. *Extradition to and from Canada.* New Orleans: Hauser Press, 1960.

Lawson, John. *A New Voyage to Carolina.* Chapel Hill: University of North Carolina Press, 1967.

Leaders in Education. New York: Science Press, 1941.

Lefler, Hugh. *North Carolina History Told by Contemporaries.* Chapel Hill: University of North Carolina Press, 1934.

_____, and Albert Ray Newsome. *The Growth of North Carolina.* New York: World Book, 1947.

_____, and _____. *North Carolina: History, Geography, Government.* New York: Harcourt, Brace & World, 1959.

Lemmon, Sarah. *North Carolina's Role in the First World War.* Raleigh: North Carolina Department of Cultural Resources, 1975.

Leonard, Stephen. *Lynching in Colorado: 1859–1919.* Boulder: University Press of Colorado, 2002.

Lewis, John. *Walking with the Wind: A Memoir of the Movement.* New York: Simon and Schuster, 1998.

Lincoln, Eric C., and Lawrence H. Mamiya. *The Black Church in the African-American Experience.* Durham, NC: Duke University Press, 1990.

Logan, Frenise A. *The Negro in North Carolina 1876–1894.* Chapel Hill: University of North Carolina Press, 1964.

Lynching Is Wholesale Murder. Association of Southern Women, 1937.

Lyons, James E. *In the Beginning Faith: Oral History of Barber-Scotia College.* Concord, NC: Barber-Scotia College, 1976.

Madigan, Tim. *The Burning: Massacre, Destruction and the Tulsa Race Riot of 1921.* New York: St. Martin's Press, 2001.

Madison, James. *A Lynching in the Heartland: Race and Memory in America.* New York: Palgrave Press, 2003.

Makers of America: Biographies of Leading Men of Thought and Action, the Men Who Consti-

tute the Bone and Sinew of American Prosperity and Life. Washington, DC: B.F. Johnson, 1915–1917.

McGovern, James T. Anatomy of a Lynching: The Killing of Claude Neal. Baton Rouge: Louisiana State University Press, 1982.

Moore, John Hammond. South Carolina in 1880. Orangeburg, SC: Sandlapper Publications, 1989.

Myrdal, Gunnar. An American Dilemma: The Negro Problem and Modern Democracy. New York: Harper & Brothers, 1944.

Newbold, N. Five North Carolina Negro Educators. Chapel Hill: University of North Carolina Press, 1939.

Norrell, Robert. Reaping the Whirlwind: The Civil Rights Movement in Tuskegee. New York: Alfred A. Knopf, 1985, 1998.

North Carolina. Adjutant General. Annual Report of the Adjutant-General of the State of North Carolina for 1923–1924. Raleigh: North Carolina Adjutant General's Department, 1924.

Orr, Oliver. Charles Brantley Aycock. Chapel Hill: University of North Carolina Press, 1961.

Oshinsky, David. Worse Than Slavery: Parchmen Farm and the Ordeal of Jim Crow. New York: Simon and Schuster, 1996.

Ovington, Mary. The Walls Came Tumbling Down. New York: Harcourt Press, 1974.

Paschal, Andrew, ed. A W.E.B. Du Bois Reader. New York: Macmillan, 1971.

Payne, Charles. I've Got the Light of Freedom: The Organizing Tradition and the Mississippi Freedom Struggle. Berkeley: University of California Press, 1995.

Pitre, Merline. In Struggle Against Jim Crow: Lula B. White and the NAACP, 1900–1957. College Station: Texas A&M University Press, 1999.

Powell, William S. Dictionary of North Carolina Biography. Chapel Hill: University of North Carolina Press, 1979.

Powledge, Fred. Free at Last. New York: Harper-Collins, 1991.

Prather, Leon H. We Have Taken a City: Wilmington Racial Massacre and the Coup of 1898. Wilmington, NC: NU World Enterprises, 1984.

Raper, Arthur F. The Tragedy of Lynching. Chapel Hill: University of North Carolina Press, 1933.

Raper, Horace, and Thornton W. Mitchell. The Papers of William Woods Holden. Raleigh: Division of Archives and History, 2002.

Reed, Christopher. The Chicago NAACP and the Rise of Black Professional Leadership 1910–1966. Bloomington: Indiana University Press, 1997.

Rimanelli, Marco, and Sheryl L. Postman, eds. The 1891 New Orleans Lynchings and U.S.-Italian Relations: A Look Back. New York: Peter Lang Publishing, 1992.

Robinson, Armstead, and Patricia Sullivan, eds. New Directions in Civil Rights Studies. Charlottesville: University Press of Virginia, 1991.

Ross, Joyce. J.E. Spingarn and the Rise of the NAACP, 1911–1939. New York: Viking Press, 1982.

Rusher, Tom. Until He Is Dead: Capital Punishment in Western North Carolina History. Boone, NC: Parkway Publishers, 2003.

Salmond, John. Gastonia 1929: The Story of the Loray Mill Strike. Chapel Hill: University of North Carolina Press, 1995.

Seligmann, Herbert. The Negro Faces America. New York: Harper & Brothers, 1920.

Sernett, Milton. Bound for the Promised Land: African-American Religion and the Great Migration. Durham, NC: Duke University Press, 1997.

Shapiro, Herbert. White Violence and Black Response: From Reconstruction to Montgomery. Amherst: University of Massachusetts Press, 1988.

Sharpe, Bill. A New Geography of North Carolina. Raleigh: Sharpe Publishing.

Shay, Frank. Judge Lynch: His First Hundred Years. New York: I. Washburn, 1938.

Sher, Julian. White Hoods: Canada's Ku Klux Klan. Vancouver: New Star Books. 1983.

Sieber, H.A. Holy Ground: Significant Events in the Civil Rights-Related History of the African-American Communities of Guilford County, North Carolina, 1771–1995. Greensboro, NC: Tudor Publications, 1995.

Skinner, Elliott P. African-Americans and U.S. Policy Toward Africa, 1850–1924. Washington, D.C.: Howard University Press, 1992.

Smead, Howard. Blood Justice: The Lynching of Mack Charles Parker. New York: Oxford University Press, 1986.

Stockley, Grif. Blood in Their Eyes: The Elaine Race Massacres of 1919. Fayetteville: University of Arkansas Press, 2001.

Sullivan, Patricia. Days of Hope: Race and Democracy in the New Deal Era. Chapel Hill: University of North Carolina Press, 1995.

Sweet, Frank W. Legal History of the Color Line: The Rise of the One Drop Rule. Palm Coast, F.L.: Backintyme Publishing, 2005.

Taylor, Alrutheus Ambush. The Negro in South Carolina During Reconstruction. Washington,

DC: Association for the Study of Negro Life and History, 1924.

Taylor, Arnold. *Travail and Triumph: Black Life and Culture in the South Since the Civil War.* Westport, CT: Greenwood Press, 1976.

Teatero, William. *John Anderson, Fugitive Slave.* Kingston, ON: Treasure Island Books.

Thorne, J. William. *North Carolina in the 19th Century: The Great Ecclesiastical Trial of J. William Thorne.* Ridgeway, NC: J. William Thorne, 1874.

Tolnay, Stewart, and E.M. Beck. *A Festival of Violence: An Analysis of Southern Lynchings, 1882–1930.* Urbana: University of Illinois Press, 1992.

Traylor, Ken, and Delas M. House. *Asheville Ghosts and Legends.* Asheville, NC: Haunted America, 2006.

Turner, J. Kelly, and J.N.O. Bridgers. *History of Edgecombe County, North Carolina.* Raleigh: Edward & Broughton Printing, 1920.

Tushnet, Mark. *The NAACP's Legal Strategy Against Segregated Education 1950.* Chapel Hill: University of North Carolina Press, 1987.

Tuttle, William. *Race Riot: Chicago in the Red Summer of 1919.* New York: Atheneum, 1974.

Twelvetrees, Harper, ed. *The Story of the Life of John Anderson, the Fugitive Slave.* London: Burns, 1863.

Tyson, Timothy B. *Radio Free Dixie: Robert Williams & the Roots of the Black Power.* Chapel Hill: University of North Carolina Press, 1999.

Wadelington, Charles, and Richard Knapp. *Charlotte Hawkins Brown and Palmer Memorial Institute.* Chapel Hill: University of North Carolina Press, 1999.

Walls, William. *The History of the African Methodist Episcopal Zion Church.* Charlotte, NC: African Methodist Episcopal Zion Publishing House, 1972.

Warren County Heritage Book Committee, eds. *Warren County Heritage.* Waynesville, NC: Warren County Heritage, 2002.

Watson, C.H. *Colored Charlotte.* Charlotte, NC: African Methodist Episcopal Zion Publishing House, 1915.

Weares, Walter B. *Black Business in the South: A Social History of the North Carolina Mutual Life Insurance Company.* Urbana: University of Illinois Press, 1973.

Weaver, John. *The Brownsville Raid.* College Station: Texas A&M University Press, 1992.

Wedin, Carolyn. *Inheritors of the Spirit: Mary White Ovington and the Founding of the NAACP.* New York: Wiley, John, 1998.

Wellman, Manley W. *The County of Warren, North Carolina 1586–1917.* Chapel Hill: University of North Carolina Press, 1959.

Wexler, Laura. *Fire in a Canebrake: The Last Mass Lynching in America.* New York: Scribners, 2003.

White, Walter. *A Man Called White: The Autobiography of Walter White.* Athens: University of Georgia Press, 1995.

_____. *Rope and Faggot: A Biography of Judge Lynch.* Notre Dame: University of Notre Dame Press, 2001.

Whitfield, Stephen. *A Death in the Delta: The Story of Emit Till.* Baltimore: John Hopkins University Press, 1992.

Williams, Lillian. *Strangers in the Land of Paradise.* Bloomington: Indiana University Press, 1999.

Williamson, Joel. *After Slavery: The Negro in South Carolina During Reconstruction, 1867–1877.* Hanover, NH: University Press of New England, 1990.

Wilkins, Roy, and Tom Mathews. *Standing Fast: The Autobiography of Roy Wilkins.* New York: Da Capo Press, 1994.

Wilson, Sandra, ed. *In Search of Democracy: The NAACP Writings of James Weldon Johnson, Walter White and Roy Wilkins (1920–1977).* New York: Oxford University Press, 1999.

Wimberley, Ronald, and Libby Morris. *The Southern Black Belt: A National Perspective.* Lexington: University of Kentucky Press, 1997.

Winks, Robin. *The Blacks in Canada: A History.* Montreal: McGill-Queens University Press, 2nd ed., 1997.

Winston, Robert. *It's a Far Cry.* New York: Henry Holt, 1937.

Wormster, Richard. *The Rise and Fall of Jim Crow.* New York: St. Martin's Press, 2003.

Wright, George. *Life Behind a Veil: Blacks in Louisville, Kentucky, 1865–1930.* Baton Rouge: Louisiana State University Press, 1988.

Wyatt-Brown, Bertram. *Southern Honor: Ethics and Behavior in the Old South.* New York: Oxford University Press, 1982.

Zangrando, Robert. *The NAACP Crusade Against Lynching, 1909–1950.* Philadelphia: Temple University Press, 1980.

Zuber, Richard. *North Carolina During Reconstruction.* Raleigh: Division of Archives North Carolina Department of Cultural Resources, 1969.

Articles

Abrams, Douglas Carl. "Irony of Reform: North Carolina Blacks and the New Deal." *North Carolina Historical Review* 66, no. 2 (April 1989): 149–79.

Alexander, Roberta Sue. "Hostility and Hope: Black Education in North Carolina During Presidential Reconstruction 1865–1867." *North Carolina Historical Review* 55, no. 2 (April 1976): 107–27.

Autrey, Dorothy. "Can These Bones Live: The National Association for the Advancement of Colored People in Alabama, 1918–1930." *Journal of Negro History* 82, no. 1 (Winter 1997): 1–12.

Baldhaber, Michael. "A Mission Unfulfilled: Freedmen's Education in North Carolina, 1865–1870." *The Journal of Negro History* 77 (Fall 1992).

Balonoff, Elizabeth. "North Carolina Legislators in the North Carolina General Assembly." *North Carolina Historical Review* (April 1972).

Beatty, Bess. "Textile Labor in the North Carolina Piedmont: Mill Owner Images and Mill Worker Response, 1830–1900." *Labor History* 25 (Fall 1984): 485–504.

Catledge, Tony W. "Sitting in Josiah's Chair." *Biblical Recorder* (November 2005).

Connor, R.D. "The Ku Klux Klan and Its Operations in North Carolina." *North Carolina University Magazine* 30 (April 1900).

Du Bois, W.E.B. "The Talent Tenth: Memorial Address." In *A W.E.B. Du Bois Reader*, ed. Andrew Paschal, 34–41. New York: Macmillan, 1971.

Eisenberg, Bernard. "Only for the Bourgeois? James Weldon Johnson and the NAACP, 1916–1930." *Phylon* 43, no. 2 (June 1982): 110–25.

Ellis, Mark. "W.E.B. Du Bois and the Formation of Black Opinion in World War I: A Commentary on the Damnable Dilemma." *Journal of American History* 81, no. 4 (March 1985): 1584–90.

Falk, Stanley. "The Warrenton Female Academy of Jacob Mordecai, 1809–1818." *North Carolina Historical Review* 35, no. 3 (July 1958): 281–98.

Ford, Lacy K. "Rednecks and Merchants: Economic Development and Social Tensions in the South Carolina Upcountry, 1865–1900." *Journal of American History* 71 (September 1994): 294–318.

Gavins, Raymond. "Fighting for Civil Rights in the Age of Segregation: The NAACP In North Carolina During the Age of Segregation." In *New Directions in Civil Rights* Studies, ed. Armstead L. Robinson and Patricia Sullivan, 105–25. Charlottesville: University Press of Virginia, 1991.

Goerch, Carl. "Discovering Warren County." *The State* 8, no. 10 (3 August 1940): 1–6.

Gorn, Elliot. "Gouge and Bite, Pull Hair and Scratch: The Social Significance of Fighting in the Southern Backcountry." *American Historical Review* 90 (1985).

Hamilton, Donna Cooper. "The National Association for the Advancement of Colored People and New Deal Reform Legislation: A Dual Agenda." *Social Service Review* 68 (December 1944): 488–503.

Hanchett, Thomas W. "The Rosenwald Schools and Black Education in North Carolina." *North Carolina Historical Review* 65, no. 4 (October 1988): 387–444.

Hepburn, Sharon. "Following the North Star: Canada as a Haven for Nineteenth-Century American Blacks." *Michigan Historical Review* 25 (Fall 1999).

"Historical Chronology of the North Carolina Bureau of Investigation 1937–2005." North Carolina State Bureau of Investigation, Raleigh, North Carolina. 2007.

"Historical Summary of the North Carolina State Bureau of Investigation 1937–Present." North Carolina Department of Justice.

Hopkins, Stella. "Textiles' Dark Legacy." *Business Monday* (24 November 1997): 10D–12D.

Hoveland, Carl, and Robert Sears. "Minor Studies of Aggression: Correlations of Economic Indices with Lynching." *Journal of Psychology* 9 (1940).

Huber, Patrick J. "Caught Up in the Violent Whirlwind of Lynching: The 1885 Quadruple Lynching in Chatham County, North Carolina." *North Carolina Historical Review* 75, no. 2 (April 1998): 135–61.

Inborden, T.S. "Jos. K. Brick Agricultural, Industrial and Normal School." *The American Missionary* 55, no. 3 (July 1901): 142–47.

Inscoe, John. "The Clansmen on Stage and Screen: North Carolina Reacts." *North Carolina Historical Review* (April 1987).

Ireland, Robert. "The Campaign for Good Roads and Good Men." *North Carolina Historical Review* (April 1991).

Jordan, William. "The Damnable Dilemma: African-American Accommodation and Protest During World War I." *Journal of American History* 81, no. 4 (March 1985): 1562–83.

Landon, Fred. "Amhersburg, Terminus of the

Underground Railroad." *Journal of Negro History* 10 (January 1925).

Lawrence, R.C. "Lynchers of the Law." *The State* 12, no. 47 (21 April 1945): 6, 7, 26.

"Lynching & Anti-Lynching" *Time* (26 April 1937).

Meir, August, and John Bracy, Jr. "The NAACP as a Reform Movement, 1909–1965: To Reach the Conscience of America." *Journal of Southern History* 59 (February 1993).

Mobley, Joe. "In the Shadow of White Society; Princeville, a Black Town in North Carolina, 1865–1915." *North Carolina Historical Review* (July 1986).

Moore, Christopher. "The Varieties of Black Experiences: By 1850s, Blacks Were a More Rooted Permanent and Diverse Part of the Canadian Population Than the Fugitive Slave Narratives Might Suggest." *The Beaver: Exploring Canada's History* (June–July 2002).

Olsen, Otto. "The Ku Klux Klan: A Study in Reconstruction Politics and Propaganda." *North Carolina Historical Review* 34 (July 1962): 340–63.

O'Reilly, Kenneth. "The Jim Crow Policies of Woodrow Wilson." *Journal of Blacks in Higher Education* (Autumn 1997).

Phillips, Charles. "Exploring Relations Among Forms of Social Control: The Lynching and Execution of Blacks in North Carolina." *Law & Society Review* 21 no. 3 (1987): 361–73.

Postel, Danny. "The Awful Truth." *The Chronicle of Higher Education* 68 no. 44 (12 July 2002): A14–A16.

Prather, Leon. "We Have Taken a City: A Centennial Essay." In *Democracy Betrayed: The Wilmington Race Riot of 1898 and its Legacy*, ed. David Cecelski and Timothy Tyson, 15–43. Chapel Hill: University of North Carolina Press, 1998.

Richardson, William. "No More Lynchings: How North Carolina Solved the Problem." *The American of Reviews* 69 (January–June 1924): 401–404.

_____. "North Carolina Crushes Mob Rule." *Dearborn Independent* (April 10, 1926).

Rowland, Robin. "With Intent to Kill Matthew Bullock." *Hamilton This Month* (April 1989).

Savitt, Todd. "Training the Consecrated, Skillful, Christian Physician: Document Illustrating Student Life at Leonard Medical School, 1982–1918." *The North Carolina Historical Review* 65, no. 3 (July 1998): 250–77.

Toby, Jeffers. "A History of Blacks in Hamilton." *Hamilton Spectator* (18 February 1993).

Weaver, John. "Black Man, White Justice: The Extradition of Matthew Bullock, an African-American Residing in Ontario, 1922." *Osgood Hall Law Journal* 34, no. 4 (1996): 627–60.

Weber, Ralph. "Riots in Victoria. 1860." *Journal of Negro History* (January 1971).

Wells-Barnett, Ida. "Lynching Law in America." *Arena* (9 January 1909).

Whalen, Robert. "Recollecting the Cotton Mill Wars: Proletarian Literature of the 1929–1931 Southern Textile Strikes." *The North Carolina Historical Review* 65. no. 4 (October 1998): 370–98.

White, George. "The NAACP and Residential Segregation in Louisville, Kentucky, 1914–1917." *Register of the Kentucky Historical Society* 41. no. 2 (1979): 39–53.

"With Intent to Kill Matthew Bullock." *Hamilton This Month* (April 1989).

Web Sources

Handbook of Texas Online, December 10, 2006, http://www.tsha.etwxas.edu/handbook/online/articles/LL/jgll.html.

Norlina Online, 13 April 2005, http://www.norlina.com/history.html.

The Roaring 20s and the Root of American Fascism, Part 5: Preachers & Klansmen, http://www.spiritone.com; http://www.u-s-history.com/pages/h1381.html.

African-American History, Microsoft Encarta Online Encyclopedia 2007, http://encarta.msn.com.

Unpublished Materials

Amick, Dorothy Hayes. "Direct Action by Rock Hill Negroes in Protest Against Segregation, 1957–1962." M.A. Thesis, Winthrop University, 1970.

Andrews, Columbus. "Warren County, North Carolina: Economic, Social, Civic." Ph.D. Thesis, University of North Carolina, 1932.

Baradell, William. "An Analysis of the Coverage Given by Five North Carolina Newspapers of the Three Events in the Civil Rights Movement in the State." M.A. Thesis, University of North Carolina, 1990.

Biggs, Thomas. "Fort Mill: Transition from Farming to a Textile Community, 1880–1920." M.A. Thesis, Winthrop College, 1984.

Bogue, Jesse Parker. "Violence and Oppression in North Carolina During Reconstruction 1865–1873." Ph. D. Thesis, University of Maryland, 1973.

Buggs, Patricia. "The Negro in Charlotte, North Carolina as Reflected in the *Charlotte Ob-*

server and Related Sources, 1900–1910." M.A. Thesis, Atlanta University, 1976.

Charles, Cleophus. "Roy Wilkins, the NAACP and the Early Struggle for Civil Rights: Towards the Biography of a Man and a Movement in Microcosm, 1901–1939." Ph.D. Thesis, Cornell University 1981.

Chujo, Ken. "The Black Struggle for Education in North Carolina, 1877–1900." Ph.D. Thesis, Duke University, 1988.

Cobb, Turney E. "Race Relations in Edgecombe County, North Carolina 1700–1975." Honor's Thesis, University of North Carolina, 1975.

Darling, Marsha. "The Growth and Decline of the Afro-American Family Farm in Warren County, North Carolina, 1910–1960." Ph.D. Thesis, Duke University, 1982.

Davis, Gregory. "A Multi-Disciplinary Critique of the Protest Accomodationalist Analysis of the Black Church and Black Leadership Styles with an Analysis of the Leadership Styles of Dr. Reginald Armistice Hawkins." Ph.D. Thesis, University of Michigan, 1985.

Dillard, Geraldine. "The Negro in the Political, Economic, and Social Development of Charlotte, North Carolina, 1890–1900." M.A. Thesis, Atlanta University, 1972.

Dowdy, Lewis, Jr. "The Impact of the Philosophies of the Presbyterian Church, U.S.A., Booker T. Washington, and W.E.B. Du Bois on the Educational Program of Johnson C. Smith University." Ph.D. Thesis, Rutgers University, 1989.

Earnhardt, Elizabeth. "The Critical Years: The North Carolina Commission on Interracial Cooperation, 1942–1949." M.A. Thesis, University of North Carolina, 1971.

Hazel, David. "The National Association for the Advancement of Colored People and the National Legislative Process: 1940–1954." Ph.D. Thesis, University of Michigan, 1957.

Jones, William Powell. "The NAACP, the Cold War and the Making of the Civil Rights Movement in North Carolina." M.A. Thesis, University of North Carolina, 1996.

Leach, Damaria. "Progress Under Pressure: Changes In Charlotte Race Relations 1955–1965." M.A. Thesis, University of North Carolina, 1976.

Lockhart, Walter. "Lynching in North Carolina." Ph.D. Thesis, University of North Carolina, 1972.

Magruder, Nathaniel. "The Administration of Governor Cameron Morrison of North Carolina, 1921–1925." Ph.D. Thesis, University of North Carolina, 1968.

Moore, Linda. "The Emergence of the NAACP: An Analysis of Interorganizational Linkage Using Social Movement Theory." Ph.D. Thesis, Texas Women's University, 1994.

Newkirk, Vann. "The Greensboro Massacre, the Communists and Black Relationships." M.A. Thesis, Winthrop College, 1991.

Patterson, Maxine. "The Influence of the NAACP on Federal Educational Policy from 1955–1965." Ed.D. Thesis, Memphis State University, 1984.

Piehl, Charles. "White Society in the Black Belt, 1870–1920: A Study of Four North Carolina Counties." Ph.D. Thesis, Washington University, 1979.

Sides, Margaret. "Harry Golden's Rhetoric: The Persona, the Message, the Audience." M.A. Thesis, Northern Illinois, 1988.

Stokes, Allen Heath, Jr. "Black and White Labor and the Development of the Southern Textile Industry, 1880–1920." Ph.D. Thesis, University of South Carolina, 1977.

Thomas, Clarence. "The Journalistic Civil Rights Advocacy of Harry Golden and the Carolina Israelite." Ph.D. Thesis, University of Florida, 1990.

Walker, Lewis. "The Struggles and Attempts to Establish Branch Autonomy and Hegemony: A History of the District of Columbia Branch, National Association for the Advancement of Colored People, 1912–1942." Ph.D. Thesis, University of Delaware, 1979.

Index